Call of Duty

THE STERLING NOBILITY OF ROBERT E. LEE

J. STEVEN WILKINS

GENERAL EDITOR, GEORGE GRANT

LEADERS IN ACTION SERIES

CUMBERLAND HOUSE

PUBLISHING INC.

Copyright © 1997 by J. Steven Wilkins

Published by
CUMBERLAND HOUSE PUBLISHING, INC.
431 Harding Industrial Drive
Nashville, Tennessee 37211
www.cumberlandhouse.com

General Editor: George Grant

All Scripture quotations, unless otherwise indicated, are taken from the King James Version.

Cover photo: Robert E. Lee, Valentine Museum, Richmond, Virginia

Library of Congress Cataloging-in-Publication Data

Wilkins, J. Steven, 1950–
   Call of duty : the sterling nobility of Robert E. Lee / J. Steven Wilkins
      p.   cm. — (Leaders in action series)
   Includes bibliographical references (p.).
   ISBN: 978-1-68162-068-8

   1. Lee, Robert E. (Robert Edward), 1807–1870—Military Leadership. 2. Command of troops. I. Title. II. Series.
E467.1.L4W65 1997
973.7'3'092—dc21
[B]   97-8180
                                                                CIP

5 6 7 8 9 10 11 — 09 08 07

To Matt, Jeremy, Bray, Jordan, and Caleb,
with the earnest prayer that they might be true gentlemen

and to Charity,
that she might love, honor, and obey such a man.

TABLE OF CONTENTS

FOREWORD

BY GEORGE GRANT

Samuel Johnson once quipped, "Any man honored by both his enemies and his compatriots is a man worthy of our closest attentions—for in him you may be sure to find authenticity. After all, authenticity is the rarest of all human traits."

By any standard, Robert E. Lee was an authentic man—worthy of our closest attentions.

A little over a century ago, he was a marvel of unimpeachable character. Today, he is a marvel of universal admiration. History has bestowed the latter distinction precisely because history has confirmed the former.

That is quite a remarkable feat in this age of relentless debunking when all too few figures emerge from the past unscathed and untainted. But it is an even more remarkable feat in light of the epoch in the past from which General Lee emerged. The fiercely uncivil War between the States not only divided the nation then; it continues to divide us now. Indeed, few polarizing episodes from the past continue to so fervently stir our passions, pique our interests, and arrest our attentions as does this one.

Almost every aspect of the conflict splits our opinions and our loyalties into opposing sides. About how and why the war began there is little agreement. About what its objectives actually were there is little accord. About which side was morally right and which was morally wrong there is little consensus. About who its villains and who its champions were there is little concurrence. About which side possessed constitutional warrant there is little consonance. About the relative virtues and vices of General Lee's contemporaries, rivals, and companions—Sherman, Hood, Stuart, Grant, and even Lincoln—there is little harmony. Indeed, about the merits of this, that, or the other strategy there is little but fractious disagreement.

But somehow General Lee has escaped all such carping and bickering. Though the war he fought in, the cause he fought for, the men he fought with, and the nation he fought to defend are all subsumed in intractable controversy, there is clear consensus when it comes to him: he was a great man, a proven stalwart, and a leader of sterling nobility. No ifs, ands, or buts about it.

According to liberal and conservative alike, according to Southerner and Northerner alike, according to great and small alike, and according to common and elite alike—General Lee was a man without parallel or peer. The experts, academicians, and historians all speak with startling unanimity. According to English historian Paul Johnson, "General Lee has accomplished in both life and death what few, indeed, hardly any have ever accomplished in all of the annals of history: ubiquitous respect, renown, and acclaim." And Czech poet Klaus Leveric has said, "Robert E. Lee is an inspiration to all peoples and all nations simply because he embodies the hopes and dreams of all virtuous men everywhere."

How can this be? What possible explanation is there for this unexpected paradox?

In this brilliantly succinct study, Steven Wilkins answers these questions and more. He delves into the life and career of General Lee in search of the seeds of greatness—and his search is by no means found wanting.

As I read the manuscript of this book—the fifth volume in a series of leadership sketches—I found myself yearning for a whole new generation of leaders influenced by the character of General Lee. And I found myself hoping that, through the agency of this inspiring work, this yearning might well be fulfilled.

ACKNOWLEDGMENTS

N o book comes into existence by the author's efforts alone. There are often hundreds of people who have had a significant role to play in its production. After going through the entire process, I now realize the tremendous sense of obligation an author feels to all who have helped. And thus, I understand more than ever how important "Acknowledgments" are. It would be the height of ingratitude not to mention those who have had such a big part to play in the production of this book.

I am not one who "craves" to write. Honestly, I avoid it as much as possible. The chief reason I did not avoid this project is George Grant. George's faithful friendship, unfailing optimism, unswerving vision, and steady encouragement have made this book a reality. Without his kindness, persistent prodding, and stirring example, it would never have been written.

I also must mention all the folk at Highland Books who were always supportive and did everything possible to assist me every step along the way. Heather Armstrong's good cheer and Nancy Drazga's patience and gifted editorial work were invaluable.

Many friends have contributed in uncountable ways in helping me to understand the past and present: George Calhoun (keeper of the Mount Olive Tape Library), Mark Duncan (companion in the ministry and faithful guide through the battlefields of Virginia), Bill Hart (fellow admirer of Lee), Michael Hill (courageous scholar and Christian gentleman),

Otto Scott (author and cultural critic extraordinaire), Lloyd Sprinkle (pastor and publisher of long-forgotten but vitally important books), and Tom Trice (who took me on my first visit to Lee Chapel).

I have had the immeasurable privilege of being surrounded with a "multitude of counsellors" who have been faithful to encourage and exhort: Jim Bordwine, Walter Bowie, Tom Ellis, Sonny Peaster, Franklin Sanders, Steve Schlissel, Mickey Schneider, Byron Snapp, Douglas Wilson, and Tony Tosti.

The congregations of the Covenant Presbyterian Church in Forest, Mississippi, and the Westminster Presbyterian Church of Vancouver, Washington, have been a tremendous blessing and were influential in helping me to grapple with the history of our country from a Christian perspective.

I cannot forget my wife Wendy. Never has a man had such a faithful friend and companion. My six children (Matt, Jeremy, Bray, Jordan, Caleb, and Charity) are my greatest earthly joy. My parents (Mr. and Mrs. J. M. Wilkins) and my mother-in-law (Mrs. J. D. Hilleke) have been inestimable blessings and indispensable supports.

Special thanks also must be given to the elders (Hewitt Carter, Danny Keyes, Dale Peacock, and Bill Smith) and the congregation of the Auburn Avenue Presbyterian Church. Brothers and sisters all, faithful and gracious, staunchly supportive.

This book owes its existence to the love, support, kindness, and generosity of these gracious saints. May God look upon all with mercy and continue to them His uncountable and immeasurable blessings.

Deo Vindice
St. Valentine's Day, 1997

INTRODUCTION

*A*fter completing his magisterial four-volume biography of Lee, on which he labored for more than ten years, the great Southern author Douglas Southall Freeman stated: "I have been fully repaid by being privileged to live, as it were, for more than a decade in the company of a great gentleman."

Truly, for anyone who knows Robert E. Lee, the term "gentleman" comes immediately to mind. For Lee the term encompassed diligence, respect for authority, honorable conduct, and faith in Almighty God. Lee manifested these qualities to a degree equaled by few men in history. Indeed, his entire life—from his early years with his mother, through his education at West Point and his years as a professional soldier and educator—was the life of a gentleman.

Lee was, by turns, a loving son, diligent student, devoted husband, faithful father, obedient soldier, courageous officer, decisive general, and dedicated educator. In all of these roles he was a stirring example to those around him. Seldom has there been a man who evoked such love and loyalty; rarely has a man commanded such admiration and respect.

The greatness of Lee was impossible to ignore. His sterling character was recognized by friends and adversaries alike. At his death, tributes came from his homeland, from abroad, and even from the North. *The New York Sun's* Charles A. Dana wrote: "[I]n the death of General Lee an able soldier, a sincere Christian, and an honest man has been taken from the earth."

The testimonial in *The New York Herald* acknowledged that

> [I]n [Lee] the military genius of America was
> developed in a greater extent than ever before.
> In him all that was pure and lofty in mind and
> purpose found lodgment. He came nearer the
> ideal of a soldier and Christian general than
> any man we can think of, for he was a greater
> soldier than Havelock, and equally as devout a
> Christian.

From Canada, *The Montreal Telegraph* declared:

> Posterity will rank Lee above Wellington or
> Napoleon, before Saxe or Tureene, above
> Marlborough or Frederick, before Alexander, or
> Caesar… [Lee was] the greatest general of this
> or any other age. He has made his own name,
> and the Confederacy he served, immortal.

Tributes from abroad similarly acknowledged Lee's
legacy. An article in *The London Standard* read, in part:

> [A] country that has given birth to men like
> him, and those who followed him, may look the
> chivalry of Europe in the face without shame:
> for the fatherlands of Signey and of Bayard
> never produced a nobler soldier, gentleman,
> and Christian than Gen. Robert E. Lee.

Many know of Lee's exploits in the field of battle, but few
are familiar with his life apart from the military. For this reason, while not ignoring his military accomplishments, I have

focused upon his life before and after the War for Southern Independence: the days of preparation under the tutelage of his faithful mother; the days of training at the military academy and in the Corps of Engineers; and the days of mentoring his students, both at West Point and Washington College. I have sought to illustrate the love and care he exhibited to his wife and children; his never-failing concern for his soldiers, his students, and the people of his land; his patient submission to the providence of God; his patriotism, sound judgment, personal courage, gentle humor, and spotless integrity; his keen sense of honor and his willing sacrifice. These are the aspects of Lee that need to be better known, so that the whole man and the impact he made on his times may be clearly seen.

Lee's life was one that needs no defense; it was a life full of deeds that require no justification. It would be easy to deify this man who led a life of such stunning nobility, to make him into an almost imaginary figure of mythic proportions. However, it would be a great mistake to do so. The value of studying the life of Robert E. Lee lies in seeing that he was in one profound way no different from every other person who comes into the world. Lee described himself in these words: "I am a poor sinner, trusting in Christ alone for salvation." It was this awareness of his own insufficiency and of his need for the grace and mercy of God that formed the foundation of his extraordinary character.

Our country is presently nearly devoid of the manhood Lee embodied. The primary reason for this is that we as a people have lost the faith that alone can produce true manliness. Nothing has more effectively "unmanned" the present age than unbelief. Until we see men again embracing with their whole hearts the true religion, we shall be doomed to live in a land filled with and led by unholy children (Isaiah 3).

It is my prayer that our children and grandchildren will live to see true godliness restored. That, above all, is why this book has been written.

CHRONOLOGY OF
ROBERT E. LEE'S LIFE

1807   Robert E. Lee is born on January 19 at Stratford, Westmoreland County, Virginia, the fourth son of General Henry Lee and Ann Hill Carter Lee.

1813   Henry Lee leaves in the summer for the British West Indies, never to return.

1818   Henry Lee dies on March 25, on Cumberland Island, in the home of Revolutionary War hero Nathaniel Greene.

1825   Robert leaves home in July to enter West Point.

1829   Lee graduates from West Point in June without a single demerit, is commissioned brevet second lieutenant in the Corps of Engineers.

1831   On June 30, Robert E. Lee marries Mary Anne Randolph Custis at Arlington.

1831   The Lees move into officers' quarters at Fortress Monroe in August.

1832   On September 16, Custis Lee is born.

1836   Lee receives his first promotion to first lieutenant of the Engineers in September.

1844   Lee is given the opportunity to work with Major General Winfield Scott on the board of visitors for the military academy at West Point.

1846   The Mexican War begins on April 25 with a clash between Mexican and American troops near the Rio Grande.

1846   On August 19, Lee receives his orders to report to Brigadier General John E. Wool in San Antonio.

1847   Lee joins the staff of General Winfield Scott in February.

1847	Mexico City falls to American troops in September.
1848	The Treaty of Guadalupe Hidalgo is signed on February 2, ending hostilities.
1848	Lee returns home to his family in June.
1852	On September 1, Lee becomes the ninth superintendent of the United States Military Academy.
1853	On July 17, Lee receives confirmation in the Episcopal Church with his two daughters, Mary Custis and Anne.
1855	Lee appointed to take command of the 2nd Cavalry on April 12.
1857	On October 10, George Washington Parke Custis, Lee's father-in-law, dies.
1859	Lee receives orders on October 17 to go to Harper's Ferry to take command of the troops sent to quell the uprising led by John Brown.
1860	Abraham Lincoln elected president of the United States in November, receiving only 40% of the popular vote.
1860	On December 20, the state of South Carolina secedes from the Union.
1861	On April 18, Lee is offered command of the United States Army through an intermediary of President Lincoln, Francis Preston Blair.
1861	On April 18, the Virginia state legislature votes to secede from the Union.
1861	Lee resigns from the United States Army on April 20.
1861	Lee appointed major-general of the military and naval forces of the state of Virginia on April 23.
1861	Lee is sent to command the Confederate troops at Cheat Mountain on July 28.
1862	General Joseph Johnston is killed in battle at Seven Pines on May 31.
1862	On June 1, Lee takes command of the Army of Northern Virginia.
1863	President Lincoln issues the "Emancipation Proclamation" on January 1.
1863	On May 2, General Thomas J. "Stonewall" Jackson is wounded in the battle of Chancellorsville, and dies on May 10.

1863	On July 1, the battle of Gettysburg begins.
1863	Lee writes a letter on August 8 offering his resignation to President Jefferson Davis; the offer is refused.
1864	On March 9, Ulysses S. Grant is given command of the Army of the Potomac.
1865	The Confederate evacuation of Petersburg begins on April 2.
1865	On April 9, Lee surrenders the Army of Virginia to General U. S. Grant at Appomattox Courthouse.
1865	On April 14, President Lincoln is shot by former actor John Wilkes Booth at the Ford Theatre in Washington, D. C.
1865	Lee arrives back at his house in Richmond on April 15.
1865	On August 25, Lee accepts the position of president of Washington College, Lexington, Virginia.
1870	Lee begins a tour through the South with his daughter Agnes on March 24.
1870	On September 28, Lee attends his last vestry meeting at the Episcopal church and suffers a stroke upon arriving home that evening.
1870	Robert E. Lee dies on October 12.
1870	Lee's funeral is held in the chapel of Washington College on October 14.

PART I:
THE LIFE OF ROBERT E. LEE

As in the lives of all persons, Lee's essence was to be found not in what he said, but in what he did. There were dimensions to Lee, but his life was one long response to whatever struck him as being the call of duty.
Charles Bracelen Flood

Ask me, if you please, to paint
Storm winds upon the sea;
Tell me weigh great Cheops,
Set volcanic forces free;
But bid me not, my countrymen,
To picture Robert Lee*!*

Memorial Ode
by James Barron Hope

PROLOGUE

*T*uesday, September 28, 1870, was chilly and overcast. Rain was falling steadily by late afternoon when General Robert E. Lee prepared to leave for the vestry meeting at his church. His daughter Mildred was playing Mendelssohn's *Funeral March* on the piano. As he donned his grey military cape and took his broad-brimmed hat in his hand, he commented, "Life, that is a doleful piece you are playing!" Bending over to kiss her goodbye, he remarked, "I wish I did not have to go and listen to all that powwow."[1] But he was chairman of the vestry, and duty called.

His fellow vestrymen—among them, his personal physicians, Drs. Howard T. Barton and R. L. Madison—greeted the general as he entered the cold, damp church house. As he returned their greetings with "marked cheerfulness of manner," they never guessed that he had come so reluctantly. They did notice, however, that he seemed cold and did not remove his cape, as was his custom. As the meeting proceeded, General Lee seemed to become more tired than usual, and his face became flushed, even though the room grew colder as the evening wore on.

Finally, they reached the last item on the agenda: the pastor's salary. The Reverend Dr. William Nelson Pendleton, one of Lee's old war generals, was now his pastor. Dr. Pendleton had graduated from West Point a year ahead of Lee, but had eventually surrendered to the call of God to the ministry and resigned from the army to enter the service of the Episcopal Church of Virginia. When the war came, he was rector of the small Episcopal congregation in Lexington. After a great deal of soul-searching, Pendleton resigned his charge and enlisted in the Confederate army, not as a chaplain but as an artillery officer. After the war, it was Pendleton who had been instrumental in persuading his former commander to accept the position offered by the Washington College Board of Trustees to become president of the languishing institution.

> *One great reason why I hope you may judge favorably of this invitation is, that the destiny of our State & country depends so greatly upon the training of our young men. And now our Educational Institutions are so crippled that they need the very best agencies for their restoration and the revival of high aims in the breasts of Virginian & Southern youths.*[2]

Knowing Lee as he did, Pendleton had then included the "magic words," expressing his hope that "it might accord with your views of duty & with your tastes to accept the important trust." The reverend concluded his letter by saying, "I have thought Dear General while thus doing an important service to the State & its people you might be presenting to the world in such position an example of quiet usefulness & gentle patriotism, no less impressive than the illustrious career in the field."[3] Duty. General Robert Edward Lee had a duty to perform for the sons of the South in general, for the sons of Virginia in particular, and for the nation at large. For Lee, the call of duty was irresistible.

The amount pledged for the salary for Dr. Pendleton was short of what had been agreed upon. Upon hearing the report of the treasurer, each vestry member, according to his means, pledged to contribute a certain sum towards the deficit. When all had spoken, the total was still fifty-five dollars short. The men looked at one another and then to the chairman. In a low tone General Lee said, "I will give that sum."[4] It was far above his portion of the subscription, especially in light of the many generous contributions to the church he had already made (not to mention those to other charities), but that was Lee.

Arriving home, Lee went upstairs to hang up his cape and hat, and returned downstairs to the dining room where his dear wife Mary had been awaiting him for evening tea. Mildred was entertaining some friends in the parlor. Mary greeted him with mock indignation, saying, "You have kept us waiting a long time. Where have you been?" Lee made no reply, but took his usual place at the head of the table to pray. Mary and daughter Agnes bowed their heads, but this time they did not hear the familiar reverent tones of their husband and father giving praise to God for His bountiful care and provision. Lee opened his mouth to pray, but no words came. Confounded, he slowly took his seat.

Mary poured him a cup of tea, making the observation that he looked "so tired." Lee again tried to respond and again words failed him. He then sat up straight in his chair. Mary and Agnes stared at him, thinking that he looked just like a cadet at West Point, with one exception: he had a look of resignation on his face they had never before seen.

Mary called for her son Custis, who hurried to the general's side to ask if there was anything he could do to help. When his father made no answer, Custis threw on his coat and ran out through the heavy rain to find the doctors. Mildred came in to find her father "bowed down and looking very strange and speaking incoherently."[5]

Lee's doctors were still walking home together from the vestry meeting when Custis caught them. Within minutes they were at the house. They had General Lee's "low, single bed" brought down from upstairs and set up in the dining room. The doctors diagnosed the general's condition as "venous congestion of the brain" which, in a later day would be called "cerebral thrombosis" (a blood clot on the brain). This, along with a throat infection, had produced, in the wonderfully imprecise medical terminology of the day, "cerebral exhaustion."

The rain fell at a record rate—fourteen inches in thirty-six hours—and brought some of the worst floods in history to that region of Virginia. At the president's house on the campus of Washington College, the dining table was removed and the dining room made into a sick room. A fire was kept burning in the fireplace to take the edge off the chill. The general, though "inclined to dose" was alert and understood conversation, though he could only say a few words clearly himself. He ate soup and other bland foods and communicated chiefly in monosyllables and by nodding or shaking his head.

Though in the first few days of his sickness, his doctors were encouraged to hope for recovery, Lee himself seemed to hold no such hope. Once when Custis made an allusion to his recovery, the general shook his head vigorously and pointed upward. One of his doctors would later say, "he neither expected nor desired to recover."[6]

The vigil was attended by Agnes, who fixed the medicines and sat with her father through the night, and Mildred, who prepared his meals and stayed during the day. Mary would be rolled in her chair to the bedside that she too might be with her husband. The time was spent mostly in silence, as is usual in such situations. But how strange that silence was in the Lee household. Mildred would say, "The silence was awful! He would lay straight and motionless, gazing with that solemn unalterable look, into the flames that played on the hearth." Her father, the man who had always been so cheerful and so free with the jest, who delighted to play sweet games with his girls—provoking gales of laughter from them and filling the house with his own joy—now lay silent, uttering not a word. "Hour after hour Agnes and I would sit by him," Mildred remembered, "rubbing his dear hands in the old way he used to like—never saying a word. Now I wonder I did not read comforting passages from the Bible—did not repeat his favorite hymns—but words seemed frozen in all our mouths; he was speechless—so were we!"[7]

On Monday, October 10, Lee seemed to be suffering from constant pain for the first time in his illness. He tried to speak but could not. His eyes appealed to his helpless family who could do nothing but give him tender expressions of love and offer prayer in his behalf. It was a difficult time. Mildred would exclaim, "Oh, the horror of being helpless when he needed help!"

On Tuesday afternoon the general sank into a coma. His wife sat by his side as he, in her words, "wandered to those dreadful battlefields." In the mysterious workings of the mind, the great warrior had been taken back to those days of triumph and despair. "Tell Hill he *must* come up!" he cried. There followed the last distinct words anyone would hear from the great man's lips, "Strike the tent!"

That night Mildred was awakened by Agnes who, saying nothing, led her downstairs by the hand to their father's sick bed. Dr. Pendleton was there, repeating the liturgical prayers for the dying. Their mother sat in her wheelchair by the bed. Their brother Custis was kneeling at his father's side, and Mildred and Agnes knelt beside him. Lee was breathing "hard and painfully."

The storm, which had continued nearly unabated throughout the ordeal of the general's sickness, finally broke just as the sun arose on Wednesday morning. The family remained silent beside their stricken head. Around nine, Mildred saw that her father "seemed to be struggling." She rushed out for the doctor, but when he arrived and looked at General Lee, he walked away without saying a word. "In a moment," said Mildred, "he was dead." And so ended the life of one of the most noble men to have graced the ground of this fair country.

How firm a foundation, ye saints of the Lord,
Is laid for your faith in his excellent Word!
What more can he say than to you he hath said,
You who unto Jesus for refuge have fled?

Stanza 1
How Firm A Foundation

BIRTH AND LINEAGE

I would rather see you unlettered and unnoticed, if
virtuous in practice as well as theory, than see you
the equal in glory to the great Washington.
–Henry Lee to his sons

Robert E. Lee was born at Stratford Hall, the ancestral home of the Lee family, in Westmoreland County, Virginia. Interestingly, he was born in the same room as three of his famous relatives: Richard Henry Lee, called "The Cicero of the American Revolution;" Francis Lightfoot Lee, one of the signers of the Declaration; and Sydney Smith Lee, one of the most famous members of the young American navy. The child of a prominent family, Lee was descended from a long line of illustrious men and women famous both in this country and England. Some have traced the Lee family back to the royal Scottish family of Robert the Bruce.[8] Whether this can be done with any degree of certainty, it is indisputable that the Lee ancestry is filled with great and noble men who won the respect of their peers.

The first Lee to come to the New World was Richard Lee, "a gentleman of good position and many accomplishments,"[9] who came to Virginia as secretary and member of the King's Privy Council. After he settled, he became the secretary of the colony under Sir William Berkeley, the royal governor.[10]

Richard Lee was the father of two sons, John and Richard. John died before his father but Richard lived to become a considerable scholar. We are told that he passed his life in study (he was more often to be found in his large library than on his wide plantations),"writing his notes habitually in Greek, Hebrew, or Latin."[11] He married a Miss Corbin of England and died on March 12, 1714, leaving one daughter and five sons: Richard, Philip, Francis, Thomas, and Henry.

Henry, Richard's fifth son, took up residence on the Potomac, on land adjoining Mount Pleasant, the older Lee residence, and became a planter of "ample means." He married a Miss Bland and they had several children, the third of whom was born in 1729 and also named Henry. This Henry, who called himself "Henry the second," was so dull, says tradition, that their more outgoing son, who was R. E. Lee's father, once explained his own personality as contrasted to those of his parents by saying that "two negatives make an affirmative."[12] This is no doubt an exaggeration, for "Henry the second" actually became a man of distinction, serving as county lieutenant, burgess, member of the Revolutionary conventions, and justice of the peace.

Robert E. Lee's father, the son of "Henry the second" and also named Henry, was born on January 29, 1756. After being homeschooled, he was sent to Princeton, where he was placed under the charge of Dr. John Witherspoon. He graduated in 1773, just in time to participate in the momentous events which were sweeping the colonies to a clash of arms with Great Britain. In 1776, Patrick Henry nominated Henry Lee to command a cavalry company raised in Virginia for the service of the Continental Congress under the command of Colonel Bland.[13] It was in the army that he came into his own. "A soldier from his mother's womb," as General Charles Lee put it, Henry Lee was a vigorous man—though only five feet nine inches in height—and he had the strength and endurance to meet the demands of General Washington in the colonies' life and death struggle with Britain.

In 1777, Lee's company was placed under the direct command of General Washington. It was in Washington's army that Henry Lee became one of the most famous men of the Revolution. His accomplishments were more than notable. In January, 1778, Lee made himself the talk of the army by beating off a surprise attack at Spread Eagle Tavern. In July 1779, he captured the British fort at Paulus Hook (later called Jersey City). So skillful were his efforts, Congress declared its thanks and voted to give him a medal of honor. In November of 1780 he was made lieutenant-colonel, and in 1781 he joined General Nathaniel Greene for service in the Carolinas, where his fame and renown increased.

By the time Henry Lee reached General Greene, he was already a hero. Given the nickname "Light-Horse Harry," Lee continued in the South as he had begun in the North. He won honors at Guilford Courthouse, forced the surrender of Fort Granby, and had a major role in the surrender of Fort Conwallis in Augusta. "At the close of the Revolution," says A. L. Long, "no one had acquired a more permanent and deserved reputation than 'Light-Horse' Harry."[14] Indeed, aside from Washington himself, no man had a greater name. He became close friends with General Washington, and it was he whom the Congress named to give the eulogy at Washington's funeral. In this famous speech, Henry Lee referred to Washington with the memorable words, "First in war, first in peace, first in the hearts of his countrymen."

In 1782 Henry Lee resigned from the military. For a while all seemed well. Lee married, and four children were born within five years. In 1785 he was elected to the Virginia House of Delegates. In 1786 Lee was chosen by Henry's peers for a seat in Congress. He took an active part in the Constitutional debates, opposing Patrick Henry and helping to defeat his opposition to the proposed Constitution. He was elected governor of Virginia three times. But throughout this period, Lee—unable to resist the allure of speculation—was distracted by and preoccupied with various questionable financial ventures. They would lead to his ruin.

He invested, and lost, £8,000 in a failed venture in Mississippi. Seeking to recoup his losses, he purchased five hundred acres at the Great Falls of the Potomac, which he hoped to subdivide and sell at a sizeable profit. In spite of the support of Washington and Madison, this project, too, fell through. He failed to pay back a debt to his close friend Washington, and later—in desperation—sought "insider" information from Alexander Hamilton about the financial plans of the federal government. Hamilton kindly but bluntly refused. Though none believed Harry Lee devious, all began to lose respect for their friend and old war compatriot.

Lee began to borrow money to make ends meet at home. His precarious financial dealings caused his wife, who had been in bad health since 1788, to place her property in trust for her children, thus protecting it from the reach of her husband's creditors as well as from his own financial misjudgment. In 1790, she died. This sorrow was followed shortly afterwards by the death of his oldest son, Philip Ludwell Lee, who was only seven years old.[15]

The double bereavement pushed Lee further into the darkness. He became an opponent of the country's fiscal policy and openly opposed his friend Washington. At one point he even seriously thought of going to France and joining the revolutionary army! These plans were abandoned when he met Ann Hill Carter, the woman who became his second wife. Had Lee not met Miss Carter, he probably would have gone to France and on June 30, 1793, would have been assisting Robespierre rather than taking his wedding vows.[16] And what is more, the world would never have known the great son of this union, Robert E. Lee, who was born nearly fourteen years later, on January 19, 1807.

For a time after the marriage, Lee seemed to improve. But soon, the fever of speculation hit him again. Things went from bad to worse until finally, on April 11, 1809—after many more failed ventures—Lee was arrested and jailed for a debt of some 5,400 Spanish dollars, which had accrued interest for seven years. He did not receive his freedom until the spring of 1810, and by then, all that was left of his estate was a small bit of unsalable land.[17]

Hope now died in "Light-Horse" Harry. Helpless to provide for his family, he determined to leave the country and go to the British West Indies in order to regain his health and, one suspects, his vision. He left home in the summer of 1813, leaving behind a loving (if long-suffering) wife and five adoring children. Though little of his once fine reputation remained abroad, he was still the hero at his own fireside.

Henry Lee died in the early spring of 1818, while he was seeking to return home. He was forced by failing strength to stop at Cumberland Island, off the coast of Georgia, where the daughter of his old comrade General Nathaniel Greene resided. Refusing to allow the physician to operate, he said, "My dear sir, were the great Washington alive, and here, and joining you in advocating it, I would still resist."[18] He lingered only a short while before passing from this life on March 25, 1818. The details of his death were not known by his family until that autumn.

Although Robert was only six years old when his father left for the West Indies, Henry Lee would always hold a place of honor in his son's heart. Though knowing little of his father from personal interaction, Robert did have the letters his father had written to his older brother Carter during his self-imposed exile. Many of his father's words in these letters had a powerful influence upon his life:

> *Fame in arms or art, however conspicuous, is naught, unless bottomed on virtue.*

> *Many lads…fall into another habit which hurts only themselves and which certainly stupefies the senses—immoderate sleeping.*

> *It is hard to say whether too much eating or too much drinking most undermines the constitution.*

> *You know my abhorrence of lying, and you have been often told by me that it led to every vice and canceled every tendency to virtue. Never forget this truth and disdain this mean and infamous practice.*

> *Avoid all frivolous authors, such as novel writers, and all skeptical authors, whether religious, philosophical, or moral.*

> *Self-command…is the pivot upon which the character, fame, and independence of us mortals hang.*

And, perhaps most poignantly,

Avoid debt, the sink of mental power and the subversion of independence.[19]

Thus, Henry Lee left his sons a legacy after all, in these words of wisdom—words akin to those of the preacher in Ecclesiastes who fell from the heights of wisdom into folly and humiliation. Henry Lee had learned the truth of the wisdom he wrote about by ignoring much of it, and he desperately desired that his sons not follow in his footsteps. God granted his request. Both Carter and Robert were fine successes. No little credit for this must be given to the example of their not always wise but greatly humbled father. Such is the power of the father's example, even when that example is flawed by sin. Though Robert knew his father best through his letters, it may also be said that by this means he learned the best his father had to offer.

If Lee was ever embittered by his father's failures, he never stated it. He would remember his father as the great friend of Washington and the mighty warrior of the War for Independence. In January of 1863, while on an inspection tour of coastal defenses, Lee made a stop at Cumberland Island to visit his father's grave. General A. L. Long describes this visit:

While passing through the channel that separates Cumberland Island from the main land, the steamer stopped at the plantation wharf, and the general then asked me to accompany him on a sacred mission. After following for some distance a road shaded with live-oak and magnolia, we passed through a gate opening into extensive grounds dotted with groups of olive, orange, and lemon trees, intermingled with brilliant subtropical shrubbery. In the midst of these grounds arose an extensive pile of buildings whose unfinished state bore evidence that the design of the projector exceeded his means of execution. This was the residence of General Greene...Passing on, we came to a dilapidated wall enclosing a neglected cemetery. The general then, in a voice of emotion, informed me that he was visiting the grave of his father. He went alone to the tomb, and after a few moments of silence plucked a flower and slowly retraced his steps, leaving the lonely grave to the restless waves that perpetually beat against the neighboring shore. We returned in silence to the steamer, and no allusion was ever made to this act of filial devotion.[20]

Lee's father, in spite of all, would always be his hero.

CHILDHOOD AND EDUCATION

You cannot be a true man until you learn to obey.
                                                            –R. E. Lee

The Lee family moved to Alexandria, Virginia, in the summer of 1810, when Lee was three. Three years later, Lee's father left for the British West Indies, never to return. But he was not forgotten. No fewer than twenty members of "Light-Horse" Harry's old legion lived in Alexandria at this time and all of them remembered their old commander with great affection.

The hero of Alexandria, however, was George Washington. He had been dead more than a decade when the Lees arrived, but he was very much alive in the hearts of Alexandrians. Reminders of him were everywhere. Many still remembered his personal appearance and bearing. All this was doubly impressive to young Robert Lee, for his father's hero had been Washington, and that alone was enough to make him Robert's hero as well. Washington's example was one of the great influences on Lee's life.

The greatest influence, however, was his mother. Ann Carter Lee was the daughter of Charles Carter, a member of the wealthy and prominent Carter family. A faithful mother, like Solomon's "virtuous woman," is to be valued "far above rubies." Lee was blessed to have such a mother. William Jones says that Mrs. Lee "stayed with her household, and by womanly arts, graces, and virtues made a home for her children....Refined, cultivated, pious, and very tactful, she nobly met her obligations, and reared her children for humanity, for God, and for truth."[21]

Ann Lee was a godly and faithful mother who taught her children to honor God above all. At home, daily prayers were faithfully held, and on Sunday, attendance at the Episcopal Church of Alexandria—Washington's church—was routine.

Second only to the influence of his mother was the Reverend William Meade, the rector of the Protestant Episcopal church in Alexandria. Though Reverend Meade remained in the Alexandria church only eighteen months after the Lees arrived in town, he often returned to preach there. Meade, more than anyone else, was the leading force in restoring the credibility of the Church in Virginia from the ruin it had suffered during the War for Independence.

The Church of England in Virginia (and elsewhere in the country) was not of the high Anglo-Roman type found in England but was distinctly biased toward more Protestant/ Puritan convictions. Historian Earnest Trice Thompson has stated that "All of the ministers brought to the colony before 1624, under the auspices of the Virginia Company, were apparently Puritan in their sympathies."[22] Meade was thoroughly so and it was his spirit which dominated the Episcopal Church in Virginia. No doubt his solemn warnings of God's judgment and earnest pleadings to embrace the Savior had a salutary effect upon young Robert.

Robert's mother taught him the rudiments of reading and writing, but later, she sent him to one of the two family schools operated by the Carter family. The Carters were so numerous that they had two schools, one for the girls—located on the old family home at Shirley—and one for the boys—at Eastern View in Fauquier County. It is not known how long Lee attended the Carter family school at Eastern View, but we do know that the experience away from his mother's faithful discipline had a deleterious effect upon his behavior. When Robert returned from his first session at Eastern View, his behavior was most displeasing to his mother, who wrote to Mrs. Elizabeth Carter Randolph—in whose home the school met—to mention her displeasure over his conduct. Mrs. Randolph replied that she had found Robert an engaging child. If he was getting out of hand, she continued, the only advice she could give was "whip and pray, and pray and whip." [23]

Robert manifested in his later life the fruits of his mother's faithful discipline. A member of the family observed that Robert learned from his mother "to practice self-denial and self-control, as well as the strictest economy in all financial concerns," [24] virtues which governed him throughout his life. The fact that this was accomplished without the assistance of a husband and father makes it all the more remarkable. Truly, as William Jones notes, "Alongside of Mary, the Mother of Washington, among American women, should stand Anne, the Mother of Lee." [25]

Robert loved "sports" (riding, swimming, and hunting) and consequently he developed a strong, muscular frame. His childhood was happy, but he had cares and responsibilities that usually don't fall upon children until much later in life. He was only eleven years old when his father died in 1818, and even before that time the responsibilities of the household had fallen heavily upon him. His mother had begun the long slide into invalidism, and there were no siblings to help him with her. His sister Ann was chronically ill and often required medical treatment in Philadelphia. His brother Carter, who had graduated from Harvard in 1819, had opened a law practice in Washington and was seldom at home. In 1820, Robert's other brother, Smith, received a commission in the navy and went to sea. His baby sister Mildred was still too young to be of much help, and so the "running of the house" fell to Robert. It was his duty as a son to take up the care of all and he did so willingly.

We are told that Robert would "hurry home from his studies to see that his mother had her daily drive, and might be seen carrying her to her carriage, affectionately arranging her cushions, and earnestly endeavoring to entertain her, gravely assuring her that unless she was cheerful she would derive no benefit from her airing."[26] If she was in low spirits, he would seek to cheer her. If she was worried, he sought to bring comfort.

One of Lee's cousins said that the most impressive thing about Lee's character at this time in his life was his devotion to his mother. "He was her housekeeper, relieved her of all domestic cares, looked after the horses, rode out in the carriage with her, and did the marketing for the family."[27] Later, as her physical condition deteriorated, he was her nurse. We are told by another cousin that in Mrs. Lee's last illness, Robert "mixed every dose of medicine she took, and he nursed her night and day. If Robert left the room she kept her eyes on the door till he returned. He never left her but for a short time."[28]

The almost constant companionship Robert enjoyed with his mother was, without question, the dominant influence upon his life. Both the discipline of caring for her and the wisdom he gleaned from her molded his character. As his famous biographer, Douglas S. Freeman, has stated, "The man who was to order Pickett's charge at Gettysburg got part of his preparation for war by nursing sick women." [29]

Robert's presence and assistance was also an invaluable encouragement to his mother. When he later left for West Point, his mother remarked, "How can I live without Robert? He is both son and daughter to me." [30]

Lee's education was thoroughly Christian, and, indeed, could not have been otherwise, since all education at this time had its foundation in the Christian faith and ethic. After leaving Eastern View he entered Alexandria Academy. There he was trained following the classical model, reading Homer and Longinus in Greek, Tacitus and Cicero in Latin, and receiving instruction in mathematics, logic, and rhetoric.

In March of 1824, when Robert was seventeen years old, he received an appointment to the United States Military Academy at West Point, but was told that, because of the number of new students, he could not be admitted until July of 1825. This providence gave Robert the opportunity to take further instruction and he enrolled in a new school under the direction of Benjamin Hallowell. Hallowell later recorded,

> *He was a most exemplary pupil in every respect...He was never behind time at his studies; never failed in a single recitation; was perfectly observant of the rules and regulations of the institution; was gentlemanly, unobtrusive, and respectful in all his deportment to teacher and his fellow-students. His specialty was finishing up. He imparted a finish and a neatness, as he proceeded, to everything he undertook* [31]

This trait would stand him in good stead at West Point.

At the same time that Robert Lee set out for West Point, a little three-year-old was toddling about on his father's farm in Clermont County, Ohio. In 1825, no one would make any connection between the two boys, though they were to become two of the most famous men in the history of this country. But in 1825, life had few cares for little Ulysses Grant. Things would change.

WEST POINT

*Obedience to lawful authority is the foundation of
manly character.*

–R. E. Lee

*T*he discipline, patience, and faithfulness Lee learned
at the side of his mother was most beneficial at the
United States Military Academy. The academy in the nineteenth century was a spartan place. It was established for the
purpose of training soldiers, and soldiers had to learn to
endure hardness.

The first two months for the freshmen were spent in
tents. No classes were held, but there were four hours per day
of drill, and the rest of the day was spent in keeping camp
and tent clean and neat. At the end of August, the cadets were
moved into the barracks, four to a room, and kept on a strict
schedule from daybreak to sundown. Reveille was at dawn.
After room inspection and study, breakfast was served at
seven. Then came four hours of mathematics, an hour for dinner, and two hours of French, followed by two hours of drill

before supper at sundown. Study hours lasted until 9:30 P.M. and lights went out at ten o'clock.

Though the subjects of study changed as one advanced through the curriculum, the schedule remained the same. The food was notoriously bad and there was no heat in the winter—which led to widespread sickness among the cadets. As Freeman has noted, "To endure the life for four years was an achievement; to win good marks and to keep out of trouble was a triumph." [32] Robert Lee did both.

Lee was not a "natural genius," though he had always been a good student. His academic success came only through strenuous and dogged effort. And no student worked harder. It was during this first year that Robert learned a valuable lesson: *Success is not always dependent upon perfection.* Sometimes success comes to the one who makes fewer mistakes than the other fellow.

Final exams for the cadets consisted of a series of five oral exams of one hour each administered by a special "board of visitors." This examination board was allowed to ask the cadet any question about any subject he had studied during the year. It was an ordeal that tested the mettle of even the brightest student. Lee finished second in his class, taking top honors in artillery and tactics, and he earned in those four years not one demerit mark for a breach of rules or neglect of duty.

One might think that Lee—to have achieved such a high level of academic excellence—was a scholastic hermit who had few friends and desired none. Not so. Discipline at one's labor grants one the luxury of enjoying one's free time. Lee's garrulous personality and sincerity won him many friends— friends who not only liked him, but respected him. Joseph E. Johnston, a classmate and later Lee's compatriot at arms, described Robert in this way:

*[N]o other youth or man so united the qualities
that win warm friendship and command high
respect. For he was full of sympathy and kindness, genial and fond of gay conversation, and
even of fun, while his correctness of demeanor
and attention to all duties, personal and official, and a dignity as much a part of himself as
the elegance of his person, gave him a superiority that everyone acknowledged in his heart.*[33]

A significant influence at the academy, and one which
had a great impact on many of the students, was the labor of
the Reverend Charles P. McIlvaine, chaplain and professor of
geography, history, and ethics. He took his role as chaplain
most seriously, and each Lord's Day zealously sought the salvation and spiritual edification of the cadets. Many who came
to chapel expecting to sleep or study ended up listening spellbound as the Reverend McIlvaine preached—even though his
sermons lasted up to two hours! God blessed his work to the
hearts of many. One of Lee's classmates, Leonidas Polk, was
convinced to choose the ministry as his life-calling while sitting under the ministry of McIlvaine. Lee was always a
reverent and willing attendee at worship. No doubt the God of
grace used the ministry of His Word through McIlvaine to
reinforce the teachings Robert had heard many times from his
mother—teachings that would touch him even more strongly
later in his life.

In all four of his years at the academy, Lee had been
listed as one of the "distinguished cadets." As a class leader, he
was given the privilege of choosing the branch of the service
in which he desired to be commissioned. He requested the
Engineer Corps, which utilized the subjects that had captured
his imagination during his course of study. He was commis-

sioned a brevet second lieutenant in the Corps of Engineers, United States Army. In mid-June of 1829, he climbed aboard a steamship to go home for a two-month furlough.

Lee was twenty-two years old, five feet seven inches tall, handsome, gallant, disciplined, and he had been given the best education and training his country could offer. His preparation was now complete, and he was ready to begin his time of service.

SORROW AND JOY

Never marry unless you can do so into a family that
will enable your children to feel proud of both sides
of the house.

                    –R. E. Lee's advice to J. B. Hood

*T*he summer of 1829 should have been one of the happiest in Robert Lee's life. Newly graduated with honors from the military academy, newly commissioned as brevet second lieutenant, his life lay before him, shining like a brightly polished diamond with all its wondrous possibilities and adventures. But, as it turned out, this period was to be one of the saddest of his life.

When he arrived home he found his mother extremely ill. He immediately took up his old duties as her nurse and watched her anxiously as she declined day by day. Finally, on July 10, she died. Ann Carter Lee was fifty-six. The sad business of disposing of the property and distributing his mother's personal effects was finally completed by the end of the month, when Robert left to visit relatives.

In God's providence, however, times of great sorrow are often accompanied by times of great joy. So it was with Robert during this season. It was during the sojourn in northern Virginia at the home of the Randolphs in Eastern View that Robert's heart was captured by his future bride, the belle of Arlington. Arlington was the home of George Washington Parke Custis, grandson of Martha Washington—through one of her four children by her first husband, John Daniel Parke Custis—and adopted son of the great general. Mr. Custis built Arlington after the death of his grandmother in 1802, and moved in with his new bride, Mary Lee Fitzhugh, in 1804. Of their four children, only Mary Anne Randolph Custis survived infancy. When Robert came to visit in August 1829, she was twenty-one years old. The relationship flourished, and nearly two years later they were married at Arlington on a rainy June 30, 1831.

Mr. Custis had approved the marriage reluctantly, not because of any concern about Robert's character but because of Lee's precarious financial condition. Custis was fully aware of the Lee family's financial difficulties and was concerned that the young second lieutenant might not be able to support his daughter in the style to which she had become accustomed. It had become clear, however, that his daughter was more than willing to take that risk, and so he did not stand in the way.

The couple was married by the Reverend Reuel Keith, the Episcopal minister of Christ Church in Alexandria and principal of the newly established Episcopal Theological Seminary. Lee later remarked that Reverend Keith "had few words to say, though he dwelt upon them as if he had been reading my death warrant." [34]

Lee was gloriously happy and the month-long honeymoon went by all too fast. His marriage was to be one of the great turning points in his life.

The new Mrs. Lee was in many ways the exact opposite of her husband. He was orderly and nearly uncompromising in his concern for neatness. Mary, on the contrary, was careless and neglectful to the point of untidiness, even in her personal appearance. He was fanatically prompt; she, chronically late. He was often reserved and kept his opinions to himself; she was outspoken and frequently quick to voice her views (even when they were not her husband's). He was always careful to plan and avoid the impulse of the moment; she was whimsical and sometimes shockingly impulsive. Once, rising from an illness in which she had been confined to her bed, Mrs. Lee found her hair so hopelessly tangled that she took up the scissors and cut it off![35]

Despite these shortcomings, Lee was devoted to her. Following the example and precept of the Savior, he was always thinking of how to minister to her rather than being concerned with his own wants. He gladly overlooked her worst characteristics and gloried in her better ones. And her love for him was equal to his for her. One observer noted, "Although she was never awed by his presence, she had for his character a respect that became in time a positive reverence."

Lee's love for his bride would be manifested in innumerable ways throughout his married life, but nothing would more clearly reveal it than his care for her. Mary Lee developed an infirmity equal to—some say even greater than—that of Robert's mother, and spent the latter years of her life an invalid, utterly dependent upon the loving assistance of her husband. He always insisted on having the honor of wheeling his wife into the dining room for meals and also around the grounds of the college when they took their regular constitutionals. His favorite exercise in the evenings was reading aloud to her and his daughters.

It is important to note that by this marriage Robert Lee became connected with the Washington family. "When he married Mary Custis, he married Arlington as well."[36] The strong ties that Lee had always felt for the father of our country—because of his own father's close friendship with Washington—were now strengthened into an unbreakable bond. Many of Washington's personal effects were present in the home—lanterns, china, camp equipment, a bookcase, and even some of Washington's clothes and the bed in which he died. Living among Washington's effects was like living in the very shadow of the hero himself.

Edward Lee Childe notes in his biography of Lee, "This marriage in the eyes of the world, made Robert Lee the representative of the family of the founder of American liberty."[37] To the people of the South, Lee would be viewed as a worthy heir.

Fear not, I am with thee, O be not dismayed;
I, I am thy God, and will still give thee aid;
I'll strengthen thee, help thee, and cause thee to stand,
Upheld by my righteous, omnipotent hand.

Stanza 2
How Firm a Foundation

Preparation for Prominence

"Charity should begin at home." So says ___. No,
charity should have no beginning or ending.
–R. E. Lee

The newlyweds moved into the officers' quarters at Fortress Monroe in August 1831. For the next fifteen years, Lee was assigned to one engineering project after another. For six years he served as junior construction engineer at the fort. He then spent four years as an office assistant in Washington D.C. before being assigned to St. Louis. The current of the Mississippi was eroding the banks and depositing sediment in a way that blocked navigation. Lee's job was to divert the river so that this process ceased and the river remained navigable. This was a complex problem but Lee successfully accomplished the feat (and thus may be justly credited for making St. Louis a city with a future). This secured his first promotion to first lieutenant of the Engineers in September of 1836. Two years later he was made a captain. In 1841, Lee was called to New York to supervise the repair of some of the defenses of New York Harbor. There he remained for five years.

There were challenges in his work, but it was not the exciting, thrilling business young men always seem to envision for themselves. His days were made up of dull routine and mundane tasks which were decidedly humdrum. Lee had to learn to "glory in the grind" of an everyday duty—the common experience of most who pass through this life. Lee, however, made the most of the occasion.

He learned during these years an essential lesson, a lesson that is one of the distinguishing marks of maturity: *Work goes best when one does it heartily and faithfully without complaint.* How many there are who have yet to learn this basic lesson! In Lee's case, he was merely putting into practice things he learned earlier in his life, both at home and in school.

A second important lesson he learned at this time was the art of getting along with others (especially those who were quite different). An essential quality of a great leader is the ability to lead men whose perspectives on life are different from his own. Lee often found himself called upon to direct men with whom he had very little in common. Here again he had occasion to apply a childhood lesson: *Regardless of birth or social status, men ought to be treated with respect.* We are, in the Scripture's words, "to esteem others better than ourselves." From the humblest laborer to the chief of the Corps, he treated all with respect and demonstrated genuine interest in them—winning, in return, their loyalty.

His sincerity and humor, his integrity and honor prompted from others the very attitudes he demonstrated toward them. He did not remain aloof from the men and, consequently, they viewed him as both leader and friend. One of his companions would say of him at this time, "He was one with whom nobody ever wished or ventured to take a liberty, though kind and generous to all his subordinates, admired by all women, and respected by all men. He was the model of a soldier and the beau ideal of a Christian man."[38]

It was during this time as well that God gave the Lees the blessing of children. Captain Lee learned as much from being a father as he did from his experiences in the Corps. His first child, Custis, was born on September 16, 1832. Two years later, Mary arrived. On May 31, 1837, a second son, William Henry Fitzhugh (affectionately nicknamed "Rooney"), became part of the family. Two years later a second daughter, Anne Carter, was born. Anne was followed two years later by a third daughter, Eleanor Agnes. The third son, Robert, Jr., entered the rapidly growing family on October 27, 1843, and the fourth girl, Mildred, was born in 1846. Altogether, the Lees had seven children in fourteen years. The Lord had blessed them mightily.

Lee did not take fatherhood lightly. In spite of his other responsibilities, he gave himself to training and caring for all his brood as a man conscious of the eternal issues involved. The interest he took in his children was intense and often (for him) painful. Every sickness was a matter for anxiety, every injury an agony.

Lee realized from the outset the importance of a godly example. He was not a stern disciplinarian (though not at all averse to the appropriate application of the rod), but by precept and example sought to inculcate into his high-spirited sons those qualities of self-control, disciplined labor, and honor—the indispensable traits of a *gentleman* that had been so much a part of his own upbringing.

The Southern concept of a gentleman has been frequently discussed but seldom fully understood. The idea is rooted in the Biblical expectations of a man, which are that a man should not be merely one who is virile and masculine in the external sense, but one who fears God first, and secondly, devotes himself to serving his fellow men. The Southern ideal of a gentleman was a composite of that godliness and nobility one finds in the heroes of the Scripture and history. A gentleman was to be bold without becoming insensitive; courageous without forgetting to be gentle; principled without becoming stubbornly inflexible; passionate but not fanatical; courteous but not hypocritical; chivalrous but never inappropriately familiar with ladies.

The examples set before Southern children were many and varied. Preeminent among them was George Washington, but there were also the burning and shining lights of other ages: the Scottish patriots William Wallace and Robert the Bruce; the Christian martyrs memorialized by Foxe; and Knox and Calvin, the great servants of Christ during the Protestant Reformation. These and many more gave flesh and bones to the concept of gentleman, and gave a vivid if somewhat indefinable vision of what was expected of men.

The young men of the Lee household had one more example to add to the long list of gentlemen, one who would have more influence than any other: their own father. And he would become the example not only for them, but for untold thousands of children, both here and abroad.

It was during this season that another significant event occurred in the life of Lee. In 1844, the board of visitors for the military academy at West Point, previously responsible for giving the final examinations, was abolished in favor of a special army commission appointed by the President. Lee was appointed to the first of these commissions and had the privilege of spending a fortnight at the academy with a group of some of the most distinguished soldiers in the country. It was at this time that he became acquainted with the commanding general of the nation's army, Major General Winfield Scott. Lee had, no doubt, met General Scott in his many visits to Washington, but this was the first occasion on which they had worked together.

Scott was without question the leading military figure of the day and had a physical frame to fit his reputation. He stood fully six feet five inches and weighed more than 230 pounds. Though often overbearing and somewhat pompous in manner (consequently nicknamed old "Fuss and Feathers" by those around him), General Scott was an able man and Lee grew to respect him deeply. The feeling was mutual. As the general observed the young captain, his admiration grew. Lee did not seek to impress him with flattery and he was certainly no sycophant. In fact, when he believed it was warranted, Lee disagreed with him. This he did with as much grace as insight.

First impressions, the saying goes, are often most important. The impression made on General Scott was one not soon to be forgotten. In the following year, events would begin to move in such a way that this favorable impression made upon the country's first soldier would have significant repercussions in the life of Robert Lee.

THE MEXICAN WAR

Fame which does not result from good actions and
achievements for the good of the whole people is not
to be desired. Nero had fame... Who envies him?

–R. E. Lee

The year 1845 was dominated by one issue: Texas. The long dispute between the people of Texas and Mexico finally came to a head with the annexation of the Texas territory by Congress in December of that year. The debate had been heated. The New England states, fearing the increased political power which this action would give to the South, threatened to secede from the Union if Texas was annexed. In an anti-annexation convention held in Boston, the famous abolitionist William Lloyd Garrison stated that the annexation of Texas would constitute sufficient reason for the New England states to withdraw and form their own country.

Congressmen, both North and South, were divided on the issue, but finally approved annexation in the face of Mexican threats. Determined to defend its claim to Texas by arms, on

April 25, 1846, near the Rio Grande, Mexico first clashed with American troops. Two more engagements took place early in May before Congress declared war on Mexico on May 13. Twenty thousand volunteers were called for from the Southern states. All Washington was astir with the preparations. Plans, appointments, assignments, and expeditions were made as the rush to war began.

Meanwhile, Lee found himself mired in dull routine at Fort Hamilton in New York, waiting to see if he would be allowed to take part in the campaign. He realized that if he were not called to support the war effort, he would likely grow old holding obscure posts with perfunctory duties. The best positions would doubtlessly be reserved for those who distinguished themselves during the war. "They would have fame; he would have slippers and old age on the porch at Arlington."[39] He would become merely another old, forgotten army officer.

For three months he waited, hope growing dimmer every day. Then finally, on August 19, 1846, Lee received the long-anticipated order to report to Brigadier General John E. Wool in San Antonio (then called San Antonio de Bexar), Texas, for duty in Mexico. Lee arrived in Texas a month and two days later. His life was to be changed forever.

Lee quickly distinguished himself in Mexico, as he had in all other assignments. He instructed the soldiers on the building of bridges and the repairing of roads, while excelling in reconnaissance. It was during this time that Lee performed what General Scott would later call "the greatest feat of physical and moral courage performed by any individual" during the war.

It happened just before the battle of Contreras. Scott had learned by means of Lee's reconnaissance that the Mexican forces could be attacked from the rear, but this position could only be obtained by crossing a pathless and rugged volcanic field called the "Pedregal." The field was filled with blocks of lava—with razor sharp edges jutting up and out of the ground—as well as crevasses in which a man could be mortally injured. Under the best of conditions it was a dangerous task to cross this land.

Scott determined to carry out the dangerous movement and Lee and his engineers led the 3,300 men across the treacherous ground. The painful march brought the division to the decisive point by nightfall, and a council was held to determine the next movement. The council arrived at its decision around nine o'clock and desired to communicate the plans to General Scott, necessitating a recrossing of the Pedregal. A storm was raging and the darkness would be impenetrable—apart from lightning flashes. Crossing the Pedregal under such conditions seemed an insurmountable obstacle. Lee did not hesitate. When the desire to communicate with Scott was mentioned, he volunteered to take the message, even though he had only crossed that part of the Pedregal once and the weather conditions and the darkness would make landmarks unrecognizable.

Lee and his companions literally felt their way across the treacherous and uneven field. When they reached Scott's headquarters at Zacatepec, they learned to their dismay that the general had returned to San Augustin. Though exhausted, Lee proceeded on to San Augustin with his message. Then, in his third journey in less than twenty-four hours, he accompanied an injured officer—General David Twiggs—back across the Pedregal before he was finally able to rest. It was, all in all, an amazing performance.

In February, 1847, General Scott took Lee into his small circle of advisors, which he called his "little cabinet." As a result of the privilege of participating in Scott's "cabinet" meetings, Lee gained invaluable ideas about strategy and warfare. But the benefit was mutual. Jefferson Davis, who was also part of the army at that time, later wrote, "History will record, as Scott himself nobly admitted, that Lee was Scott's right arm in Mexico."

In March, General Scott determined to move inland, capturing Vera Cruz. Vera Cruz was a walled city surrounded by natural and man-made barriers. To capture it was no easy proposition. Should the city be stormed or should it be taken by siege? The plan settled upon by the "little cabinet" was to batter the walls with artillery until a breach was made, and then to enter the city. With the crucial aid of Lee's reconnaissance once again, a decision was made to move the heavier ship's artillery to shore to use against the walls. The city was reduced by the end of the month.

Scott had hoped that the capture of Vera Cruz would bring about a willingness on the part of the Mexican government to enter into peace negotiations. This was not to be, and when it became plain that the Mexicans had determined to continue their resistance, Scott boldly determined to advance to Mexico City.

Victory was achieved at Cerro Gordo on April seventeenth and eighteenth. The next day the army entered the city of Jalapa, where General Scott set up headquarters and awaited reinforcements before going on to Mexico City. They waited none too patiently until August 7th, when (future president) Franklin Pierce arrived with 2,500 men. The American force now numbered around 10,700. Scott decided to abandon his lines of supply and to live off the country while searching for Santa Anna and heading for the capital. It was a risk that paid off handsomely. Mexico City fell in September of 1847. The Treaty of Guadalupe Hidalgo ended hostilities on February 2, 1848.

During this last stage of the campaign, Lee again distinguished himself as a superior soldier. His service was unparalleled. He had volunteered for dangerous service, gained indispensable information by reconnaissance, fought fearlessly, and through it all, remained aloof from the in-fighting and jealousies that at times broke out among the officers. His service won the admiration of all, but especially of the commanding general. According to E. D. Keyes, a general who was close to Scott, the commander had an "almost idolatrous fancy for Lee, whose military genius he estimated far above that of any other officer of the army." Scott pronounced Lee the "very best soldier [he] ever saw in the field," and he would later remark that if the nation could preserve the life of Robert E. Lee, it would be cheap, even if it cost five million dollars per year.[40]

This judgment is all the more impressive when one remembers that among the men who fought in the American force were some of the most gifted soldiers in this country's history. The names of some would later become household words: P. G. T. Beauregard, George B. McClellan, J. B. Magruder, Thomas Jonathan "Stonewall" Jackson, Joseph E. Johnston, and many more. Indeed, except for John Pope, every one of the commanders who would later lead the Army of the Potomac for the United States, and many of the Southern officers, served in the Mexican War under Scott.

But much more important for Lee's future than General Scott's approbation were the lessons learned from Scott in the Mexican War. It was here Lee learned the value of "audacity," of taking a daring course when the advantage is yours. In Mexico, the Americans fought a distinctly inferior force. Lee would later determine that this same quality could be a tremendous advantage when facing a superior foe as well.

Scott was a careful planner but did not seek to plan in detail. His concern was to set the overall plan, to acquaint his corps commanders thoroughly with that plan, and to insure that the troops arrived at the right place at the right time. The details of the battle, however, were left to his field commanders. The demands of battle require officers who are able to make adjustments to fit the changing situations facing their men. It was Scott's view that officers ought to be trusted in this regard rather than to be locked into a detailed plan that pretends to anticipate all the vicissitudes of the battlefield. Lee would later follow this same procedure, some would say to the injury of the Southern forces.

Further, Lee learned the value of good, accurate information, the significance of communication, and the importance of fortification to the forming and execution of strategy. Each of these factors played a vital role in every battle Lee witnessed in Mexico, and they would all play an important role in his battle strategy in the future.

By 1848, Lee had been promoted to the rank of major, then lieutenant colonel, and finally colonel "by brevet"—the latter awarded for his extraordinary valor. Lee had become a genuine hero, like his father before him. But there was nothing of the braggart in him. If anything, his native reserve had deepened into an even more serious humility. In Mexico he had come face to face with death and had come away a changed man. He became more aware of his own sins and failures as a man before God and in his earthly responsibilities. Writing to his wife on April 25, 1847, he stated:

> *This morning I attended the Episcopal service within the fort…The minister was a Mr. McCarty, the chaplain of the Second Brigade, First Division. Many officers and soldiers were*

> *grouped around. I endeavored to give thanks to*
> *our Heavenly Father for all his mercies to me,*
> *for his preservation of me through all the dan-*
> *gers I have passed, and all the blessings which*
> *he has bestowed upon me, for I know I fall far*
> *short of my obligations.*[41]

Battle has a way of clarifying a man's vision. The things that are truly important are seen in high relief against those things that are often viewed as vital but which are, in reality, trivial. It was during one of the battles in the Mexican War that Lee thought of his children and of his responsibility as a father to protect and care for them. In a letter to Custis, his eldest son, he wrote,

> *I thought of you, my dear Custis, on the 18th in*
> *the battle [of Cerro Gordo], and wondered, when*
> *the musket balls and grape were whistling over*
> *my head in a perfect shower, where I could put*
> *you, if with me, to be safe. I was truly thankful*
> *that you were at school, I hope learning to be*
> *good and wise. You have no idea what a*
> *horrible sight a battlefield is.*[42]

Lee returned home at the end of June to a joyful reception from his family. His youngest son, Robert, had insisted upon wearing what he considered his most handsome suit—a blue gown dotted with white diamonds—for this special occasion. There were other friends present for the homecoming as well, and when the brevet colonel arrived, all greeted him warmly. After a few moments, Lee began asking for his youngest son. "Where is my little boy?" he exclaimed. Seeing a smartly-dressed child who looked about the age of Robert, he took him up in his arms and began smothering him with kisses. There was a shout of laughter from the other children and a sound of distress from one little boy in particular. The Colonel had picked up not his youngest son, but the child of Armistead Lippit, a family friend who was visiting. Having been away from his family for almost two years, Lee had not recognized his own son.[43]

Lee had changed as well. Flecks of grey now salted his hair and lines creased his formerly youthful face and brow. The children stared at him, seeking to reconcile the vision they had had of him while he was away with the reality of his presence with them now. Lee was perfectly happy, however, as a letter to his brother demonstrates.

> *Here I am once again, my dear Smith, perfectly surrounded by Mary and her precious children, who seem to devote themselves to staring at the furrows in my face and the white hairs in my head. It is not surprising that I am hardly recognizable to some of the young ones around me and perfectly unknown to the youngest. But some of the older ones gaze with astonishment and wonder at me, and seem at a loss to reconcile what they see and what was pictured in their imaginations. I find them, too, much grown, and all well, and I have much cause of thankfulness and gratitude to the good God who has once more united us.*[44]

Superintendent at West Point

*Hold to your purity and virtue. They will sustain
you in every calamity.*

–R. E. Lee

*I*n September of 1848, after brief duty in Washington,
Lee was assigned to Baltimore to supervise the
building of a new fort that was needed to secure the harbor
defenses. Although construction was actually delayed until
the new year, by the following September, Lee was well settled into the routine of the work.

Though there were the usual frustrations in his work, the
time in Baltimore was a happy one for Lee. He was able to
have his family with him and they all enjoyed meeting new
friends. Everyone—the girls especially—delighted in the
larger social circles the change of scene afforded.

All went along normally until the spring of 1852. In May,
Lee received orders to transfer to West Point and take over
superintendency of the military academy. Lee protested that
he did not believe himself qualified for such an appointment,

but his protest had no effect upon his superiors. His ability was held in such high esteem that his own humble judgment of his gifts was insufficient to persuade them that his appointment was a mistake. The orders were finalized and the Lee family set out for West Point on August 23.

He little suspected it, but Robert E. Lee had done his last service in the Engineer Corps of the United States Army. On September 1, 1852, he became the ninth superintendent of the United States Military Academy.

Lee never viewed his position as superintendent as purely administrative. He was keenly, even painfully, aware of his role as an example and leader to the young men. It was his job not merely to see to the efficient running of the academy, but also to be an inspiration and encouragement to the cadets to be not only good soldiers, but men of integrity and true gentlemen.

This was a particular burden because of the condition of the cadets themselves. In recent years, many young men had been sent to the academy ill prepared. Discipline had been hampered by politics. Young men from more prominent families had been restored to duty after they had been justly dismissed. The curriculum was too crowded, yet some important subjects received no attention at all. The job also involved a number of things that were irksome to Lee—among them, paperwork and correspondence.

But Lee faithfully gave himself to the task. His first step was openly to identify himself with the living God and His Church. Lee, primarily because of his mother's faithful instruction and example, had always felt a dependence upon God. He had been baptized in the Episcopal church, catechized by Reverend William Meade, and had always faithfully attended worship. However, he had never been confirmed. His war experience and his view of God's goodness to him and his family impressed upon him the need to confess the faith that was in him. Thus, on July 17, 1853, with his two daughters, he was confirmed. To Lee it was a vow never to be broken. If God had been so gracious to him, he must live faithfully for Him.

There was no spectacular "conversion" experience for Lee. He had, rather, an increasingly strong attraction to the Savior whom he had known of from his youth. From the time of his confirmation, his faith and devotion to Christ became more overt and increasingly the dominant aspect of his life.

Lee was beloved and respected by the young men of the academy. They knew him to be just and dreaded having to appear in his presence to answer for misconduct. Lee confessed to Jefferson Davis, the new secretary of war and his superior at West Point, that the cadets "did exceedingly worry him." There are quite a few incidents that illustrate these "worries" and also testify to the effect Lee had upon the youth under his charge.

Lee was once called upon to deal with an eccentric young man his comrades called "Curly." He almost completely disdained all subjects he deemed boring, but in the subject of "drawing" he stood first in his class. Lee sought to deal patiently with the young man, out of consideration for the appeals of his Scots mother, but to no avail. "Curly" began to pile up demerits and was soon dismissed from West Point. When an appeal of his dismissal was denied, "Curly" was forced to return home. The young man's name was James McNeil Whistler and his famous portrait of his patient mother would later be prized as one of the finest examples of American art. In spite of his expulsion, Whistler always spoke highly of both Lee and the academy.[45]

Lee was just but never unreasonable. Once there was an incident involving Cadet Archibald Gracie Jr. of New York.

Gracie possessed a powerful frame and loved to aggravate smaller cadets during dress parade. He succeeded one day in provoking Wharton Green, who flew into him and started a furious fight. Gracie was on the losing end of the battle (and it was getting worse by the minute) when a professor stopped the fight and demanded Gracie's name. While the professor was taking this down, Green calmly walked away from the scene. When the instructor asked for the name of his companion in battle, Gracie refused to give Green's name, protesting that he was "no informer."

Gracie was put under arrest and the whole affair was reported to Superintendent Lee. The next morning, as Lee was perusing the reports, Cadet Green entered his office. "Colonel Lee, Mr. Gracie was yesterday reported for fighting on the parade ground, and the 'other fellow' was not."

"Yes sir," replied Lee. "And I presume you are 'the other fellow'?"

"I am, sir," said Green, "and I wish to submit the case in full for your consideration. Don't you think it very hard on him, Colonel, after getting the worse of the fracas, to have to take all of the penalty?"

"Admitted," said Lee. "What then?"

"Simply this, sir. Whatever punishment is meted out to him, I insist on having the same given to me."

"The offense entails a heavy penalty."

"I am aware of the fact, Colonel, but Mr. Gracie is not entitled to a monopoly of it."

At this, Lee smiled. "No sir; you will get neither report nor penalty for this and neither will Mr. Gracie get the latter. I will cancel the report. Don't you think, Mr. Green, that it is better for brothers to dwell together in peace and harmony?"

"Yes, Colonel, and if we were all like you, it would be an easy thing to do."[46]

Both Green and Gracie honored the memory of their noble superintendent, who was able to show both justice and mercy.

Eleven years later, while in the horrifying trenches around Petersburg, Lee saw Mr. Gracie once again. Desiring to see the disposition of the enemy, and momentarily forgetting the fact that sharpshooters were targeting any man who exposed any part of his body above the trenches, Lee stepped up on the "firestep" in order to get a better view. Before the sharpshooters could fire, a young man jumped up between General Lee and the enemy rifles to protect him. His name was Archibald Gracie.

"Why Gracie, you will certainly be killed," Lee protested.

"It is better, General, that I should be killed than you. When you get down, I will," Gracie replied. At this, Lee smiled and stepped down.[47]

The interest Lee took in the training of these young men is remarkable. He knew them all personally. If a cadet was negligent in writing home, Lee wanted to know the cause. In the case of illness, the superintendent made sure the family was promptly notified. On those rare occasions of tragedy, it was Lee who wrote the sympathetic note of condolence. He kept close tabs on those men who were careless and struggling academically, calling them to his office for an early morning session of fatherly admonition and encouragement. In all this, Lee learned valuable lessons in motivation and leadership of the young men who would in a short time be under his command in far more trying circumstances.

It was also during this time that Lee had the rare opportunity to study. He read widely and copiously, and his studies ranged from books on grammar, geography, architecture, military law, and the science of warfare to biographies and histories. The volumes most frequently consulted were those dealing with Napoleon's Italian campaign of 1796 and the American War of Independence.

Lee spent two and a half years at West Point, carrying the cadets on his heart and spending many hours considering how he might best promote their education and training. On April 12, 1855, he received orders to go to Louisville, Kentucky, to take command of the new 2nd Cavalry, whose colonel was not able to report for duty. It was the kind of service needful for the army, but dreaded by most men because of its hard, unpleasant, and lonely character. Lee obeyed without complaint.

While stationed in Kentucky, Lee was often called upon to serve on military courts martial. Because of his good sense and fair-mindedness, he was a natural choice. This duty often required him to travel great distances (he served on courts from Kansas to Pennsylvania before being transferred with his unit to Texas) and was wearisome and depressing for him. In this duty, too, however, Lee profited. He gained insight about how men who are small-minded or who possess weak characters often respond to army life, and why they fall into temptations and lapses of duty. The insight thus gained served him well later.

When through the deep waters I call thee to go,
The rivers of woe shall not thee overflow;
For I will be with thee thy troubles to bless,
And sanctify to thee thy deepest distress.

Stanza 3
How Firm A Foundation

DAYS OF SORROW

Misfortune nobly borne is good fortune.

–One of Lee's favorite sayings,
from *The Meditations of Marcus Aurelius*

*L*ife rolled on with the uneventful duty in Texas until
October of 1857. On October 21, news reached Lee
that his father-in-law had died at Arlington on October 10.
George Washington Parke Custis was seventy-seven at his
death. He had survived his wife by almost four-and-a-half
years. To Mrs. Lee, bedridden with illness, was now added the
burden of grief. No male member of the family was home to
take care of the necessary business. Hence, it was necessary
for Lee to take a leave of absence and return home.

Lee reached Arlington on November 11, and it was perhaps the saddest of all his homecomings. The greatest shock
of all was the condition in which he found his wife. Mrs. Lee
had been in fairly good health when he had left home in
1856. She had told him of her illness, but had not told him
how serious it was. Arthritis had almost totally incapacitated

her right hand and arm and was slowly spreading through the rest of her body. She was now barely able to move around the house.

Lee was the only executor qualified to administer Mr. Custis' will, and this too brought troubles. His father-in-law had left over $10,000 in debts and almost no money with which to operate Arlington, which had, in recent years, become greatly dilapidated. The amount of work that needed to be done coupled with the financial tangle forced Lee to request an extension of his leave to December of 1858. Lee the soldier became Lee the farmer.

The work at Arlington was as frustrating as it was difficult, and Lee made progress slowly. His wife's physical condition improved somewhat, but elsewhere there was little about which to be encouraged. Lee wrote to his son Rooney, "I am getting along as usual, trying to get a little work done and to mend up some things. I succeed very badly." [48]

As the fall of 1858 wore on, Lee realized that he was still not in a position to leave. Much work still remained on the farm and Mr. Custis' will had yet to be probated. Accordingly, he requested an additional year of leave, which was granted.

The spring of 1859 brought more disheartening news. The court again adjourned without addressing the Custis will, financial pressure was mounting, the girls were suffering from a malady and needed care, and on top of all, Mrs. Lee's condition was again as bad as it had been when he had returned from Texas. Lee kept up a cheerful appearance but he was greatly burdened. "I have no enjoyment in life now but what I derive from my children." [49]

The morning of October 17, 1859, brought an abrupt change to the routine at Arlington. Lieutenant J. E. B. Stuart arrived with an order for Lee to report immediately to the secretary of war. A mysterious insurrection had taken place at

Harper's Ferry, Virginia. Trains had been stopped, firing had been heard, and the rumor was that a number of strangers had entered the town to incite a slave uprising. Troops had been ordered to Harper's Ferry from Fort Monroe, a detachment of marines had been sent from Washington, a group of Maryland militiamen had volunteered their services, and Lee was ordered to take command of them all.

The "insurrection" was, of course, the famous raid on Harper's Ferry by John Brown, the radical abolitionist and terrorist. He and his sons were fanatically devoted to the cause of abolitionism. He did not believe in non-violent opposition, however. Taking as his motto "Without shedding of blood there is no remission of sin" (Hebrews 9:22), Brown ignored the fact that the passage refers to Christ's sacrifice and instead determined that it gave him a license to go on a murderous rampage to promote the crusade against slavery. Financed by six wealthy Unitarians (the so-called "Secret Six"), he had already made bloody raids in Kansas. His targets were not always slave owners; indeed, the first victims of Brown's madness had been non-slaveholders whom Brown had killed in cold blood, dragging them from their beds in the middle of the night. His purpose was not to bring vengeance but to promote terror. Now he had come South to provoke what he hoped would be a bloody slave rebellion.

Early on Sunday morning, October 16, 1859, Brown led a small contingent of twenty-one men—sixteen white and five black—into Harper's Ferry to capture the federal arsenal. Having captured a number of prominent citizens as hostages (among them, Lewis W. Washington, grandnephew to the father of our country), they were planning to hold out until news of the venture inspired an uprising among the slaves in the area. Brown assumed that when the slaves heard of his exploits, they would rush to his aid, and, when they came, he would arm them with guns and begin the great campaign of liberation throughout the South.

At one A.M. on October 17, the express train from Baltimore stopped at Harper's Ferry to exchange passengers. The conductor and engineer, hearing a report that the tracks were blocked, walked down the track and were driven back by shots from Brown and his men. Then Haywood Shepherd, the Negro baggage master at Harper's Ferry, ventured out and was hit and mortally wounded by one of the bullets. Thus, ironically, the first casualty of John Brown's "crusade for freedom" was a free black man.[50] By the time Lee arrived from Washington—at eleven P.M.—Brown and his men had taken over the railroad's engine house on the edge of town, not far from the river.

Lee surrounded the engine house and decided on his plan. He would send Lieutenant Stuart up to the engine house with a proposal for surrender. If Brown refused, Stuart was immediately to give a signal to the troops to storm the house and attack the insurgents with bayonets. Lee specified that no shots were to be fired, lest the hostages be injured.

The next day, on October 18, at seven o'clock in the morning, Stuart advanced under a flag of truce and was met at the door by an old man whom he immediately recognized as John Brown. Stuart read Lee's terms. Brown began demanding concessions and advanced a counter proposal. Before Stuart could tell "Ossawatomie" Brown that there would be no consideration given to other terms, one of the hostages, hearing the discussion, cried out, "Never mind us, fire!" It was the voice of Lewis Washington. Lee, recognizing the voice, replied quietly, "The old revolutionary blood does tell!"[51]

After a few more minutes of this fruitless exchange, Stuart stepped back and gave the signal to the troops to storm the engine house. Sledge hammers had no effect upon the door. A ladder lying nearby was then used as a battering ram and a hole was made in the door, through which Lieutenant Israel Green stepped into the house. Major W. W. Russell followed him. The next man who entered—a private—was shot and mortally wounded. The fourth was struck in the face by another bullet. The entire detachment of twelve men was soon inside and the operation was over only three minutes after Stuart's signal.

Four of Brown's men were dead from wounds received the previous day. One more lay dying, and Brown himself had been seriously wounded by Green. All of the hostages were uninjured. Colonel Washington, however, refused to come out of the house until he was brought a pair of gloves to hide his dirty hands.[52]

This event did not affect Lee's view of the dispute over slavery. He had already seen enough to know that the radicals in the North would stop at nothing in their efforts to bring about social revolution in the South. What was surprising, however, was the reaction of the North to the deeds and execution of John Brown. Lee and the rest of the South were shocked to see this murderer and revolutionary lionized by members of the church, the press, and the intelligentsia.

Rather than receiving deserved condemnation, Brown was portrayed as a martyr to a holy cause. Across the North church bells tolled; minute guns fired salutes; ministers preached laudatory sermons; and thousands grieved in silent memorial to this "holy victim" to liberty's cause. Theodore Parker, a prominent Unitarian minister, pronounced Brown "not only a martyr...but a saint." A member of the clergy in Roxbury, Massachusetts, declared that Brown had made the word treason "holy in the American language." Henry David Thoreau pronounced Brown "a crucified hero" and Ralph Waldo Emerson declared that Brown would "make the gallows as glorious as the cross."

Henry Wadsworth Longfellow wrote in his diary that the day of Brown's execution would be "the date of a new Revolution, quite as much needed as the old one." Indeed, when Virginians hanged John Brown, he said, they were "sowing the wind to reap the whirlwind, which will come soon."[53]

Charles Eliot Norton of Harvard stated, "I have seen nothing like it." Few had. The canonization of John Brown was a turning point in American history. Never before had lawlessness been praised or terrorism sanctified. More than a few wondered what would be the result. Lee believed the adulation of Brown to be a portent of much evil to come. He was right.

SECESSION

A Union that can only be maintained by swords and bayonets, and in which strife and civil war are to take the place of brotherly love and kindness, has no charm for me.

–R. E. Lee

*J*ohn Brown's raid on Harper's Ferry sent shock waves through the South. The alarm increased as it became known that Brown had been financed by six wealthy and prominent Northerners.[54] The election of 1860 became the chief indication to many in the South of what the future would hold for them in the old union.

Abraham Lincoln was the presidential nominee of the Republicans, now styled throughout the South (and indeed, the entire nation) as "Black Republicans" for their sympathy with the abolitionists. The Democratic party had split over the issue of slavery. Meeting in Charleston, South Carolina, the Southerners refused to remain in the convention when an anti-slavery plank was added to the platform over their objections.

With the Southern delegates gone, Stephen Douglas, the favorite for the nomination, could not get enough votes to gain the nomination. The convention took fifty-eight ballots in an attempt to agree upon a nominee, but all failed to give a majority to one man. It was thus with great anger and frustration that the convention adjourned to reconvene six weeks later in Baltimore.

In Baltimore, the Northern delegates were angry and the Southern men were equally belligerent. When the Northerners again refused the South's request to include a plank supporting the right of Southerners to take their slaves into the new territories, the Southerners again walked out of the convention. The latter, along with delegates from the upper South, organized their own convention and nominated John C. Breckenridge as their candidate. The "loyalists" nominated Douglas and each side went home blaming the other for the certain defeat that awaited them in the presidential election.

Meanwhile, the old Whig party—under the name of the Constitutional Union Party—decided to run its own candidate, nominating the Tennessee planter John Bell for president and Edward Everett of Massachusetts for vice-president. Ignoring the dispute over slavery, the Whigs adopted the resolution that they would "recognize no political principle other than *the Constitution...the Union...and the Enforcement of the Laws.*"[55] The Whig strategy was to deny an electoral victory to Lincoln by winning the states in the upper South and taking enough of the lower North to deny Lincoln a majority in the electoral college. It was a bad strategy.

Lee, who had never paid much attention to national politics, feared the consequences of a Lincoln victory and believed that Judge Douglas should withdraw from the race and throw his support to Breckenridge. He had no delusions that this would happen, however. He wrote, "Politicians I fear are too selfish to become martyrs." [56]

Lee had good reasons for his apprehensions. The South, even prior to 1860, had begun to speak of secession from the Union. Just as New England states had threatened secession no fewer than five times prior to 1860 over federal policies, so the same rumblings began in the South. Secession was viewed as the only alternative that could preserve the integrity and freedom of the individual states. As the election drew near, this alternative seemed all the more attractive. A North Carolina congressman stated, "No other 'overt act' can so imperatively demand resistance on our part as the simple election of their candidate." [57]

The four-way race divided the vote enough for Lincoln to win with only forty per cent of the popular vote. Only John Quincy Adams had gained a lower percentage of the popular vote and still achieved victory in a general election. Lincoln was a truly regional president: his name did not even appear on the ballot in the ten states of the lower South. Even in the North, he was viewed as the representative of a revolutionary faction. He was not the choice of the majority, but in the sometimes strange world of presidential politics, he was the winner.

The New Orleans Delta stated that no one could any longer be deceived by the claims of the Republicans to be a moderate party: "It is, in fact, essentially a revolutionary party." [58] Charles Francis Adams, whose father and grandfather had been defeated in their presidential bids by Southern slaveholders, wrote, "The great revolution has actually taken place...The country has once and for all thrown off the domination of the Slaveholders." [59]

The election of Lincoln proved the last straw for the South. On December 20, 1860, the South Carolina legislature passed an ordinance of secession "dissolving the union now subsisting between South Carolina and other States." This began the exodus from the Union of the so-called "Cotton States." Mississippi followed on January 9, 1861. Florida left the Union the next day and Alabama the next, on January 11. Eight days later, Georgia seceded. Louisiana withdrew on January 26 and Texas on February 1.

At first, Lee had little sympathy for the states who threatened and then carried out this action. Though he saw plainly the inequities in the Northern policies with regard to the South, he loved the Union and was loth to see it torn apart. He wrote, in December of 1860, "Feeling the aggressions of the North, resenting their denial of the equal rights of our citizens to the common territory of the commonwealth, etc., I am not pleased with the course of the 'Cotton States,' as they call themselves." [60]

In January, 1861, he wrote to his son Custis,

> *As an American citizen, I take great pride in my country, her prosperity and institutions, and would defend any State if her rights were invaded. But I can anticipate no greater calamity for the country than a dissolution of the Union.*[61]

He had little sympathy with secession at this time:

> *Secession is nothing but revolution. The framers of our Constitution never exhausted so much labor, wisdom and forbearance in its formation, and surrounded it with so many guards and securities, if it was intended to be broken by every member of the Confederacy at will...It is idle to talk of secession.*[62]

Yet with all his love for the Union, he had no desire to defend a union held together by force. "Still, a Union that can only be maintained by swords and bayonets, and in which strife and civil war are to take the place of brotherly love and kindness, has no charm for me." His undying allegiance was with his state: "If the Union is dissolved, and the Government disrupted, I shall return to my native State and share the miseries of my people, and save in defense will draw my sword on none."[63]

Lee's views, as recorded above, deserve some comment. It is plain that prior to the war, Lee did not view secession as a right of the states. Later, this view would change decidedly: with the experience of war, after continued discussion with other men about the constitutional rights of the states, and upon his own reflection, Lee came to believe that the actions of the Southern states were thoroughly justified, and he fully embraced the Southern constitutional argument. In 1866, he would write to Chauncey Burr, the great constitutional scholar: "All that the South has ever desired was that the union, as established by our forefathers, should be preserved; and that the government, as originally organized, should be administered in purity and truth."[64]

Also, it was Lee's conviction that no state should be forced to remain in the Union. He believed that the union was basically voluntary and could not rightly be held together by force. This was the common view of the day for both North and South. President Buchanan himself held an identical view, as did the famous Northern newspaperman, Horace Greeley. Lee was very fearful that the actions of the Lincoln government to preserve the Union would end in the destruction of liberty. In a letter to his friend A.G. Brackett, who was later to be a colonel in the Southern army, he stated: "I fear the liberties of our country will be buried in the tomb of a great nation."[65]

Finally, to understand Lee's convictions at this time, it is important to know that he believed quite clearly that his first allegiance was not to the nation but to his state. Prior to the war, it was commonplace for individuals to regard themselves first as citizens of their particular states, and only secondarily as citizens of the United States. For most, your state *was* your "country." The outcome of the war diminished the power of the states and eradicated the sense of allegiance to one's state so thoroughly that today this allegiance is utterly foreign to most Americans. Yet for Lee, Virginia was his "home country." When his country left the Union, he had no choice but to follow.

After Lee had received orders to come to Washington, he encountered one of his officers, Captain George B. Cosby, at a spring where he had stopped for dinner (what Northerners call "lunch"). As they conversed, Captain Cosby offered his opinion that Lee was being called back to Washington to confer with the leaders about a campaign against the South. Lee said that he feared Cosby was right and that if he was, Lee would resign his position. Cosby wrote,

> *He further said that he had confidence that Virginia would not act on impulse, but would act as she had in the past, and would exhaust every means consistent with honor to avert civil war. That, if she failed and determined to secede, he would offer her his services. That he had ever been taught that his first allegiance was due his mother State; that he fervently hoped that some agreement would be reached to avert such a terrible war... but under no circumstance could he ever bare his sword against Virginia's sons. As he spoke his emotion*

brought tears to his eyes, and he turned away
to avoid showing this emotion which was
greater than he afterwards showed when he lost
or won some great battle.[66]

Robert E. Lee had a great love for the Union, but he always remembered that he had been a Virginian long before he had become a soldier.

THE DECISION

Lee is the greatest military genius in America.
                                        –General Winfield Scott

*L*ee was still on duty in Texas when, on February 1, 1861, the Texas legislature voted to secede from the Union. Three days later, Virginia elected delegates to a convention for the purpose of considering secession. Of the delegates elected, those who opposed secession outnumbered those who favored it by a two to one margin. The same day, at the request of Virginia, a peace conference met in Washington in an effort to allay the tensions which were rising in both the North and the South.

When orders came for Lee to report to the general in chief in Washington, hope still remained that war would be avoided. Lee was to be in Washington by April 1.

What exactly Winfield Scott and Robert Lee discussed for three hours in this meeting has never been fully revealed. It was no secret that General Scott had the highest opinion of Lee's ability as an officer. Many have concluded that General

Scott offered Lee command of the Union forces should war come and Lee remain loyal to the Union. In later years, a relative of Mrs. Lee stated that Mrs. Lee herself believed that such an offer had been made during this meeting. Charles Anderson also related a conversation he had had with General Scott in which the general confirmed that he was authorized to offer Lee command of the armies of the United States. Lee, however, denied that he and General Scott discussed this.

Lee *was* offered the command of the Northern forces, though it did not come through General Scott. Lee affirmed in a letter to Reverdy Johnson, dated February 25, 1868, that indeed he had been offered command from President Lincoln himself, through the intermediary of Mr. Francis Preston Blair. Lee states,

> *I never intimated to any one that I desired the command of the United States Army; nor did I ever have a conversation with but one gentleman, Mr. Francis Preston Blair, on the subject, which was at his invitation, and, as I understood, at the instance of President Lincoln.*[67]

This meeting with Blair took place on April 18, 1861, in the Blair family home across the street from the War and Navy Building on Pennsylvania Avenue. Blair had received authorization from President Lincoln to speak to Lee on the subject of taking command of the Union forces. Here was the opportunity of a lifetime. Lee was offered command of an army of almost 100,000 men, with the full support of the government and the assistance of some of the ablest military men in the country, plus the rank of major-general. It was enough to make even the most principled of men waver. But Lee apparently never hesitated:

After listening to his remarks, I declined the
offer he made me, to take command of the
army that was to be brought into the field; stat-
ing, as candidly and as courteously as I could,
that, though opposed to secession and deprecat-
ing war, I could take no part in an invasion of
the Southern States.[68]

Long before this, Lee had decided what duty required of him, and the allure of supreme command did not tempt him to change what under more calm circumstances he had come to understand was the path of honor. Allegiance to the nation could never take precedence over allegiance to one's native state. The states, as the basic political units in this country, both pre-dated and created the Union. State loyalty was demanded first and last. Blair tried in vain to persuade Lee otherwise, but to no avail.

Lee immediately went to General Scott's office to inform him of the offer and to give him his reply: "I went directly from the interview with Mr. Blair to the office of General Scott; told him of the proposition that had been made to me, and my decision."[69] Scott replied, "Lee, you have made the greatest mistake of your life; but I feared it would be so."[70] Scott went on to say that it was his opinion that Lee should resign his position in the army.

The next morning, April 19, while Lee was on business in Alexandria, the news came that Virginia had seceded. It was confirmed by the Washington papers that evening. The decision had been made and Lee now had but one thing to do. The morning of April 20, Lee determined to convey his decision to the army. Downstairs, Mary Lee heard her husband pacing in his room and, she thought, falling on his knees in prayer. In a brief note to Simon Cameron, the secretary of war, Lee wrote out his resignation:

Arlington, Virginia (Washington City P.O.)
20 April 1861.
Hon. Simon Cameron
Secty of War

Sir:
I have the honor to tender the resignation of
my commission as Colonel of the
1st Regt. Of Cavalry.

Very resp'y Your Obedient Servant.
R. E. Lee
Col 1st Cav'y.

There was no rancor, no bitterness, and no resentment, but there was pain. Lee had no doubt about where his rightful allegiance lay, but he had no desire to fight against the flag he had served for so many years. Writing to General Scott on the same day, he stated his difficulty in resigning from a service to which he had devoted, in his words, "all the best years of my life and all the ability I possess." [71]

When he came downstairs, he calmly said to his wife, "Well, Mary, the question is settled. Here is my letter of resignation and a letter I have written to General Scott." Mary Lee was not surprised. She, too, understood the call of duty. A man's first obligation is always to his home, family, and countrymen. Robert E. Lee loved America, but he was first and foremost a Virginian.

Before the day closed, Lee took up the pen to write one more letter, this time to his sister:

With all my devotion to the Union and the feel-
ing of loyalty and duty of an American citizen,
I have not been able to make up my mind to
raise my hand against my relatives, my chil-
dren, my home. I have therefore resigned my
commission in the Army, and save in defense of
my native state, with the sincere hope that my
poor services may never be needed, I hope I
may never be called on to draw my sword.[72]

The Call of the South

I did only what my duty demanded. I could have
taken no other course without dishonor.

–R. E. Lee

Lee was not one who rejoiced over secession and the prospects of war, as did so many in the South. He was not so foolish. He understood that if the Union forces came against the South it would mean unthinkable devastation and bloodshed. The overwhelming force and matériel the Union could bring against the South would make war a most difficult prospect for the new Confederate nation. He knew the projections for a short war were overly optimistic. He wrote to Mrs. Lee, "The war may last ten years."(73)

In such circumstances a man can only do what he judges to be right and trust God for the results. It was preeminently his trust in God that upheld him now. He would write to his old friend, Reverend Cornelius Walker,

I shall need all your good wishes and all your prayers for strength and guidance in the struggle in which we are engaged and earnestly and humbly look for help to Him alone who can save us, and who has permitted the dire calamity of this fratricidal war to impend over us. If we are not worthy that it should pass from us, may He in His great mercy shield us from its dire effects and save us from the calamity our sins have produced.[74]

Lee would have had little time for celebration even if he had been so inclined. On Sunday, April 21, the day after his resignation, he was met outside his church after the worship service by three men, who conveyed to Lee the news that he would be soon called to Richmond to confer with the governor. The official message came that evening. Lee set out for Richmond the next morning.

When he left Arlington on the morning of April 22, it probably never entered his thoughts that he would not set foot in that stately mansion again. He was fifty-four years old, stood a little over five feet seven inches, and weighed around 170 pounds. As far as we know he had suffered only one illness—and that not a serious one—in the whole of his life up to that time. He had been trained in the school of experience as well as in the classroom. He was fit to lead and the time had come.

The governor, at the recommendation of his advisory council, offered Lee the appointment of commander of the military and naval forces of Virginia with the rank of major-general. Lee accepted and the Virginia convention of delegates approved the appointment. On the 23rd of April, Lee was officially presented to the convention at the capitol to acknowledge his appointment. Lee was abashed at the reception he was given and, after accepting the appointment, replied, "I would have much preferred had your choice fallen on an abler man. Trusting in Almighty God, an approving conscience, and the aid of my fellow-citizens, I devote myself to the service of my native State, in whose behalf alone will I ever draw my sword."[75] That same day, Lee opened a temporary office in the Richmond post office.

Preparing a people for war is not easy under the best of circumstances. This is especially so when the people are foolishly overconfident. The problems facing Virginia were those facing the entire Confederacy: the preparation of a navy to combat the North's dominant sea-power; the organization, training, mobilization, and disposition of troops; the production of weapons and ammunition; the securing of competent officers; the organization of general staff; and many other problems associated with preparing to face a vastly superior foe.

The world had changed greatly since the last major war in the previous century. Troops could be moved more than five times as rapidly as a century earlier. Telegraphic communications had revolutionized the transmission of information. Weapons were far more accurate and, consequently, far more deadly. In a very real sense, the coming war would mark the transition to modern warfare. The old world was coming to a close.

When Virginia by popular vote ratified the Ordinance of Secession, Lee became a general in the Confederate States of America and was assigned to assist President Jefferson Davis. At this time the Confederacy was in the process of moving its capitol from Montgomery, Alabama, to Richmond, Virginia. With secession, all the Virginia forces and resources were delivered over to the Confederate government. Lee had done a remarkable job. The entire mobilization had taken less than eight weeks.

He had done all he could do to prepare his people for war. Now they had nothing left to do but to commit themselves into the hands of God. "In God alone must be our trust," he wrote to Cassius Lee. When asked during this time by a minister if he was sanguine of results, Lee replied, "I am not concerned with results. God's will ought to be our aim, and I am quite contented that [H]is designs should be accomplished and not mine." [76]

When through fiery trials thy path-way shall lie,
My grace, all sufficient, shall be thy supply;
The flame shall not hurt thee; I only design
Thy dross to consume and thy gold to refine.

Stanza 4
How Firm A Foundation

THE WAR BEGINS

That beautiful feature of our landscape has ceased
to charm me as much as formerly. I fear the mischief
that is brewing there.
  –R. E. Lee, speaking of the capitol building
  as he viewed it from across the Potomac

*A*lmost before Lee could get settled in as assistant
to President Davis, the war began with two
engagements that seemed to confirm even the most highly
inflated expectations of the South. On June 10, a small group
of 1400 Confederate soldiers met and defeated seven regi-
ments of Federal forces at Big Bethel. This was followed in
July by the smashing triumph over the federal armies at
Manassas. One Southerner really could whip a hundred
Yankees! This euphoria would soon be tempered by the sober-
ing realities of war.

Lee was ordered to remain in Richmond during
Manassas, and for the first time he experienced the anguish
of having to await reports from the field to know what was

happening and how the fight was progressing. When at last the message came from President Davis that a glorious victory had been won, Lee rejoiced. "I almost wept for joy at the glorious victory achieved by our brave troops," he wrote to his old friend Johnston. No little part of the credit for the victory should have been given to Lee. Almost one fourth of the men in the field were troops that had been raised, trained, and equipped under his direction. In addition, he had been responsible for much of the strategy and the positioning of the forces. These efforts, however, were hidden from the public eye and he received no acknowledgment for them. His prestige was forgotten. At the end of the month he received an assignment that nearly destroyed his military career.

On July 28, Lee was sent to western Virginia to organize the troops there who had suffered defeat and lost their commanding general. He had no written orders. His task was simply to reorganize, not to command. The public, assuming he had been sent to take over command, expected great things. They were disappointed.

Lee was not given sole authority over the troops. Authority and responsibility were divided between himself and General W. W. Loring, a younger man, but one who took Lee's arrival as an indication of a lack of confidence in his leadership. Loring was not bashful about showing his displeasure at Lee's presence. Without written orders, Lee judged the best thing to do was to seek to placate Loring and avoid a dispute. This was the wrong decision. The Southern troops were routed in what came to be called the Battle of Cheat Mountain.

A number of factors contributed to the disaster Lee experienced at Cheat Mountain in western Virginia: sickness among the soldiers (measles), bad weather (the roads were quagmires, making travel most difficult), and the demoralization, inexperience, and lack of discipline of the soldiers themselves. But nothing so hindered the operation as Loring's jealousy.

Lee's tact, as well as his conviction that quarrel was an unworthy course for true gentlemen, led him to bear with Loring far longer than was wise or good. Even after he received the confirmation of his promotion to the full rank of general, Lee continued to go to great lengths to avoid a clash. In other circumstances this is a commendable trait. In times of war, however, it is often a notable weakness. Lee's gentleness gave others the impression that he was indecisive and weak, and made him susceptible to intellectual bullying. His personal humility and sense of duty kept him from treating Loring with the bluntness that is sometimes necessary in dealing with those with inflated egos and stubbornly-held opinions.

Lee's disappointment was profound, though he remembered that all depended upon the sovereign disposal of God, who always does all things for His glory and man's good. His disappointment was no doubt sharpened by the fact that the newspapers, confident of victory and fueled by false rumors of a great triumph, published editorials proclaiming the certainty of victory. As Freeman put it, "It was bad enough to have failed; it was worse to have failure presented as victory and to be lauded for it." [77]

Typically, Lee assumed full responsibility for the failure of the action. He even refused to relate to President Davis what had happened, until Davis promised that nothing would be said or done about the failure of those who had not carried out orders. Lee never used his position to shift blame (even when he could have done so legitimately) or to jeopardize his men in order to enhance his reputation.

From Cheat Mountain, Lee removed to the Kanawha River Valley, where a federal army was threatening an advance. Opposing this force were two small Confederate detachments under the command of Henry Wise and John B.

Floyd. Neither man was trained militarily but that was not the biggest problem. Before the war, both had been politicians who often fought on opposite sides of issues! They despised one another and spent most of their efforts and energies writing each other nasty letters.

When Lee arrived, he reconciled the two men and got their troops ready to oppose a federal assault. Finally, after days of tense waiting, the federal forces withdrew. This brought more criticism upon Lee. Why had he allowed them to get away? And when he realized what had happened, why had he not pursued and routed them?

Lee was later asked about this decision by General William E. Starke. He explained that his troops had been more than seventy miles from their base, the roads were nearly impassable because of the rain, and—consequently— it was impossible to secure sufficient food for them. "But," General Starke noted, "your reputation was suffering, the press was denouncing you, your own state was losing confidence in you, and the army needed a victory to add to its enthusiasm."

Lee smiled sadly, "I could not afford to sacrifice the lives of five or six hundred of my people to silence public clamor." [78] And that, to Robert E. Lee, settled it. For him, there were some things more important than one's reputation.

LEE TAKES COMMAND

It is well that war is so terrible—we should grow too fond of it!

                                                    –R. E. Lee

L ee's star had fallen and he received a great deal of criticism for his role in the Cheat Mountain and Kanawha Valley engagements. Nevertheless, early in November, President Davis assigned him to command the forces on the coast of South Carolina. The federal navy had assembled a large fleet off the coast and was threatening action. Lee's job was to defend this area. This appointment was not received with general favor by the public. He was called "Granny" Lee for his apparent reluctance to engage in fighting. He was too much a "theoretical soldier," people said.

Lee had little trouble accomplishing the goals of his assignment: the federal commander was overly cautious, and slow to make any move that might result in an armed engagement. Lee spent the time shoring up the defenses on the coast, especially in Charleston.

On the second of March, Lee was recalled to Richmond, where President Davis named him to conduct, under his supervision, all the military operations of the Confederate armies. This order did what no order ought ever to do: namely, give tremendous responsibility, yet withhold the necessary authority to carry it out. President Davis, concerned with maintaining his own constitutional authority as commander in chief, left only matters of detail to Lee. Though Davis was careful to counsel with Lee in matters of strategy, he never completely gave him a free hand to initiate or direct any particular operation. It was a period of thankless service and once again Lee proved his character by giving himself to the task without complaint.

But the restlessness of being away from the action grew in Lee until it was well-nigh unbearable. The war had been going on now for over a year and he had spent most of the time in vital but—for a soldier—uninspiring work. Finally, on the morning of Saturday, May 31, Lee found himself with no duties to keep him at his office. The previous weeks had been a flurry of activity in an effort to prepare for the defense of Richmond, which was seriously threatened by Union armies. All had been made as ready as could be with the Confederacy's limited manpower and resources, and now there was nothing for Lee to do but wait. And that was one thing he did poorly.

Unable to stand the silence and separation from the action, Lee determined to ride with some of his lieutenants to General Johnston's headquarters. Upon arriving, it was evident that an action was underway. Detachments of men were hurrying down the road past the headquarters toward Seven Pines (or Fair Oaks) where the federals had drawn a line. Soon, Lee saw a familiar figure coming on horseback. It was the president himself. Jefferson Davis, another old soldier, could not stay behind the lines in Richmond either. General Johnston hurried off to the battle and Lee and the president were left alone.

Sporadic firing had been heard but soon it broke out in earnest. Davis hurried to his horse and headed toward the sound of battle, Lee following. Before they knew it, they were both in a scene of intense firing and high confusion. Several members of the Confederate Congress were there as well, but no one knew what was happening—other than the obvious fact that the two armies were engaged in a hotly contested struggle. Men pled with Davis to leave his dangerously exposed position. But to this counsel he was in no wise inclined to assent. Soon, news came that General Wade Hampton had been shot, and almost on the heels of this message came another: General Johnston had been terribly wounded, possibly fatally.

Only later did Davis and Lee learn the details of what had happened. The news was not good. The battle had been poorly planned and executed. The commanding general, Johnston, was obviously in no condition to lead the forces. As night fell, there was only one option for President Davis. In one of the most momentous orders he would ever give, Davis quietly said, "General Lee, I shall assign you to the command of this army. Make your preparations as soon as you reach your quarters. I shall send you the order when we get to Richmond." [79] On June 1, 1862, Lee headed out with his staff for the battlefield as commanding general of the Army of Northern Virginia.

The news of General Johnston's replacement initially received a cool reception. In many quarters, Lee's military ability had become suspect. Was he aggressive enough to command the army? Could he command the confidence of the men? Lee ignored the criticism, both implied and explicit, and set about the task of defending the South. Though few realized it at the time, the war would not be the same from this point forward. One Northern correspondent later reported:

> *The shell...which wounded...General Johnston, although it confused the Rebels, was the saddest shot fired during the war. It changed the entire Rebel tactics. It took away incompetence, indecision and dissatisfaction and gave skillful generalship, excellent plans and good discipline...Before the battle of Fair Oaks, Rebel troops were sickly, half fed and clothed, and had no hearts for their work... [After Lee took command] the discipline became better; they went into battles with shouts, and without being urged, and, when in, fought like tigers.*[80]

THE CATASTROPHIC LOSS

It is a terrible loss.
                    –R. E. Lee in a letter to Custis Lee after
                    the death of Stonewall Jackson

The story of the war is a sad and often recounted one. I will not try to cover what has been done so thoroughly and so ably by others, but there were a number of significant turning points which historians have noted, and one in particular that had an incalculable effect upon the Southern war effort in general and Lee's leadership in particular.

The great initial victories experienced after Lee was made commanding general of the Army of Northern Virginia were, taken together, the first great turning point of the war. Lee's famous Seven Days campaign, in the summer of 1862, foiled McClellan—who was in position to strangle the Confederacy—and gave the South the hope of complete success. Europe realized for the first time that the Confederacy might be able to defend its independence, and serious thought was given to granting diplomatic recognition and other support to the South. By September of 1862, according to the French foreign secretary, "not a reasonable statesman in Europe" believed the North could win.[81]

But this great success was followed by the repulse at Sharpesburg (or Antietam) of the Confederate invasion into the North. Though militarily this battle was a draw, strategically it was a failure. This failure caused Europe to hesitate in its support for Southern independence and forestalled diplomatic recognition of the Confederacy. It may also have even prevented Democratic victories in the Northern elections of 1862, which would surely have hindered Northern efforts in the war. Further, it stirred President Lincoln to pursue a course he had been reluctant to take earlier: to make the war a crusade against slavery.

On September 22, five days after the battle of Antietam, Lincoln called his cabinet into session and announced his plan to issue the Emancipation Proclamation. This was a brilliant political move, though it brought no practical benefits to the slaves themselves. The Proclamation freed no slaves in the North, or in the border states, or in those sections of the South under Union control. It only proclaimed the freedom of the slaves who lived in those parts of the South where Lincoln's authority was not recognized.

Though impotent in regard to its stated object, it bore much fruit in the political sphere. It gave the nations of Europe another reason to hesitate in their consideration of Southern support. It also had the deadly effect of changing the purpose of the war from an effort to preserve the Union to one of subjugation and destruction of the South. Lincoln told an official of the Interior Department after the publication of the Proclamation: "[T]he character of the war will be changed. It will be one of subjugation...The [old] South is to be destroyed and replaced by new propositions and ideas."[82]

From this point on, though the South would gain impressive victories, the tide had turned—and turned decisively in favor of the North. One of the key factors in this stark reversal of fortune came—ironically—during one of the South's most spectacular victories, the battle of Chancellorsville.

This magnificent victory was largely the result of the daring decision on the part of Lee to divide his forces in the face of an overwhelming federal army. Jackson took 28,000 men around the right flank of the Union army, leaving Lee to defend three and one-half miles of front with only 14,000 men. It is a battle still studied by students of military strategy, and it may well have been the battle which cost the South the war.

In the midst of the flanking action, General Jackson rode forward with some of his staff and was fired upon by his own men, who had mistaken him for the enemy. Jackson was wounded severely by three balls in the left arm and one through his right hand. His horse bolted and he was knocked to the ground, causing further injury. Suffering severe pain, he was carried back to the rear. Captain R. E. Wilbourn brought the news to General Lee. At his mention of Jackson's wound, Lee gave an audible groan and seemed nearly to break into tears. He turned to Wilbourn in great emotion and said, "Ah, captain, any victory is dearly bought which deprives us of the services of General Jackson, even for a short time!"[83]

The next day, May 3, when it was evident that the army had won perhaps its most thorough victory yet, Lee received a brief dispatch from Jackson that had been dictated after awakening from the operation in which his left arm had been amputated. Upon reading it, Lee sent the following message to Jackson:

*General:— I have just received your note,
informing me that you were wounded. I cannot
express my regret at the occurrence. Could I
have directed events, I would have chosen for
the good of the country to be disabled in your
stead. I congratulate you upon the victory,
which is due to your skill and energy.*[84]

On the seventh of May, Reverend B. T. Lacy arrived at headquarters with the news that General Jackson was worse. There was fear now that his wounds might prove fatal. Lee could not admit the possibility of Jackson's death. He could not imagine God taking away Jackson at the time of the South's greatest opportunity. He told Pastor Lacy, "Give [Jackson] my affectionate regards, and tell him to make haste and get well, and come back to me as soon as he can. He has lost his left arm, but I have lost my right."[85]

On Friday, May 8, more bad news came. Jackson was weaker, pneumonia had been contracted, and its effects were being felt. Jackson was experiencing mild delirium. Saturday's news was no better. The doctors believed the outlook was hopeless. In his anxiety and helplessness, Lee realized there was only one thing he could do: pray. That evening, while the army slept and Stonewall suffered, Robert E. Lee was on his knees begging God to spare his friend and brother in Christ.

The next morning was a beautiful Sabbath, and Lee had declared it as a day of thanksgiving for the victory gained. Lee rushed to the chaplain who had just come from Guiney's Station where Jackson was struggling for life. The doctors had given up all hope. Lee couldn't believe it. "Surely, General Jackson must recover, God will not take him from us, now that we need him so much. Surely he will be spared to us, in answer to the many prayers which are offered for him!" After the service, Lee again spoke with Reverend Lacey: "When you return, I trust you will find him better. When a suitable occasion offers, give him my love, and tell him that I wrestled in prayer for him last night, as I never prayed, I believe, for myself."[86]

Later that afternoon, as Lee considered a dispatch from the War Department, there was a stir outside his tent. A messenger then stepped in and handed him a small piece of folded paper. Lee took the paper, unfolded it, and read that Stonewall had died.

The loss was stunning. So affected was Lee that when he spoke of Jackson to General W. N. Pendleton, days later, he broke down in tears and wept unabashedly. Jackson could not be replaced. Lee had said of him, "Such an executive officer, the sun never shone on. I have but to show him my design, and I know that if it can be done, it will be done. No need for me to send or watch him. Straight as the needle to the pole he advanced to the execution of my purpose."

"Great and good" were the words that he resorted to over and over again to describe Stonewall. "I had such implicit confidence in Jackson's skill and energy that I never troubled myself to give him detailed instructions. The most general suggestions were all that he needed."[87] He wrote to his son Custis, "It is a terrible loss. I do not know how to replace him. Any victory would be dear at such a cost."[88]

The Scripture teaches us that though the child of God may sorrow, he does not sorrow as the world, which has no hope. Lee did not despair. In his general order announcing Stonewall's death, he said:

> *The daring, skill, and energy of this great and*
> *good soldier, by the decree of an all-wise*
> *Providence, are now lost to us. But while we*

mourn his death, we feel that his spirit still
lives, and will inspire the whole army with his
indomitable courage and unshaken confidence
in God as our hope and our strength.[89]

Lee knew the loss of Jackson was a tremendously heavy one, but not even he at that time knew how heavy it would be. He wrote to his wife on the day after Stonewall's death, "I do not know how to replace him. God's will be done! I trust He will raise up some one in his place."[90] This was not to be. Jackson was perfectly suited to Lee's style of command. Not one of his other officers was of equal spirit or skill. Without Jackson, Lee was forced to depend even more heavily upon an increasingly headstrong and moody Longstreet.

To replace Jackson, Lee had to turn to Major General R. S. Ewell. Ewell, a fine soldier, was not a man who operated well under the kind of vague orders Lee liked to give his generals. Under Jackson, Ewell had formed the habit of obeying his orders to the letter and never exercising discretion. This practice, though perhaps a commendable quality in a subordinate, was not the spirit Lee required in his generals, and it—along with Longstreet's refusal to follow orders—would prove deadly at Gettysburg. It would not be until then that Jackson's absence would be felt in all its severity. But by then it would be too late.

After the war, during a long ride in the country with a friend, Lee remarked, "If I had had Stonewall Jackson at Gettysburg we should have won a great victory."[91] As it was, however, Gettysburg became the Confederate Waterloo.

GETTYSBURG

It's all my fault. I thought my men were invincible.
                                                        –R. E. Lee

*T*he battle of Gettysburg may well have been the decisive turning point of the war. A victory here would
not only have been a major blow to the Northern army but
would also have severely damaged the popular opinion of
Lincoln's war policies and given the "peace faction" in the
North ammunition to increase the pressure for a negotiated
settlement of the war.

In spite of the loss of Jackson, Lee was confident about the
prospects for victory. Prior to the battle, while he maneuvered
his troops into position, he pointed to Gettysburg on the map
and noted to General Isaac Trimble, "Hereabout, we shall probably meet the enemy and fight a great battle, and if God give
us the victory, the war will be over and we shall achieve the
recognition of our independence." [92] It was not to be.

Many reasons for the Confederate defeat at Gettysburg
have been set forth. Lee took full responsibility, as was his

wont, but a careful consideration of the battle indicates that the fault was not exclusively his to bear. Three major factors can be noted which contributed significantly to the loss.[93]

The first reason has to be the absence of the intelligence that was usually supplied by the cavalry. General J. E. B. Stuart, whom Lee often referred to as "the eyes of the army," was nowhere to be found. When, on the 18th of June, Lee had begun the move toward Pennsylvania, he had consented to a request from Stuart to harass the Northern army commanded by General Joe Hooker. Lee told Stuart that if Hooker crossed the Potomac into Maryland, he should immediately return to guard the right flank of the Southern forces as they moved north.

The debate about why Stuart was not available and what happened to him has raged ever since. What is clear is that without Stuart's reconnaissance, the army (and Lee) was blind. Stuart was not available when his services were most needed. Lee had become heavily dependent upon Stuart's information on the enemy's position, strength, and movements in planning and carrying out a battle. Without Stuart he had to operate in the dark. If Stuart had been present, Lee would have had early information about the federal positions and movements and could have avoided the disastrous consequences that followed. This was a critical loss. Without Stuart's cavalry the Southern effort was severely crippled.

The second reason for defeat was General R. S. Ewell's failure to capture Cemetery Hill on the afternoon of July 1. Earlier that day, the Confederate forces had won a surprisingly easy victory in their initial engagement around Gettysburg and had routed the federal troops. Though Lee had initially been cautious because of his lack of information, when he arrived on the field of action and saw the great advantage the early victory offered, he desired to press forward on the offensive (the tested and successful tactic of the army). Consequently, seeing the disarray of the Union troops, Lee issued orders to Ewell to capture Cemetery Hill—adding to the order the usual phrase "if practicable." Had Ewell obeyed this order immediately, the field would have been controlled by the Southern forces and the battle would have, without question, gone their way.

Ewell, however, hesitated. He had been trained under the specific, precise commands of his old general, Stonewall Jackson, who allowed for no discretion on the part of his subordinates unless absolutely compelled to do so. Lee, conversely, always trusted the judgment of his commanders and allowed room for them to exercise their discretion depending upon the circumstances of battle.

But it was this freedom that threw Ewell into confusion and indecision. Hearing conflicting and sometimes false reports from the field and not quite sure what Lee desired him to do, he hesitated and did not attack Cemetery Hill at all. As a result, the federal forces were allowed to re-form and fortify a strategic location, which proved essential to their victory. Jackson would have taken the hill without an order. Ewell couldn't decide.

The third factor in the defeat at Gettysburg was the refusal of General James Longstreet to follow Lee's orders. On July 1, Longstreet had confidently suggested an entirely different strategy than Lee's and became quite disgruntled when Lee did not agree with his views. Ever inclined to take the defensive, Longstreet was not in favor of Lee's offensive strategy. Over the next two days, he demonstrated his disagreement by his lethargic obedience to Lee's commands. Here again, Lee missed Jackson.

After the disappointment of the first day, Lee had very few alternatives on the second day. He could hold his present position and await attack. But why wait until the Union forces were at full strength? He could retreat. But this decision would almost certainly be disastrous, as he still did not know the location and strength of General Meade's troops. Only one good alternative remained: a direct attack before the enemy had time to concentrate his forces.

On the evening of July 1, Lee, in consultation with his officers (Longstreet among them), decided to attack the federal right on Cemetery Ridge early the next morning. Orders to that effect were sent to General Ewell. He was to move his men into position on the right during the night and prepare to attack first thing in the morning. Later that evening General Ewell himself rode up to inform Lee that Culp's Hill, which overlooked Cemetery Hill, was unoccupied by the enemy. If Lee allowed him to stay where he was, he could take Culp's Hill in the morning, thereby preventing the Union forces from using Cemetery Hill to fire upon the men attacking Cemetery Ridge. Lee immediately canceled his previous orders and made a new plan. Longstreet's corps would attack Cemetery Ridge and as soon as Ewell heard Longstreet's fire, he was to capture Culp's Hill. Around midnight, everything was finalized. Lee stated to his subordinates, "Gentlemen, we will attack the enemy as early in the morning as practicable" and directed them all to make the necessary preparations for prompt action the next day.[94]

Here again, Lee's practice of not giving specific commands caused trouble. Longstreet was not told precisely when to attack, nor was he told the specific point of attack. It should have been plain that General Lee desired him to begin the attack first thing in the morning, as his language had plainly indicated, but for some reason Longstreet viewed the time and place of battle on July 2 as a matter left to his discretion.

Long before sunrise on July 2, Lee arose and breakfasted. Around four A.M., he hurried to an observation post on Seminary Ridge opposite the federal position. To his relief he found that the Union army had not reinforced the ridge south of Cemetery Hill during the night. Union divisions were being rushed to the site but they had not yet arrived. If Longstreet was ready, the ridge would be taken easily and the remnant of the federal forces that occupied Cemetery Hill could be swept away. But where was Longstreet? Not only were none of his men present or deploying for battle, but there was no sign of them approaching.

Around 7:30 A.M., Longstreet arrived on the ridge where Lee was observing the field. Incredibly, he again began to argue for his plan of the previous day. Lee refused to be persuaded. While Longstreet argued, Lee watched the Union forces arrive across the valley and occupy positions along Cemetery Ridge. Every minute of delay allowed more federal troops to move into place. Longstreet left, irritated and sullen that his plan had been rejected.

By ten o'clock, there was still no sign of Longstreet. Lee was clearly agitated. "What can detain Longstreet? He ought to be in position now."[95] Lee's impatience could not be contained. He searched for Longstreet to learn what was causing the delay. When he found him around eleven o'clock he saw that he was still no closer to beginning the attack than he had been before. Lee then told Longstreet what he wanted him to do, commanding him to move against the enemy with the troops he had available, and rode off, assuming his orders would now be followed. They were not.

By noon there was still no sound of Longstreet's attack. Again, Lee rode to find out why. He found that Longstreet's columns had at last begun to move to the right into position. Lee rode with Longstreet for a short time along the march, as he always did when he desired him to hurry, until it was necessary to leave him and go to another observation point. Not until four in the afternoon was Longstreet satisfied that all was ready, by which time the Union had fortified Cemetery Ridge. The assault that should have commenced at daybreak was doomed.

The costliness of this delay on the part of Longstreet cannot be overstated. Prior to seven A.M., the Union had scarcely 20,000 men on the ridge. By nine o'clock, the number had been increased to around 58,000.[96] The delay cost the lives of thousands and almost surely prevented a stunning Confederate victory.

The day of July third dawned with hope that victory could still be secured. In spite of the mishaps of the two previous days, the troops were in high spirits. However, when Longstreet again objected to Lee's plans that morning, Lee decided to adopt a new strategy. He reasoned that if Longstreet did not have confidence in the plan, it would do no good to insist upon its implementation. Lack of faith is half of defeat. Thus, Lee once more set aside what he viewed to be best because of the objections of one of his subordinates. He decided to concentrate an attack on the federal center. This change in plan culminated in the epic "charge" of General George Pickett's men that afternoon.

Many factors contributed to the defeat, but to Lee, none of them mattered. He was the commanding general and thus it was all his fault. It was, apart from the surrender itself, Lee's darkest hour. His hopes had been dashed and, worse, many men had lost their lives. His son Fitzhugh had been wounded and captured. Everything seemed to be in ruins. On July 26, he wrote to Rooney's wife to console her in regard to her husband:

> *I can appreciate your distress at F[itzhugh]'s situation. I deeply sympathize with it, and in the lone hours of the night I groan in sorrow at his captivity and separation from you. But we*

must all bear it, exercise all our patience, and do nothing to aggravate the evil. This, besides injuring ourselves, would rejoice our enemies, and be sinful in the eyes of God. In His own good time He will relieve us, and make all things work together for our good. If we give Him our love and place in Him our trust...Colonel Chambliss commands F's brigade now. The cavalry has had hard service and is somewhat pulled down...It has lost some gallant officers and men which causes me deep grief. Indeed the loss of our gallant officers and men throughout the army causes me to weep tears of blood and to wish that I never could hear the sound of a gun again. My only consolation is that they are the happier and we that are left are to be pitied.[97]

Lee sought to make sure that the reputations of all his officers were protected in the official reports and was determined not to shift the blame for the defeat upon anyone. In his mind, no one was to blame but himself. He had, he said, expected too much of his army: "The army did all it could. I fear I required of it impossibilities."(98)

LEE RESIGNS

*I cannot even accomplish what I myself desire. How
can I fulfill the expectations of others?*

-R. E. Lee

The loss at Gettysburg was overwhelming. Lee, as
usual, took the full responsibility for the defeat.
When General George Pickett responded to Lee's order to
relocate his division with the words, "General Lee, I have no
division now," Lee's immediate response to the grief-stricken
commander was, "Come, General Pickett, this has been my
fight and upon my shoulders rests the blame. The men and
officers of your command have written the name of Virginia
as high today as it has ever been written before." [99]

Despite the frustrations of the three days' battle, Lee's initial response was maintained thereafter. When General
Wilcox came up, having brought what was left of his men
away from the front, he tried to explain to Lee the condition
of his brigade, but became overwhelmed with emotion. Lee
shook his hand. "Never mind, General, all this has been my

fault—it is I that have lost this fight, and you must help me out of it the best way you can." [100]

There were no recriminations upon the men who had failed so signally, no blame shifting, no effort to clear himself of the responsibility the commanding general has for the army. Ewell had been indecisive, Longstreet had been insubordinate, and Stuart had been absent, yet Lee still felt the responsibility for the failure was his. Lee understood both the privileges and the responsibilities of headship. Though the blame was not his, the responsibility was, because part of the responsibility of a general is to know your subordinates, and to see to it that orders are obeyed. Consequently, the burden of the failure fell upon him and no one else.

Lee insisted that his subordinates cast no blame in their final reports. When Pickett filed a report with strong complaints about the lack of support his men had received, Lee returned it with the admonition, "You and your men have covered yourselves with glory, but we have the enemy to fight and must carefully, at this critical moment, guard against dissensions which the reflections in your report would create. I will, therefore, suggest that you destroy both copy and original, substituting one confined to casualties merely. I hope all will yet be well." [101]

He was determined to do everything in his power to protect the reputations of all concerned. In a letter to President Davis, he explained, "I know how prone we are to censure and how ready to blame others for the non-fulfillment of our expectations. This is unbecoming in a generous people, and I grieve to see its expression." He desired to bear the blame alone:

> *No blame can be attached to the army for its*
> *failure to accomplish what was projected by me,*
> *nor should it be censured for the unreasonable*

expectations of the public—I am alone to
blame in perhaps expecting too much of its
prowess and valour…with the knowledge I
then had, & in the circumstances I was then
placed, I do not know what better course I
could have pursued.[102]

These were not mere words. After giving more careful thought to the outcome of Gettysburg, Lee determined that he should ask to be relieved of command. On August 8, from Orange Courthouse, he wrote to President Davis that he was aware of criticism in the public journals. He continued:

I therefore, in all sincerity, request Your
Excellency to take measures to supply my
place. I do this with the more earnestness
because no one is more aware than myself of
my inability for the duties of my position. I
cannot even accomplish what I myself desire.
How can I fulfill the expectations of
others?…Everything, therefore, points to the
advantages to be derived from a new comman-
der, and I the more anxiously urge the matter
upon Your Excellency from my belief that a
younger and abler man than myself can readily
be obtained. I know that he will have as gal-
lant and brave an army as ever existed to
second his efforts, and it would be the happiest
day of my life to see at its head a worthy
leader—one that would accomplish more than
I could perform and all that I have wished. I
hope Your Excellency will attribute my request

to the true reason, the desire to serve my country, and to do all in my power to insure the success of her righteous cause.[103]

It didn't take Davis long to make a decision on this request. He responded, "To ask me to substitute you by some one in my judgment more fit to command, or who would possess more of the confidence of the army, or of the reflecting men of the country, is to demand an impossibility." [104]

Years later, when reminded of this, one of the veterans commented, "The army would have arisen in revolt if it had been called upon to give up General Lee." [105]

The Great Revival

I salute the Church of God!
—R. E. Lee's greeting to one of
the chaplains in the Confederate army

*T*he fact that the army maintained its high morale after the defeat at Gettysburg may be attributed to two not altogether unrelated factors: 1) the great revival of the winter of 1863-64, and 2) the example of its commanding general.

The revival actually began in 1862 and continued to sweep through the Army of Northern Virginia for the next two years. Men by the thousands were brought to true repentance and faith in the Lord and Savior of mankind. Nearly every brigade went to the trouble of erecting a log chapel in which nightly meetings were held, and men crowded in to hear fervent and faithful ministers of the gospel speak of the way of life which "robbed the *minnie* of its terror." It is estimated that over 15,000 men were converted during the winter of 1863-64 alone. Perhaps never in the history of man has there been a more fervent and reverent army than that under Lee's command in the last year of the war.

Lee did all he could to encourage the movement of God's Spirit. He regularly stopped to participate in the impromptu prayer meetings that occurred with frequency throughout the camps. He attended the services on the Lord's Day faithfully, and even, when time allowed, attended the meetings of the chaplains. He sought carefully to preserve Sundays for worship, that the men might not be unduly distracted from the things of God. He issued a general order to protect as far as possible the observance of the Sabbath among the troops (General Order No. 15, dated 7 February 1864):

> *II. To this end he [the commanding general] directs that none but duties strictly necessary shall be required to be performed on Sunday, and that the labor, both of men and animals, which it is practicable to anticipate or postpone, or the immediate performance of which is not essential to the safety, health or comfort of the army, shall be suspended on that day.*

> *III. Commanding officers will require the usual inspections on Sunday to be held at such time as not to interfere with the attendance of the men on divine service at the customary hour in the morning.*

> *They will also give their attention to the maintenance of order and quiet around the place of worship, and prohibit anything that may tend to disturb or interrupt religious exercises.*[106]

Lee took great interest in hearing reports of the progress of the revival among his men. Once, after two of the chaplains had finished a report to him about the work, one said, "I think it right that I should say to you, General, that the chaplains of this army have a deep interest in your welfare, and that some of the most fervent prayers we offer are in your behalf." Lee flushed deeply at this remark and tears filled his eyes. "Please thank them for that sir," he replied, "I warmly appreciate it. And I can only say that I am nothing but a poor sinner, trusting in Christ alone for salvation, and need all the prayers they can offer for me." [107]

The centrality of this revival in maintaining morale is seen in light of the extreme lack of supplies from which the army suffered during this period. There were thousands of men who had no shoes by the end of October 1863. Only fifty men in one regiment had decent shoes, and a brigade that had been sent out on picket duty had to leave behind several hundred men who could not march because of the condition of their shoes. The winter of 1863-64 was particularly cold and caused severe suffering.

The shortage of food was an even more serious problem. For a two-day period during that winter the men had no food at all. Even when there was food, the daily rations were barely enough to keep grown men afoot. Northerners who complained about the rations given to the men in Andersonville had to be reminded after the war that those rations were sometimes greater than what was given to the Southern army in the field. The reasons for the severe shortages were many, foremost among which were the blockade of Southern ports and the destruction of the food supply by the Union army. It was under these adverse conditions that Lee labored to get provisions for his men.

Lee himself set an example for the men to follow. All luxuries that were sent to him were immediately dispatched to hospitals and other particularly distressed troops. His own midday meal was commonly a small amount of boiled cabbage in salt water. If food was especially abundant, he would sometimes have his favorite meat, a joint of mutton. If then urged to have a second helping, he would decline by saying, "I would really enjoy another piece, but I have had my allowance." [108]

In addition to the problem of feeding the men, there was the problem of finding food for the numerous animals who did such difficult and necessary service for the army. The difficulties were enough to make great men quail.

These problems made the odds against his army even greater than the raw numbers indicate, and these numbers in themselves were bad enough. In March of 1863, Lincoln called for 700,000 more troops. Lee could not hope to have even 65,000 when the spring action began.

The situation was desperate, but Lee trusted in God. He wrote to his son, "Our country demands all our strength, all our energies. To resist the powerful combination now forming against us will require every man at his place. If victorious, we have everything to hope for in the future. If defeated, nothing will be left for us to live for…My whole trust is in God, and I am ready for whatever He may ordain." [109]

The Beginning of the End

*I fear they may continue to make these changes till
they find someone whom I don't understand.*
                    –R. E. Lee remarking on the changes of
                    commanding generals made by the North

With the appointment on March 9, 1864, of
Ulysses S. Grant to the command of the Army
of the Potomac, the North finally had a man who was willing
to do what was necessary to end the war. Grant's strategy was
simple: take advantage of the superiority in men and supplies
and bring pressure to bear on the South at every point. Grant
knew the South could not defend itself over an extended front
pressed consistently for an extended period of time.

A critical aspect of this plan was the wholesale resort to
total war, i.e. war upon the civilian population—with the
purpose of demoralizing both the Southern troops and the
people of the South. It was to be a war of attrition. Grant
knew he did not have to win battles: all he had to do was
injure the Confederate troops and continue to do so. He could

afford to lose men; Lee could not. Grant's brutal, sledge-hammer tactics would batter the Southern troops and people into submission. In the spring of 1864, the strategy began.

It was a horrible season: the Wilderness, Spotsylvania, Cold Harbor. Grant suffered incredible losses: nearly 18,000 in the Wilderness, another 18,000 at Spotsylvania, 7,200 (in only thirty minutes) at Cold Harbor. In less than a month, the Army of the Potomac lost more men than Lee had in his entire army when the campaign began. But Grant did not withdraw. He continued to press Lee, continually shifting his army around the Confederate right, constantly applying pressure. It was a strategy that Lee could do little about because of his shortage of men.

At one point Lee was asked by a visitor, "General, if [Grant] breaks your line, what reserve have you?"

"Not a regiment," Lee replied, "and that has been my condition ever since the fighting commenced on the Rappahannock. If I shorten my lines to provide a reserve, he will turn me; if I weaken my lines to provide a reserve, he will break them."

Not even Lee could overcome the overwhelming numbers the North was able to place on the field. And to this problem add the others: his artillery was inferior, the horses of his cavalry were worn out and broken down, he had lost men who had been critical to his earlier successes (Stonewall and J. E. B. Stuart in particular), and he himself had been incapacitated by illness. The obstacles to victory were well-nigh insurmountable.

Grant pressured Lee to take up a defensive line around Petersburg. It was to be his last stand. The winter at Petersburg was the most depressing of all. The freezing temperatures and meager provisions conspired together to attack the cheerful, fighting spirit that had characterized the

Southern army. Lee set the example for his men. He often had less to eat than others. An Irish member of the British Parliament who visited Lee's headquarters during this time reported that Lee's dinner consisted of two biscuits, one of which he shared with his distinguished visitor.

As Christmas approached, the ladies of Richmond determined to give the soldiers at least one good meal during the holidays. Appeals for food went out to all the merchants and farmers, and word spread through the trenches of the feast to come. A soldier in the Eighteenth Georgia described what happened:

> [O]ur mouths "watered" till January 1, 1865. On that day all who were able to do so got up very early. The army was to do nothing. The ladies were to do all. They would provide all vehicles, and the "goodies" would be taken right along the lines and distributed to the half-famished men by dainty hands. And we waited. What a long day that seemed to be! We whiled away the tedious hours by telling stories and cracking jokes! Noon came, then two, four, eight, ten, and twelve o'clock, and still no "goody" wagon. Being still a little weak, I became tired and lay down and went to sleep with the understanding that those on watch would call me when our dinner arrived. It was after 3 A.M. when a comrade called and told me that a detail had just gone out to meet the precious wagon and bring in our feast. But oh what a disappointment when the squad returned and issued to each man only one small sandwich made up of two tiny slices of bread and a thin piece of

ham! A few men ventured to inquire, "Is this all?" But I think they were ashamed of themselves the next moment. After the "meal" was finished a middle-aged corporal lighted his pipe and said: "God bless our noble women! It was all they could do; it was all they had." And then every man in that old tent indulged in a good cry. We couldn't help it.[110]

The suffering and deprivation of the troops was painful for Lee, and he knew that the worst was yet to come. Again he took refuge in the rock that is higher. "My reliance," he wrote to President Davis, "is in a Power which will cause all things to work together for our good." He wrote to his wife, who at this time was severely crippled, "I pray daily and almost hourly to our Heavenly Father to come to the relief of your and our afflicted country. I know He will order all things for our good, and we must be content."[111]

The situation was grim. Lee had approximately 35,000 men fit for duty. Grant had over 150,000. When all the forces available to each side were totaled, the odds got no better. The Union could muster over 280,000 men while Lee, at most, could gather 65,000. The options before Lee were only three: seek terms with the enemy, attack Grant at a "weak" point and hope somehow to break through his line, or retreat. At the end of March it was decided to begin the retreat.

Lee wrote to his wife, "I think General Grant will move against us soon—within a week, if nothing prevents—and no man can tell what may be the result; but trusting to a merciful God, who does not always give the battle to the strong, I pray we may not be overwhelmed. I shall, however, endeavour to do my duty and fight to the last."[112]

THE END COMES

I shall…endeavour to do my duty and fight to the last.

> –R. E. Lee, in a letter to Mrs. Lee,
> February 22, 1865

The plan was to move west to Amelia Court House and secure the supply of food that Lee had ordered for his starving men. The army would then turn south to join Joseph E. Johnston's force, which was opposing Sherman. The southward turn never took place.

The retreat was a nightmare. On the night of April 2, 1865, when the evacuation of Petersburg began, only 12,000 troops were able to move. Though the troops were in amazingly good spirits, the roads were terrible and travel was slow. Lee was forced to take a more circuitous route and thus had more ground to travel than did Grant, who could move in a direct line to cut off the Southern retreat.

Arriving at Amelia Court House on the morning of April 4, Lee found ammunition and ordnance supplies, but no food!

This left him no choice but to seek food for his men. Lee sent an order to Richmond as well as a request to the citizens in the surrounding area, but the next morning the foraging wagons returned almost empty. The people had next to nothing to give or sell to the army. The country had been stripped of both food and provender.

The lack of food was a catastrophe. Not merely capture, but starvation now became a real possibility. Only one option remained: march toward Danville to meet the provisions that had been ordered from there. Lee didn't know it at the time, but the train from Danville had gone past the meeting point and, mysteriously, continued on toward Richmond—where it had been captured by Union troops.

Lee ordered the army forward but, finding the federal forces blocking the way south, he was forced to veer northwestward toward Lynchburg. The next day, April 6, nearly one-third of Lee's force was trapped by federal troops at Sayler's Creek and surrendered. The remnant of the army headed on to Farmville, then continued on towards Appomattox Station, where they hoped to find food at last. The Union forces were rushing to cut off the line of retreat. They would win the race.

On the afternoon of April 7, Lee received the following message:

> *General: The results of the last week must convince you of the hopelessness of further resistance on the part of the Army of Northern Virginia in this struggle. I feel that it is so, and regard it as my duty to shift from myself the responsibility of any further effusion of blood, by asking of you the surrender of that portion of the C. S. Army known as the Army of Northern Virginia.*

Very respectfully, your obedient servant,
U. S. Grant
Lieutenant-General
Commanding Armies of the United States

Lee read the note silently and passed it to General Longstreet, who was sitting nearby. Longstreet read it and responded, "Not yet." Lee made no response but took a piece of cheap, ruled note paper and quickly wrote this answer:

> *7th Apl '65*
> *Genl*
>
> *I have recd your note of this date. Though not entertaining the opinion you express of the hopelessness of further resistance on the part of the Army of N. Va.—I reciprocate your desire to avoid useless effusion of blood, & therefore before considering your proposition, ask the terms you will offer on condition of its surrender.*
>
> *Very respy your obt. Servt*
> *R. E. Lee*
> *Genl*

Lee continued to press on toward Appomattox. The evening of April 8, after receiving another communication from Grant, Lee called his last council of war. Generals John B. Gordon, Fitz Lee, and Longstreet were present. Lee explained the situation as he knew it and then asked their advice. None of the men were about to counsel surrender. Their advice was to attack as soon as possible and seek to break through the Union forces. If this proved impossible, once begun, there would be only one other alternative left: surrender. The orders were given. Gordon's men would lead the charge.

As Lee was about to lie down for a few hours' rest before the action, one of Gordon's staff returned to ask a question on a point the general had failed to address in his orders. Where would General Lee like him to halt and camp tomorrow night? It was as though he had no doubt of success. Once again the odds would be overcome. Once again, there would be a glorious victory. "Tell General Gordon I should be glad for him to halt just beyond the Tennessee line," replied the weary Lee.[113] The Tennessee line was over 175 miles away.

The ninth of April—Palm Sunday—came with the stroke of midnight. The last effort was to begin at one o'clock. As the men gathered their meager belongings for one last charge, the hope began to stir again. It may seem incredible to many of us today that men in such hopeless circumstances would be willing not merely to attempt a battle but actually begin to be confident of success. But it was so. Soon a lone voice was heard singing a portion of the so-called "Texas Bible" (a very rough paraphrase of Ecclesiastes):

> *The race is not to them that's got*
> *The longest legs to run*
> *Nor the battle to that people*
> *That shoots the biggest gun.*

The attack actually began a little after five o'clock that morning. Gordon, with only 2000 men, went forward and passed through the village of Appomattox Courthouse. His men drove back the enemy and captured two guns, but just as they swung around to cover the advance of the wagons, they discovered a large body of federal infantry to the rear of their right flank. The Union advantage in sheer numbers was too much to overcome. Gordon's men fought valiantly, but despite all their efforts, they were slowly surrounded. He sent word to Lee that he could do nothing unless "heavily supported" by Longstreet. "I have fought my corps to a frazzle," Gordon reported. Longstreet, unknown to Gordon, was engaged in holding off two corps of the Union forces in Lee's rear.

When Lee heard Gordon's message, he replied, "Then there is nothing left me but to go and see General Grant, and I would rather die a thousand deaths." [114] The men around him were thunderstruck. Could it be that the end had come? One said, "Oh, General, what will history say of the surrender of the army in the field?" "Yes, I know they will say hard things of us: They will not understand how we were overwhelmed by numbers. But that is not the question, Colonel: The question is, is it right to surrender this army. If it is right, then I will take all the responsibility." [115]

But it was a bitter pill. "How easily I could be rid of this and be at rest!" spoke Lee, as he looked over his last battlefield. "I have only to ride along the line and all will be over!" Then after a pause for calm reconsideration, he stated, "But it is our duty to live. What will become of the women and children of the South if we are not here to protect them?" [116]

It is impossible to describe the death of a dream. Even to make the attempt seems melodramatic, or maudlin. The emptiness, the darkness, the bleakness of a dream's demise surpasses description. Wild ideas come into the mind. Desperation clings to the last tattered threads of hope as it flies inexorably away. Such was the experience of the men of the South. They had dreamt of independence. They had fought, beyond all expectation, a stunningly brave and ferocious fight.

And they had, at certain times, been so close to gaining their goal. But now the dream was gone. Darkness enveloped their souls. Even many of their enemies pitied them. One New Hampshire soldier sat with his comrades watching the greatly outnumbered and surrounded Confederates, and later remembered how he and all his friends had "pitied and sympathized with these courageous Southern men who had fought for four long and dreary years, all so stubbornly, so bravely and so well, and now, whipped, beaten, completely used up, were fully at our mercy—it was pitiful, sad, and seemed to us altogether too bad." [117]

Lee had written Grant that he would meet him at ten o'clock. By the time negotiations were finished, it was determined to meet at a place of Lee's choosing to discuss terms of surrender. The place chosen was the house of Major Wilmer McLean. Major McLean had moved to this place in central Virginia from a farm on the fields of Manassas, where the first battle of the war had been fought. Desiring to avoid the battles, McLean had removed to Appomattox, and now, in the strange workings of providence, was about to see the war that began in his fields end in his parlor.

Lee arrived first, around one o'clock. He took a seat close to a small table in the corner of the parlor, and there waited. The half-hour prior to General Grant's arrival was perhaps the longest of his life. About 1:30 P.M., the Union commander arrived.

Ulysses S. Grant had resigned from the army in 1854— a decision forced upon him as a result of his undisciplined lifestyle and habitual drunkenness. In the next six years Grant failed to succeed first as a farmer, then as a real estate salesman, and finally, as a clerk in his father's shop in Galena, Illinois. The outbreak of the war gave Grant the opportunity to re-enter the army, where his courage and resolve won the confidence of the president and landed him in the position of commander of the most powerful army in the world. Now he was about to receive the surrender of one of the most famous generals and armies in history.

Grant entered the room dressed in a private's tunic with a general's shoulder straps attached. His clothing was mud-splattered, and one of his buttons was in the wrong hole. The two men greeted each other and took their seats, as Grant's staff found places along the walls of the room, "very much as people enter a sick chamber where they expect to find the patient dangerously ill." [118]

Grant opened the conversation by referring to a previous meeting between himself and Lee during the Mexican War. He continued to reminisce, in an effort to break the tension and awkwardness of the moment. After a time Lee spoke, "I suppose, General Grant, that the object of our present meeting is fully understood. I asked to see you to ascertain upon what terms you would receive the surrender of my army."

Grant wrote out the terms in his order book and, to Lee's great relief, repeated the terms he had mentioned the previous day, promising to parole all of the men, and adding that the men would be allowed to return to their homes undisturbed by United States authority. Lee requested one further provision, that the men be allowed to keep their horses, since, in the Confederate army, they had used their own horses. Left unspoken was Lee's knowledge that, the South having been stripped of all draft animals, the horses would be of crucial importance in the effort to rebuild. Grant consented to this amendment.

Lee requested that Grant receive all the Union prisoners, stating that they were badly in need of food. Grant responded that he would be pleased to have his men returned and would take steps to have Lee's army supplied with rations. "Of about how many men does your present force consist?" Grant asked. Lee hesitated, and then said, "Indeed, I am not able to say. My losses in killed and wounded have been exceedingly heavy, and besides, there have been many stragglers and some deserters." Grant offered to send 25,000 rations—more than double the number of Lee's men—asking if Lee thought that would be sufficient. "I think it will be ample," said Lee, "and it will be a great relief, I assure you." The rations Lee had been searching for—first from Richmond, then from Farmville, and finally from Lynchburg—had all been captured by Union forces.

The papers were soon signed, and Lee took up his hat and walked out the door. Several Union officers were resting on the porch and, upon Lee's appearance, jumped to their feet and saluted. Lee returned the salute and pulled on his gauntlets, while looking in the direction where his army waited. Those valiant men, who were totally ignorant of the fact that he had just surrendered them to their foes—what would they say? Lee, in a voice choked with emotion, called for Traveller, mounted slowly, and with a "long, low, deep sigh, almost a groan in its intensity," turned in the direction of his lines.[119]

As Lee began to ride slowly away, Grant came down the steps and started across the yard. Suddenly realizing that Lee was leaving, he stopped and took off his hat. Every other Union soldier did the same. Lee lifted his hat in silent salute and turned through the gate into the road. Grant stood silently watching the great man ride away. One of his staff said to him, "This will live in history." Grant made no reply, but stood watching until Lee was out of sight.

The Return Home

We may be annihilated, but we cannot be conquered.

—R. E. Lee

*A*s Lee rode back toward the lines, the men—spotting their hero—began their characteristic cheers for him. But this time things were different. There was something about his manner and expression that stopped the cheers in their throats. Slowly, the unthinkable began to enter their minds. "General," some cried, "are we surrendered?"

Lee tried to ignore the question, but his men began to crowd around him, pulling off their hats in respect. Lee removed his hat as he acknowledged his faithful warriors with their "frenzied, famished faces." "Men," he said, "we have fought the war together, and I have done the best I could for you. You will all be paroled and go to your homes until exchanged." Tears welled in his eyes as his fabled self-mastery failed him. All he could manage was a choking "good-bye" as he again sought to move on toward the orchard which was serving as his temporary headquarters.

As the word spread, most of these hardened veterans wept openly; others walked as if in a daze, unwilling to believe that the Army of Northern Virginia had surrendered. To some it seemed the end of the world itself. "Blow, Gabriel blow!" one man cried. "My God, let him blow, I am ready to die!" [120]

"General, we'll fight 'em yet! General, say the word and we'll fight 'em yet! We'll go after 'em again!" the men yelled as if to assure their leader that they still had all confidence in him and to demonstrate their unwavering allegiance to him. The men crowded around him, hoping to touch him and express their love. Lee was overwhelmed.

Lieutenant Colonel W. W. Blackford later recorded the unforgettable scene:

> [T]wo solid walls of men were formed along the whole distance. Their officers followed, and behind the lines of men were groups of them, mounted and dismounted, awaiting his coming...As soon as he entered this avenue of these old soldiers, the flower of the army, the men who had stood to their duty through thick and thin in so many battles, wild, heartfelt cheers arose which so touched General Lee that tears filled his eyes and trickled down his cheeks as he rode his splendid charger, hat in hand, bowing his acknowledgments. This exhibition of feeling on his part found quick response from the men whose cheers changed to choking sobs as, with streaming eyes and many evidences of affection, they waved their hats as he passed. Each group began in the same way, with cheers, and ended in the same way, with sobs,

all along the route to his quarters. Grim,
bearded men threw themselves on the ground,
covered their faces with their hands and wept
like children. Officers of all ranks made no
attempt to conceal their feelings, but sat on
their horses and cried aloud...One
man...extended his arms, and with an
emphatic gesture said, "I love you just as well
as ever, General Lee!"[121]

The cheers of the men were heard by the Northern troops, and some mistakenly reported that it was the sound of jubilation over the news of the surrender. That, it was not. It was the voice of jubilation, true enough, not over the surrender, but for the captain who had surrendered and who was still "the commander of their hearts." [122]

The next day Lee published his last order to his troops:

Headquarters Army Northern Virginia,
April 10, 1865

After four years of arduous service, marked by
unsurpassed courage and fortitude, the Army of
Northern Virginia has been compelled to yield
to overwhelming numbers and resources. I need
not tell the survivors of so many hard-fought
battles, who have remained steadfast to the
last, that I have consented to this result from
no distrust of them; but, feeling that valor and
devotion could accomplish nothing that could
compensate for the loss that would have
attended the continuation of the contest, I have
determined to avoid the useless sacrifice of

*those whose past services have endeared them
to their countrymen. By the terms of the agreement, officers and men can return to their
homes, and remain there until exchanged.
You will take with you the satisfaction that
proceeds from the consciousness of duty faithfully performed; and I earnestly pray that a
merciful God will extend to you [H]is blessing
and protection. With an unceasing admiration
of your constancy and devotion to your country, and a grateful remembrance of your kind
and generous consideration of myself, I bid you
an affectionate farewell.*

R. E. Lee, General.

Lee did not attend the ceremony of the stacking of arms on the morning of April 12, but he did not leave Appomattox until the surrender was fully over and his faithful men had started for home. That afternoon, he headed for home, and for Lee, that now meant Richmond. All of the property owned by Lee and his wife had either been confiscated or destroyed by the Union forces, and Mrs. Lee and their daughters were now living in Richmond in a house provided for them by Scottish philanthropist John Stewart. Accompanying Lee were Colonels Taylor, Marshall, and Cook—the latter in an ambulance because of sickness.

He had left home four years earlier, with the cheers of citizens flush with visions of glory ringing in his ears. He returned now to a broken country. The people of Virginia, like the citizens of the South in general, had little or nothing left. Lee's personal loss in terms of property was nearly total. Arlington had been confiscated by the federal government;

the White House, another family farm, had been burned to the ground by Union soldiers; and the third family farm, Romancoke, was situated in an area so ravaged by the war that there was not even a fencepost left standing for eight miles around. Lee was nearly bankrupt.

On April 15, Lee arrived in Manchester, across the James River from Richmond. The rain was pouring down. He was soaking wet and splattered in mud. A Baptist minister who happened to see him pass through town recorded his impression of Lee:

> *The horseman himself sat on his horse like a master; his face was ridged with self-respecting grief; his garments were worn in the service and stained with travel; his hat was slouched and spattered with mud…Even in the fleeting moment of his passing by my gate, I was awed by his incomparable dignity. His majestic composure, his rectitude and his sorrow, were so wrought and blended into his visage and so beautiful and impressive to my eyes that I fell into violent weeping.*[123]

Word spread quickly through the city that Lee was coming. As he rode from the river to his residence at 707 Franklin Street, the crowd grew thicker with each block. The people began to cheer, and so moving was the scene that even the federal soldiers scattered among the residents joined in. Lee acknowledged all politely, but did not stop.

By the time he reached his home, the people were again crowded around him to greet him, touch him, and speak a word of encouragement. Lee grasped as many hands as he could as he slowly made his way to the iron gate in front of the house. Nearly overcome with emotion, he mounted the steps to his front door, turned to the crowd and bowed, and entered in. The battles over, he unbuckled his sword for the last time.

E'en down to old age all my people shall prove
My sovereign, eternal, unchangeable love;
And when hoary hairs shall their temples adorn,
Like lambs they shall still in my bosom be borne.

Stanza 5
How Firm a Foundation

In Richmond

We failed, but in the good providence of God appar-
ent failure often proves a blessing.

–R. E. Lee

We can little imagine the difficulty Lee's men faced after the surrender in leaving behind the life they had led and the cause for which they had fought for four years. Added to this difficulty was the debt they felt they owed to General Lee. It was as if they could not return home without conveying to him their gratitude and love. Hardly a day passed without old officers or soldiers stopping by his residence in Richmond to say goodbye.

One day, General Lee had decided to use the entire day to catch up on the mountain of correspondence that had poured in from all over. All visitors were to be turned away with the explanation that he had such an "arrearage of correspondence that he must dispatch it." Soon however, a tall, ragged Confederate soldier with his left arm in a sling came up the front steps. He was met at the door by Custis Lee.

"I am sorry," Custis told him, explaining the situation.

The soldier hesitated, and then said that he belonged to Hood's Texas brigade, that he had followed General Lee for four years and was about to set out (on foot) for Texas. He had hoped, he said, to be able to shake his old commander's hand and bid him goodbye. But if he couldn't, he couldn't, and it couldn't be helped. With this, the old soldier turned to go back down the steps.

It was too much for Custis to bear, and he called the soldier back, saying that General Lee might make an exception in his case and that he would see. With this, Custis ushered him into the parlor and went upstairs to speak with his father. Colonel Clement Sullivane, who was serving as an aide to Custis Lee, wrote about what happened next:

> *Presently I heard the stately step of General Robert E. Lee descending the stairway. As we both arose on his entrance into the room, he bowed gravely to me and then advanced to the Texan, with his hand extended. The poor fellow grasped it, looked General Lee straight in the eye, struggled to say something, but choked and could not, and, wringing Lee's hand, he dropped it as he burst into tears; then, covering his face with his arm, he turned away and walked out of the room and the house. General Lee gazed after him for a few moments motionless, his fine, deep, dark eyes suffused and darkened with emotion, and then, again gravely bowing to me, he left the room and returned upstairs. Not a single word was spoken during the meeting by any of the three participants.[124]*

Lee's old soldiers often viewed his safety and security as their personal responsibility. Not long after the surrender, the rumor spread that Lee himself was to be arrested—as Jefferson Davis had been. This was too much for some of his faithful men. One day, shortly after the surrender, two ragged veterans appeared at the door of the Lee home.

"General," the spokesman for the group said when Lee entered the room, "I'm one of your soldiers, and I've come here as the representative of sixty of my comrades who are too ragged and dirty to venture to see you. We are all Virginians, general, from Roanoke County, and they sent me here to see you on a little business. They've got our President in prison, and now—they—talk—about—arresting—*you.* And, general, we can't stand—we'll never stand and see that. Now, general, we men have got about two hundred and fifty acres of land in Roanoke—very good land, too, it is sir—and if you'll come up there and live, I've come to offer you our land, all of it, and we men will work as your field-hands, and you'll have very little trouble in managing it with us to help you. And, general, there are near about a hundred of us left in old Roanoke, and they could never take you there, for we could hide you in the hollows of the mountains, and the last man of us would die in your defense." [125]

"You would not have your general run away and hide," Lee replied, deeply moved by the fact that these men who had nothing left in this world but their land would be willing to give it all up for him. "He must stay and meet his fate." [126] He went on to explain that his parole protected him, and that he was depending upon General Grant's word for the maintenance of that agreement. At length he was able to persuade the good men that it would be impossible to accept their generous offer. Lee then insisted that the veterans take some of his own clothes for themselves and their comrades.

One day, in the summer of 1865, Lee's daughter Mildred was sitting with her father when the front door bell rang. Lee opened the door and there stood a tall, gaunt man dressed in homespun and covered in dust. As Mildred told it, this man "grabbed the General's extending hand and said, 'General Lee, I followed you four years and done the best I knowed how. Me and my wife live on a little farm way up on the Blue Ridge Mountains. We heard the Yankees wasn't treating you right, and I come down to see 'bout it. If you will come up thar we will take care of you the best we know how as long as we live.'"

The old veteran was holding both of Lee's hands as he said this, tears streaming down his cheeks. Lee was so taken aback by this man—who had traveled over a hundred miles to offer him shelter—that tears filled his eyes as well. At a loss for something to say, Lee began to search among the presents friends had left in the front hall for something to give to this man. He finally spied a box that he knew contained a new suit. Handing the box to the man, the general said, "My friend, I don't need a thing. My friends all over the country have been very kind and have sent me more clothes than I can possibly use, so I want to thank you for coming and give you this new suit."

Mildred described what happened next:

> *The man snatched his hand from General Lee,*
> *crossed his arms, straightened himself, and said,*
> *"General Lee, I can't take nothin' offen you."*
> *After a few moments he relaxed, put one hand*
> *on the box and said, "Yes I will, General, I will*
> *carry them back home, put them away and*
> *when I die the boys will put them on me."*[127]

Incidents like these were too numerous to count. It was these encounters which made life after the war so difficult for

Lee. He grieved over the plight of the old soldiers and the people of the South who had so valiantly stood with the army and had suffered the loss of all things.

If the anguish in the South was great, as great was the anger directed toward her by many in the North. While the majority of Northerners were in favor of reconciliation with the South, hotheaded revolutionaries, full of the wine of victory, sought to carry forward policies more akin to the French radicals under Robespierre than anything ever seen in this country.

Hatred towards the South intensified after President Lincoln's assassination. More than one called for retribution to be given to the "enemies of the people." Congressman George W. Julian of Indiana declared in a speech that he, if he were in charge, would hang Jefferson Davis "in the name of God." He went on to say that it was an outrage that Lee was left at liberty, and were it his decision, Lee would be hanged as well. The lands of prominent Southerners should be divided among the blacks and a former plantation owner should not be left even enough land "to bury his carcass in."[128]

An orator in a meeting held in the Customs House of New York City stirred the crowd to a frenzy with the chant, "Hang Lee! Hang Lee!" The proposals for the punishment of Lee and other Southern leaders were many and varied. In early June, Lee was indicted by a federal grand jury for the crime of treason, among the punishments for which was death by hanging. Though never brought to trial, the possibility weighed heavily upon him. It was a most uncertain time. Yet Lee remained quiet.

Lee steadfastly refused to be drawn into disputes, or to respond to slanders against himself. He was accused of many things, but one of the most painful to him was the slanderous allegation that he had mistreated his slaves. This libel was prominently revived in *The Baltimore American* in 1866, and many of Lee's friends urged him to respond and set the record straight. Lee refused. As he wrote in explanation to one of his friends,

> *The statement is not true but I have not*
> *thought proper to publish a contradiction,*
> *being unwilling to be drawn into a newspaper*
> *discussion, believing that those who know me*
> *would not credit it and those who do not*
> *would care nothing about it. I cannot now*
> *depart from the rule I have followed. It is so*
> *easy to make accusations against the people of*
> *the South upon similar testimony that those so*
> *disposed, should one be refuted, will immedi-*
> *ately create another; and thus you would be led*
> *into endless controversy. I think it better to*
> *leave their correction to the return of reason*
> *and good feeling.*[129]

Some have said that Lee felt no bitterness over the defeat. It is true that he never publicly expressed bitterness, and we may believe him when he assured those around him that he bore no hatred toward his former enemies. He was ever careful in his public actions and statements to avoid anything that might provoke recriminations by the victorious party. But he nevertheless tasted the bitterness of the defeat of the cause of the South. And during this time he had need of encouragement from his people.

Once a young girl, who lived near the Lees in Richmond and frequently visited in the Lee household, happened upon the general in an unguarded moment when he was feeling particularly keenly the sense of loss suffered by the South.

The expression on Lee's face provoked the young lady to ask, "Why will you look so heartbroken?"

"Why shouldn't I?" Lee replied, "My cause is dead! I am homeless—I have nothing on earth."

"Yes you have," said the girl, "You have got a plenty of love and admiration!"[130]

The love of the people of the South was undoubtedly a great encouragement to Lee on more than one occasion. He had given himself in their defense, and he would now give what was left of his life for their benefit.

A Door Opens

No man can be so important in the world that he
need not the good-will and approval of others.

–R. E. Lee

*L*ee had always had a desire to be a full-time farmer.
The peace and quiet, the solitude and tranquility of
the country were ever a strong attraction to him. They became
even more so now. Living in Richmond was like living in a fish-
bowl. Crowds gathered everywhere he went. Reporters were
ever seeking for some quote or action that might indicate his
desire to continue "the rebellion." He came to long for seclusion.

His desire to leave Richmond was also motivated by the
high cost of living in the city. Even more compelling was his
wife's health. Her condition had not improved; in fact, it had
worsened. The fresh air of the country would surely be better
for her than the congested air of the city. Lee thus determined
to search for a farm. He wrote to General Long, "I am looking
for some little quiet house in the woods where I can procure
shelter and my daily bread if permitted by the victor." [131]

The last phrase indicates something of the uncertainty that surrounded his future at this point in his life. On May 29, President Andrew Johnson had issued a proclamation offering full amnesty and pardon to all who would take a loyalty oath promising to support the Constitution and the laws of the United States. This offer excluded fourteen classes of Confederates (generals were among them). Full property rights (slaves excepted) would be restored to every man who took the oath. Those individuals who were excluded from the general pardon were free to apply individually to the president with the assurance that "clemency [would] be liberally extended as [might] be consistent with the facts of the case and the peace and dignity of the United States."

Though this offer received a mixed reaction in the South in general, Lee was heartened. His great concern had been for his men and the people of the South. Now it appeared the way had been opened for the South's recovery. President Johnson's offer opened the door to restoration without the harsh recriminations Lee had feared would come at the hands of the radicals. If the men of the South agreed to these conditions, the region might be protected from the despots and the citizens might be able to rebuild their lives and their country.

Lee did not foresee the radical reaction to President Johnson's efforts at restoration and the terrible retribution that would be exacted. At this point, every straw of hope had to be embraced.

Also, Lee knew (despite his reluctance to believe the esteem in which the people of the South held him), that many would look to him for an indication of how to respond. In his judgment there was therefore only one thing to do. He would apply for pardon according to the terms offered by the president and urge others to do the same. In answer to the charge of inconsistency he replied,

After the surrender of the Southern armies in
April, the revolution in the opinions and feel-
ings of the people became so complete, and the
return of the Southern States into the union of
all the States so inevitable, that it became in
my opinion the duty of every citizen…to cease
opposition, and place himself in a position to
serve the country. I, therefore, upon the promul-
gation of the proclamation of President
Johnson of 29th of May,…determined to com-
ply with its requirements, and applied on the
13th of June to be embraced within its provi-
sions… [T]rue patriotism sometimes requires of
men to act exactly contrary, at one period, to
that which it does at another, and the motive
which impels them—the desire to do right—is
precisely the same. The circumstances which
govern their actions change; and their conduct
must conform to the new order of things.
History is full of illustrations of this.[132]

Lee's application brought more criticism against him than anything in his life since his early military efforts in western Virginia. Men found it galling to beg pardon from the nation who had but recently devastated their homes and disembow-eled their culture. But Lee's example calmed the troubled hearts of many. "Marse Robert" would not have done it had it been truly dishonorable. Humiliating it might be, but not dis-honorable.

The example of Lee had great effect. During the early days of June, when many men wrestled over this issue, Captain George Wise, son of the former governor of Virginia, visited Lee for his advice. Lee happened to be ill at the time of the captain's visit, but Mary Lee knew the young man and allowed him to see the general anyway. Pale and tired, Lee was lying on a couch when Captain Wise entered.

"They want me to take this thing, General," he said, waving a copy of the oath in his hand. "My parole covers it, and I do not think it should be required of me. What would you advise?"

"I would advise you to take it."

"General," the veteran protested, "I feel that this is submission to an indignity. If I must continue to swear the same thing over at every street corner, I will seek another country where I can at least preserve my self-respect."

At this, Lee lay silent for a time. "Do not leave Virginia," he said quietly. "Our country needs her young men now."

Wise took the oath, but when he told his father what he had done, his father exclaimed, "You have disgraced the family!" The young Wise quickly replied, "General Lee advised me to do it." At which his father paused and said, "Oh, that alters the case. Whatever General Lee says is all right, I don't care what it is." [133]

Before Lee could find a farm to purchase, an offer came from a family friend, Mrs. Edmund Cocke, to move into Derwent, a vacant house on her estate, which was about fifty-five miles from Richmond. The Lees accepted the offer and moved at the end of June. It was a modest "tenant house" with two rooms on a second floor above the two rooms below, but it provided what Lee desired most: quiet seclusion from the eyes of the world. At least, it was *somewhat* more secluded than his home in Richmond had been: no matter where he was, Robert E. Lee attracted crowds. The affection in which Lee was held is nearly impossible to comprehend in our cynical century.

Lee's rest did not mean, however, that he forgot about the plight of the people or the travails of his comrades. He agonized over the mistreatment of President Davis at Fortress

Monroe. He groaned over the stories about the desolation of the citizens of the South that continued to come to his ears. And, most of all, he longed to do what he could to preserve the noble memory of his old soldiers—"Lee's Miserables," as they had come to be called. He wanted to write an account of the war that would preserve the truth about the men under his charge.

In a letter sent to many of his former officers to secure reports from them about various battles and movements, Lee explained his purpose: "I am desirous that the bravery and devotion of the Army of Northern Virginia be correctly transmitted to posterity. This is the only tribute that can now be paid to the worth of its noble officers and soldiers." [134] Circumstances would prevent this book from being written, but that Lee began it is further evidence of his love for his men.

Lee's time at Derwent passed uneventfully. For a while, he traveled nowhere—except to church on Sundays. Gradually, he began to take his customary rides on Traveller through the countryside (to the great delight of people who had never imagined they would ever have the opportunity of seeing Robert E. Lee with their own eyes). Little did Lee know that while he was riding about, enjoying his days, some men whom he had never met were making a decision which would alter the rest of his life.

On the afternoon of August 4, 1865, the trustees of Washington College—a small, Presbyterian school in Lexington, Virginia—met to determine what could be done to preserve the college. It was in a desolate condition. The college had been founded as Liberty Hall Academy in 1749, but its name had been changed in 1796 in honor of General George Washington, who had endowed it with one hundred shares of stock in the James River Company. Its student body had left to fight in the war in 1861, many of them joining the famous Stonewall Brigade. Along with the town of Lexington, the school had suffered severely from the occupation by federal troops in 1864. The buildings had been badly damaged; the library and laboratory had been destroyed. The school was, for all practical purposes, bankrupt. In spite of all this, the trustees—all staunch Scotch-Irish Presbyterians— were undaunted. The need was greater than ever and thus God, they believed, would make a way.

A primary purpose for this meeting of the trustees was to choose a new president. Several individuals had been nominated and the vote was about to be taken, when one of the men mentioned a bit of news he had heard from a friend of the Lee family. It seems that a young woman, while visiting with the Lees, had been told by Mary Lee, daughter of the general, that although the South stood ready to give General Lee anything he needed, what he really needed was a job by which he could earn a living to provide for his family.

The thought struck all present as most providential, and in a few minutes Robert E. Lee had been unanimously elected as the new president of Washington College. The trustees' elation over this decision lasted only momentarily, as the full realization of what they had done struck them. They had elected the most prominent man in the South—without his knowledge—to the presidency of a college which had no prestige (it was hardly known outside the Shenendoah Valley), no money, practically no student body, and hardly any usable buildings. The temerity of it all was positively breathtaking.

Ah, but blood will tell. After a brief moment of solemnity, all decided that what was done was done and, after all, nothing ventured, nothing gained. They determined to press on. A letter of invitation containing the proposed terms of the call was drafted, and a member of the board was chosen to take the invitation personally to General Lee. Judge John W. Brockenbrough was appointed for the task, but there was a problem: Judge Brockenbrough had nothing suitable to wear for the visit. His one suit was threadbare and utterly inappropriate for a meeting with General Lee. Furthermore, he had no money with which to make the trip.

Minor problems to the Scots! One of the men loaned the judge a suit and another borrowed fifty dollars from a woman in Lexington who had recently sold some tobacco from her farm. That fifty dollars—in brand new United States greenbacks—was the only cash at the disposal of Washington College, and it was all designated to the cause of obtaining the consent of the new president-elect.

So it was that Judge Brockenbrough arrived unannounced in mid-August, 1865, at the tenant house in which Robert E. Lee was staying. Lee had never met Judge Brockenbrough before, but he listened to his proposal respectfully. Although the terms were modest, considering the condition of the college, they were actually quite ambitious. A salary was proposed at $1500 per year (money which the college did not have but hoped to raise), plus one-fifth of the student fees (assuming the students who came could afford to pay), and a house and garden (which, thankfully, did exist—standing in need of only a few minor repairs).

Lee was left to consider the matter. It was evident that the college was in a low condition and that accepting this offer would place him in a situation that would involve many of those things to which he had the greatest aversion: paperwork, meetings, fund raising, public speaking, and correspondence. Yet, it was work; a work such as he had been seeking; a work that could be of great service to the people of Virginia and the South; a work that provided an opportunity to serve his former soldiers and their sons. And, most of all, it was an opportunity to affect young men for the gospel, fitting them for the great work of rebuilding a desolated country.

Lee's only reservations were his own fitness for the position and how his attachment to the college might affect its reputation. Would his presence be a boon or would it provoke hostility and opposition?

While Lee was debating these matters within himself, he received a letter from William Nelson Pendleton, his former chief of artillery, who was now the rector of the Episcopal church in Lexington. Pendleton urged Lee to accept the invitation of the college trustees. He wrote: "I have thought Dear General while thus doing an important service to the State & its people you might be presenting to the world in such position an example of quiet usefulness & gentle patriotism, no less impressive than the illustrious career in the field." [135]

Lee would not make a final decision until he had spoken with his old friend and "spiritual father" Episcopal Bishop Joseph P. B. Wilmer. Bishop Wilmer was not exactly enthralled with the prospect of a man of Lee's stature accepting the position of president in such a small, dilapidated, and undistinguished institution. "I confess," Wilmer said, "to a momentary feeling of chagrin at the proposed change (shall I say revulsion?) in his history." He urged him to realize that there were many prestigious institutions that would be delighted to have him at their head.

Lee responded characteristically. In God's providence, this was the opportunity that had opened to him. Further, did not *the cause* give dignity to the institution rather than the size of its endowment or the reputation of its scholars? The only thing he needed to know was if the bishop thought him capable of fulfilling this responsibility.

Years later, Bishop Wilmer described the rest of the interview:

> *I soon discovered that his mind soared above these earthly distinctions… I had spoken to his human feelings; he had now revealed himself to me as one "whose life was hid with Christ in God." My speech was no longer restrained. I congratulated him that his heart was inclined to this great cause, and that he was spared to give to the world the august testimony to the importance of Christian education. How he listened to my feeble words; how he beckoned me to his side, as the fulness of heart found utterance; how his whole countenance glowed with animation as I spoke of the Holy Ghost as the great Teacher, whose presence was required to make education a blessing, which otherwise might be the curse of mankind; how feelingly he responded, how eloquently, as I never heard him speak before—can never be effaced from memory; and nothing more sacred mingles with my reminiscences of the dead.[136]*

The decision was made. On August 24, Lee penned his acceptance of the invitation of the board. On September 15, 1865, Lee mounted his faithful Traveller to begin the 108-mile ride to Lexington. He would now give himself to training up young men—the president of an institution he had never seen, and which to most in Virginia was "as nearly dead as it could be."

Professor Edward Joynes later described the college and Lee's decision in these terms:

*There was absolutely nothing in this position
that could have tempted him. Not only was it
uncongenial with all the habits of his past life,
and remote from all the associations in which
he had formally taken pleasure; but it was, at
that time, most uninviting in itself. The college
to which he was called was broken in fortune
and in hope. The war had practically closed its
doors. Its buildings had been pillaged and
defaced, and its library scattered. It had now
neither money nor credit, and it was even
doubtful whether it would be shortly reopened
at all for the reception of students. The Faculty
were few in number, disorganized, and dispir-
ited... Under these circumstances the offer of
the presidency to General Lee was well nigh
presumptuous; and surely it was an offer from
which he had nothing to expect either of fortune or fame.*[137]

Lee would be offered many prestigious and well-paying
positions in the last years of his life, but he refused them all.
His life was tied to Washington College. He once refused an
opportunity to head up a "large house to represent Southern
commerce" which included both a residence in New York City
and a salary of $50,000, saying, "I am grateful, but I have a
self-imposed task which I must accomplish. I have led the
young men of the South in battle; I have seen many of them
die on the field; I shall devote my remaining energies to training young men to do their duty in life." [138] Duty had called
once again.

PRESIDENT OF WASHINGTON COLLEGE

*I consider the proper education of our youth one
of the most important objects now to be attained
and one from which the greatest benefits may be
expected.*

–R. E. Lee

*E*ven though much of the work at the college was of
the sort Lee detested, he gave himself to it with his
accustomed verve. He quickly established a daily routine.
Arising early, he walked to the college from the Lexington
Hotel, where he was staying prior to his family's arrival. He
was seated for chapel before the 7:45 A.M. starting time and
listened attentively to the sermon or exhortation given by the
minister appointed for the work. From eight A.M. until one or
two P.M. he worked in his office. The afternoons were devoted
to social duties or to rides in the country on Traveller. After
supper he usually remained in his room, retiring at ten P.M.

Running the college required stringent economy: nothing
was wasted. His years guiding an army with slender resources

had prepared him for this. Soon, however, prospects for the college began to improve. Men who respected Lee, from the North as well as the South, began to contribute to the college coffers. Enrollment increased, and within a few years Washington College was riding on the high places of the earth. From five instructors and sixty students the college grew within four years to an institution of more than twenty professors with over four hundred students.

But Lee's primary concern was always for the students themselves. Men came from all over the South to be educated at "General Lee's college." Soldiers and sons of soldiers, all became the special objects of Lee's care. The well-being of the student body and his correspondent responsibility in securing that well-being often weighed him down terribly.

His concern for the students was another fruit of his love for Christ. That which had most moved him to take the position at the college was the possibility of influencing young men toward godly manhood. Now it was his greatest burden. It was observed once, on his leaving chapel, that he was obviously affected. Asked if something were wrong, he replied, "I was thinking of my responsibility to Almighty God for these hundreds of young men."

He once remarked to Dr. William White, pastor of the Presbyterian church in Lexington, of his chief concern for the students:

> *I shall be disappointed, sir—I shall fail in the leading object that brought me here, unless these young men become real Christians; and I wish you, and the others of your sacred profession, to do all you can to accomplish this. I dread the thought of any student going away from the college without becoming a sincere Christian.*[139]

Later, in speaking with Dr. J. L. Kirkpatrick, who was professor of moral philosophy at the college, this same concern came to the fore, as Lee exclaimed, "O Doctor! if I could only know that all the young men in the college were good Christians, I should have nothing more to desire." This was said, reports Dr. Kirkpatrick, with lips quivering with emotion, both hands raised, and eyes overflowing with tears.[140]

The Christian faith pervaded all his plans for the college and its course of studies. Religion was to be inculcated through all the "schools" of the college. Though he rarely used the term "Christian" education, he did not believe there was any other education worthy of the name. Lee viewed himself as both missionary and educator and saw no conflict between the two.[141]

Lee initiated the code of honor at the college and made it the basis upon which all the students were received and governed. Once a new student requested a list of the rules of conduct for the college. Lee replied, "We have no printed rules." Lee was most unfriendly to rules which could not or would not be enforced. "Make no heedless rules," he admonished the faculty. "We must never make a rule that we cannot enforce." The only rule to Lee was the rule that had governed his own life: "We have but one rule here, and it is that every student must be a gentleman."[142]

A true gentleman, in Lee's understanding, embraced four important attributes, the first of which was manifested by diligent study. Lee could not abide idleness.

A young Georgia student, who had grown up where there was very little ice and snow, became fascinated with winter's effects. Upon learning the basics of ice skating, he determined to practice at every opportunity, even at times when his classes were in session. He soon received a summons to the president's office.

"Mr. _____," began Lee in his gentle voice, "I notice you have been absent for a number of recitations."

"Yes, sir, I was skating on North River."

"Mr. _____, if you had asked for permission to go skating, your work is very good, and I would have given you permission with pleasure. And now, Mr. _____, you know our Southern people are very poor, and to send you to college, your parents must be forced to economize, and deprive themselves of many things."

At this the boy choked up, "Stop, General Lee, you will never see me in your office again." And, true to his word, the young man never gave one cause for complaint the rest of his time at the college.[143]

A new student from North Carolina arrived at the college with a disdain for books and class both. When his first month reports came in, Lee called him into his office and went over all his grades. The student admitted that the grades were no better than he deserved and that he had no excuse for not attending his classes.

Lee, who happened to know the young man's parents, explained that he knew how much grief a poor report would bring to his family. He went on to say that if the report were to be printed in the college catalog, it would humiliate his parents. "I do not know what to do," he said, and sat for a few moments silently. Then, without a word, he tore up the paper. Upon this the boy broke down and promised to do his best to excel from that time on. Lee reported that he kept his pledge in every particular.[144]

The second mark of a gentleman was honorable conduct. A lack of discipline in morals or general deportment was to be avoided. Lee sought to encourage a sense of honor among the students. If they were indifferent or careless, intemperate or undisciplined, it brought dishonor not only upon them but their families as well. They must not only have regard for their own reputations, but regard for honoring their fathers and mothers. Nothing they did should reflect poorly upon their parents.

The third characteristic of a true gentleman was that he worshiped God faithfully. Lee was careful to be an example to the young men in this regard. He abolished compulsory chapel attendance after his first year at the college, but he was anxious that men be faithful in their attendance nevertheless. He was always promptly seated in his place, which was next to the wall on the north side of the chapel in the second pew from the front. Lee frowned on anything that interfered with worship on the Lord's Day. To Lee, the Sabbath was to be preserved as a day of rest and worship. It was the day God had set apart for Himself, and Lee believed that His honor should always take priority over man's entertainments.

The general encouraged the clergy who led the services of the college chapel to be in earnest and to speak to the hearts and consciences of his young men. He would make lists of the students who were affiliated with each denomination and send them to the local pastors, encouraging them to keep in close touch with the young men. All would be lost, in Lee's view, if the men were not faithful Christians.

The fourth gentlemanly attribute was having a respect for good order. One of Lee's favorite sayings was "Obedience to lawful authority is the foundation of manly character." And this he took most seriously. Yet, he was not unreasonable in his application of this precept.

Youth is itself enough reason sometimes to do things in an untoward way, and Lee was tolerant of innocent expressions of youthful exuberance. In the winter term of 1866-67 there was a spectacular incident which illustrates Lee's forbearance. John M. Graham, a student from Tennessee, found that someone was stealing from his wood supply. Suspecting it to be one of the janitors, he loaded one stick with gunpowder, intending to play a trick on the culprit. The next morning the stick exploded in the stove of Professor E. S. Joynes, setting his classroom afire! Little damage was done, but the professor was convinced the action was malicious. Lee mentioned it the next day in chapel, asking if anyone had information about the incident and requesting whoever might have such information to meet with him in his office that morning.

Young Mr. Graham, reasoning that the professor had in fact gotten what was coming to him, took with him a witness and appeared in the general's office. He explained his reasoning and why he had set the trap for the thief. "But General," said Mr. Graham, "I didn't know it was Professor Joynes." This provoked laughter from Lee. "Well, Mr. Graham, your plan to find out who was taking your wood was a good one, but your powder charge was too heavy. Next time use less powder." And the matter was dismissed.[145]

However, when it came to public disturbances, demonstrations which were intended to display displeasure with the ruling authorities, he was unflinching in his opposition. The students' love for the general knew no bounds and even the most timid were willing to fight to defend his honor. In the days of Reconstruction, it was not unusual for Northern hotheads to seek to bring public humiliation on former Southern leaders. Lexington, because of the presence of the Virginia Military Institute, and Washington College as well, was a target for many such agitators. One day word spread that there was to be a political meeting in town wherein the speaker intended to abuse General Lee. This inflamed the students, who decided immediately that this meeting (and holy honor) required their presence. Hearing of the plans of the students,

Lee summoned about a dozen of the leaders to his office and made it known that he desired them to avoid the meeting. In spite of the fact that this meeting with the president took place at three in the afternoon, his desire was quickly made known, and none of the students attended that evening.[146]

Thomas Nelson Page, a student of Washington College during Lee's tenure, relates the following incident:

> *It was occasionally the habit of the young orators who spoke in public at celebrations to express their feelings by indulging in compliments to General Lee and the ladies, and the reverse of compliments to "the Yankees." Such references, clad in the glowing rhetoric and informed with the deep feeling of youthful oratory, never failed to stir their audiences and evoke unstinted applause. General Lee, however, notified the speakers that such references were to be omitted. He said: "You young men speak too long, and you make three other mistakes: what you say about me is distasteful to me; what you say about the North tends to promote ill feeling and injure the institution, and your compliments to the ladies are much more valued when paid in private than in public."*[147]

Lee was master of the art of rebuking and chastising without humiliating. Indeed, so gentle was Lee's manner that one of the new students in his first visit to the president thought he was in the wrong office. "He was so gentle, kind, and almost motherly, that I thought there must be some mistake about it." Once he realized that the man to whom he was speaking was in fact General Lee, he had a different impression: "It looked as if the sorrow of a whole nation had been collected in his countenance, and as if he were bearing the grief of his whole people. It never left his face, but was ever there to keep company with the kindly smile." [148]

Lee's practice was to meet all the new students privately in his office upon their arrival. After this meeting, he ever afterward remembered their names, which proved both a grand comfort as well as, at times, a great grief. It was part of his long-held view of showing respect to the individual. Lee always made it a point to identify every student. One young man entered the college who had been introduced to the general in Baltimore some time previously—along with a host of others. To his amazement, when he entered the general's office he was recognized by Lee and greeted by name, as the president reviewed the circumstances of their previous meeting in Baltimore.

He not only remembered his students' names but kept close watch on their scholastic progress, especially if they were not doing well. In a faculty meeting Lee once expressed regret when a student's name was mentioned, saying that he was falling back in mathematics. The professor assured the general that in this case he was mistaken, that the boy was one of the best in the class. "He got only fifty-four last month," Lee insisted, and an appeal to the records of the professor proved him right. [149]

He once advised another professor who complained of the slower students in his classes, "May I give you a piece of advice, sir?…Always observe the stage-driver's rule…Always take care of the poor horses." [150] That, Lee was careful ever to do.

The Last Good-bye

I would like to go to some quiet place in the country and rest.

–R. E. Lee

*L*ee's health had never been good in the years after the war and it continued its gradual decline during his tenure at Washington College. His hair was entirely white and he walked more slowly, shoulders stooped. The tensions of the war and Reconstruction were beginning to show on him. At sixty-three, he looked and felt like an old man.

For the first ten weeks of 1870, Lee sought to carry on as usual, but it was clear to others that he was constantly in pain and suffering from severe weakness. By the spring of 1870, he confided to a friend that he could not walk up the slope from the chapel to his house without stopping to rest.

William Preston Johnson, a faculty member and one of his former soldiers, encouraged the general to take a vacation. A few days later, Lee brought up the subject to two other members of the faculty and they, in turn, called a meeting of the entire faculty to discuss the matter. It was decided that Lee should take a two-month vacation for his health. Lee agreed, and wrote to his daughter Mildred, who was visiting her brother, that he had decided to "take Agnes to Savannah, as she seems anxious to visit that city, or perhaps, she will take me. I am sorry not to be able to see you before I go but if I return, I hope to find you here well and happy." [151]

On the morning of March 24, only six days after the faculty's request that he take the vacation, Lee said good-bye to his wife and set off with Agnes for a trip south. He looked very weak and sickly. He was to take a canal boat to Lynchburg and from there go on to Richmond for the first leg of his trip. In retrospect, this was not the best decision to make. Lee needed rest most of all, and he himself had acknowledged that he would never get it if he went off on a trip. He had earlier said that he could not go to Savannah "without meeting more people than he wanted to." He did not realize how right his judgment was. A quiet trip through the South for General Robert E. Lee was, at this time in history, impossible. He little realized the love the South had for him—nor did he fully comprehend the esteem in which the region held him. He even worried about hotel rooms, never thinking that finding a place to stay would be the least of his troubles.

The trip to Lynchburg was hard on Lee and by the time he reached Richmond, he was exhausted and "a little feverish." The next day he received a thorough examination by three of the leading physicians of the city. Lee avoided the crowds while in Richmond, turning down an invitation to address the Virginia Senate and receiving only a few personal friends in his hotel room. On the afternoon of March 28, he and Agnes left for Warrenton, North Carolina, to visit the grave of his daughter Annie, who had died at age twenty-three.

They arrived unannounced at ten that evening and were invited to the home of Mr. and Mrs. John White. The next morning the general and his daughter visited the grave site. "My visit," he wrote to his wife, "was mournful, yet soothing to my feelings."[152] He and Agnes left Warrenton that evening aboard a sleeping-car, a "first" for Lee. However, the novelty, as well as the constant interruptions, conspired to keep him from sleeping.

Meanwhile, along the route word of the general's presence on the train preceded its arrival at each stop. At the station in Raleigh, scores of people waited to greet him. They cheered and chanted "Lee, Lee," until the train pulled away. The trip continued all the next day. Veterans sent fruit to his car, and restaurant proprietors served dinner and coffee to him when they realized he would not detrain. In Salisbury, a large crowd of citizens and a band greeted the train. The same occurred at Charlotte. Agnes described the scenes in a letter to her mother:

> *Indeed, I wish you could travel with papa, to see the affection and feeling shown toward him everywhere...Everywhere along the road where meals were provided the landlords invited us in and when we would not get out, sent coffee and lunches...I think we were expected to die of eating..."Namesakes" appeared on the way, of all sizes. Old ladies stretched their heads into the windows at the way-stations and then drew back and said, "He is mighty like his pictures."*[153]

It was pouring rain when they arrived in Columbia, South Carolina, but a huge crowd was waiting nonetheless.

Most stores were closed for the event, the veterans had all been mustered, and a large number of other citizens had gathered at the station house. General Lee was compelled to appear on the platform and the crowd roared its approval.

Finally, at nine-thirty in the evening, the train reached Augusta, Georgia, where they had planned to spend the night before going on to Savannah. Lee was greeted at the station by the mayor and a special committee of citizens and escorted to the Planters Hotel, where others had gathered to greet him. Lee was exhausted, having spent the last twenty-four hours practically without sleep, and decided to rest the next day in Augusta rather than set out for Savannah. But opportunities for rest the next day were few.

The next morning a reception was held in his honor. Agnes wrote, "Crowds came. Wounded soldiers, servants, and working-men even. The sweetest little children—namesakes— dressed to their eyes with bouquets of japonica—or tiny cards in their little fat hands—with their names." [154] Among the crowds was a youth of thirteen who worked his way through the throngs to see Lee. At length, he stood by his side, silently awe-struck that he, Woodrow Wilson, was in the presence of the great man.

The next day, Lee and Agnes left for Savannah. At the station the veterans gave him one last "rebel yell." At Savannah, the largest crowd yet greeted the train. They had come the previous day but had been disappointed, as Lee had remained an extra day in Augusta. Now, an even larger crowd had returned. So thick and enthusiastic was the throng that it took some time, even with escorts, to lead General Lee to the carriage that awaited him. Once he was seated, the crowd was so dense about the carriage that it couldn't move. Finally, Lee arose and bowed to the people, which brought forth a prodigious roar, and the people began to back away to allow the carriage to go on its way.

The next day, Lee met with old friends and former comrades. He mentioned to them the plight of a less fortunate comrade, General Samuel Cooper, and requested them to give thought to raising a fund for his relief. It was delightful for Lee to see these old acquaintances and to make new ones, but he was beginning to feel the strain of the trip. He wrote home to his wife, "I do not think traveling in this way procures me much quiet and repose. I wish I were back." [155]

Lee had planned to leave for Florida on April 8 for a visit to his father's grave on Cumberland Island, but Agnes became ill and they were not able to leave Savannah until April 12. On that day he and Agnes, along with Andrew Lowe, their host in Savannah, boarded the steamer *Nick King* for the leisurely trip down the Saint John's River—greeting crowds of well-wishers along the way.

When the boat docked at Cumberland Island, Lee and Agnes went ashore to the grave site. The visit was poignant but satisfying. In a letter to his wife, he wrote, "We visited Cumberland Island, and Agnes decorated my father's grave with beautiful fresh flowers....I presume it is the last time I shall be able to pay to it my tribute of respect. The cemetery is unharmed and the grave is in good order." [156]

On April 13, the boat stopped briefly at Jacksonville, where a committee from the city came aboard to give their greetings. People swarmed aboard and shook hands with Lee. So many came aboard that the *Nick King* was in danger of taking on water. The crowd continued to increase to such a degree that it was impossible for all the people to get on board to see their hero. The disappointment was so great that the officials asked Lee if he would go out on deck where he might be seen by all. Lee walked out on deck by himself, advancing to the rail with his hat in his hand. Then occurred one of the most remarkable scenes of his life. The crowd became completely silent. Starting from the front and moving back through the vast throng, men removed their hats in tribute to their beloved leader, until every last head was bare. It was as though to applaud or cheer would have dishonored the love and respect they felt for Lee. *The Jacksonville Union* reported, "The very silence of the multitude spoke a deeper feeling than the loudest huzzas could have expressed." [157]

Returning to Savannah, Lee spent a few more days there before heading on to Charleston. In Charleston, though Lee was desirous of avoiding any further demonstrations in his honor, the city's fire companies staged a colorful parade. Another reception was held. *The Charleston Courier* reported,

> *Old and young, the gray beards and sages of the country, the noble, pure, honorable, poor and wealthy, with hardly an exception, were present, and glad to do him honor. Stately dames of the old school, grandmothers of seventy, and a long train of granddaughters, all flocked around the noble old chief, glad of a smile, of a shake of the hand; and happy was the girl of twelve, or fourteen, who carried away on her lips the parting kiss of the grand old soldier.*[158]

By now, the press had begun following and reporting on what had become "Lee's triumphal tour." Invitations poured in from around the South for him to come and visit. Lee wrote to a friend, "Our kind people seem to think that I am running loose or have a roving commission to travel the country." [159]

On April 28 Lee left Charleston for Wilmington, where he spent the night in the home of George Davis, former attorney general for the Confederacy. The next day brought another reception and hundreds of well-wishers.

Lee left for the trip to Norfolk on April 30. When he arrived at Portsmouth, Virginia, to take the ferry across the Elizabeth River to Norfolk, he was met by another huge crowd at the station. Some of the young men had borrowed an old cannon—from which they fired numerous rounds in the general's honor. Roman candles, fireworks, and raucous Confederate yells alerted the folk of Norfolk that Lee had arrived and was on his way across the river. The crowds in Norfolk sought to outdo their neighbors across the river with cheers and yells. Lee was escorted to a carriage and driven off to the home of Dr. William Selden for the evening.

The next day was Sunday and Lee insisted on attending worship, as was his custom. The general requested Caroline, one of Dr. Selden's daughters, to attend with him, and off they went to Christ Episcopal Church. Caroline later wrote, "The street was lined with adoring crowds. For one block before reaching Christ Church we had almost to force our way through a narrow pathway they seemed to have left for him. Every hat was in the air, but being Sunday the homage was very quiet." [160]

From Norfolk, Lee and Agnes made their way home more quietly, stopping only to visit relatives and old friends. The impression made upon cousins, nephews, and other distant relations was as deep as any made upon the rest of the population. One young female cousin, who had never met the general before, remarked later, "We regarded him with the greatest veneration. We had heard of God, but here was General Lee!" [161]

Lee arrived home on May 28, only two months and four days after he had left for his "vacation." Though the trip had been wearisome and did little to improve his health, for Lee it was one of the most memorable seasons of his life. It was an inestimable encouragement to see that though defeated, the people of the South had not been destroyed. The trip also made him realize that which he had always modestly refused to believe: for the South, Lee was the equal of Washington.

Last Days

The Lord shall make good his loving kindness
toward me: yea, thy mercy, O Lord, endureth for
ever; despise not then the work of thine own hands.
      –from the Psalter reading for September 28,
        in the Protestant Episcopal Prayer Book

*U*pon his return to Lexington, Lee found a resolution
from the board of trustees giving Mary the new
house that had been built on the campus for the president
and providing her with an annual income in the event of his
death. Lee immediately rejected the generous gesture:

> *Though fully sensible of the kindness of the*
> *Board, and justly appreciating the manner in*
> *which they sought to administer to my relief, I*
> *am unwilling that my family should be a tax*
> *to the college, but desire that all of its funds*
> *should be devoted to the purposes of education.*
> *I know that my wishes on this subject are*

*equally shared by my wife and therefore I
request that the provisions of the fourth and
fifth resolutions may not be carried into
effect.*[162]

Normally, the board acquiesced to the general's requests. This time it made no response and did not rescind the original resolution. After Lee's death, Mrs. Lee did consent to live in the house, but she steadfastly declined to accept the annuity.

The official opening of the 1870-71 session of the college was set for Thursday, September 15. The entire student body was gathered in the chapel. General Pendleton conducted a brief worship service. Afterwards Lee arose and made a number of announcements about the classes for the term and then "expressed his earnest hope that both professors and students would attend regularly the daily prayers at the chapel." Though it was a very short spiel, it was probably the longest speech he ever gave at the college.

This year marked Lee's fifth anniversary as president of the college. How much things had changed since that fall in 1865! The old college that was to all eyes "as good as dead" was now a vibrant, vigorous example of higher education and the admiration of the South.

Lee fell quickly back into his precise and busy schedule. Breakfast, family worship, chapel at the college, visits with students (from 8:45 to 10:30 A.M.), and the routine responsibilities of the college occupied his time until dinner at two P.M. Afterwards, he took a short nap and a ride on Traveller, weather permitting. The general spent his evenings quietly at home reading and enjoying his wife and family.

On Tuesday, September 28, the general arose at his normal hour, held family prayers, and headed for his office. Only six years previous he had been in the midst of planning a surprise attack of Fort Harrison. Today his schedule involved routine office work and a vestry meeting at his church in the evening.

After seeing students, he settled down to attack his correspondence. In writing to Mr. Samuel H. Taggert, a friend from Baltimore, Lee stated "In answer to your question, I reply that I am much better. I do not know whether it is owing to having seen you and Doctor Buckler last summer or to my visit to the Hot Springs. Perhaps both. But my pains are less and my strength greater. In fact, I suppose I am as well as I shall be." [163]

The day was quite chilly, and after supper the rain began falling steadily. He probably should have stayed home, as his wife urged, but he felt keenly his duty as a vestryman and determined to go to the meeting in the church building. As there was no smaller room available, the men sat in the pews in the unheated auditorium, enduring the chill. The meeting ended around seven P.M. with Lee's generous offer to give an additional fifty-five dollars toward the pastor's salary. Fittingly, the last act of this noble man's life was one of magnanimity.

Epilogue

I look forward to better days, and trust that time and experience, the great teachers of men, under the guidance of an ever-merciful God, may save us from destruction and restore to us the bright hopes and prospects of the past.

—R. E. Lee

Word of Lee's death spread rapidly around Lexington. The stores closed; the students left their classes. Because of the flood, the news did not reach Richmond and the rest of the country until that evening. In every Southern town mourning began immediately.

The student newspaper at the college prepared this statement:

We stop our paper from going to press in order to make the saddest announcement which our pen ever wrote: our honored and loved president is no more…He died as he lived, calmly

> *and quietly, in the full assurance of the*
> *Christian's faith.*[164]

The college board of trustees, at the suggestion of the faculty, provided a vault for Lee's body in the library under the college chapel. The board further decided that Lee's name should be added to the name of the college. Thus, Washington College became Washington and Lee College.

The funeral was set for October 14 at nine A.M. Reverend Pendleton, Dr. William S. White, Stonewall Jackson's pastor, and Dr. William Jones, former chaplain in the Confederate army, all delivered eulogies. Dr. Pendleton preached from the text of Psalm 37:8-11, 28-40. After the service, Lee's body was removed from the president's house to the chapel, where it lay in state until the next day.

On the morning of October 15, a long procession of old soldiers, students, V. M. I. cadets, townspeople, and visiting dignitaries formed in front of the president's house and proceeded in grim parade through the principal streets of Lexington. The veterans wore black ribbons on the lapels of their coats. The military institute flew the flags of all the Southern states at half mast.

Many of Lee's famous officers were kept away from the ceremonies by the flood in the region. Their places were taken by the plain privates who had come down from the mountains and coves of Virginia. Fittingly, it was the men whom Lee thought the most honorable of all who came to pay their respects to the one they had followed and loved for four memorable years.

These were men of few words but solid convictions. They had been silent as they passed by his body. They had been reserved in the display of their emotions as they participated in the ceremonies of the day, but no one felt more deeply than they the realities of life and death. When the final committal had been read by Reverend Pendleton, the gathered congregation began to sing *How Firm a Foundation*, the famous hymn General Lee had loved so much in his lifetime.

Once again, the familiar sound of the singing of the Army of Northern Virginia rang across the valley. The men who had sung so many times with their general gave him his last tribute by singing at the top of their voices the praises of God and of the great salvation. The old hymn echoed off the buildings of the town, and the surrounding mountains themselves rang with the beautiful melody. It was perhaps the most fitting epitaph of all.

> *The soul that on Jesus, hath leaned for repose*
> *I will not, I will not desert to his foes;*
> *That soul though all hell should endeavor to*
>   *shake,*
> *I'll never, no, never, no, never forsake.*

PART II:
THE CHARACTER OF ROBERT EDWARD LEE

જ્જ   જ્જ   જ્જ

I have met with many of the great men of my time,
but Lee alone impressed me with the feeling that I was in
the presence of a man who was cast in a grander mould
and made of different and finer metal than all other men.
He is stamped upon my memory as being apart and
superior to all others in every way, a man with whom
none I ever knew and few of whom I have read
are worthy to be classed.
British General Garnett Joseph Wolseley

Ah! Muse, you dare not claim
A nobler man than he;
Nor nobler man hath less of blame,
Nor blameless man hath purer name,
Nor purer name hath grander fame,
Nor fame—another Lee.
from "Robert E. Lee"
Father A. J. Ryan

CHRISTIANITY

My chief concern is to try to be an humble, earnest Christian.

–R. E. Lee

*L*ee's life was, at bottom, a life of grace. Some have noted that his great rule was, like Washington before him, to be "a gentleman." This is true, but we must understand what Lee (and Washington) understood by the term. A gentleman was one who was constrained by the love of God to live in the fear of God and to love his neighbor as himself. In other words, the concept of the gentleman could not be defined without describing the Christian.

Douglas Southall Freeman states: "[Lee] could not have conceived of a Christian who was not a gentleman." To Lee, there was no contradiction between the two at all. There was no possibility of being a gentleman without first being a Christian. And there should be no such thing as a Christian who was not a gentleman.

Lee's view of himself is best captured in his response to Pastor Benjamin Lacy who, in a meeting with Lee, told him of the deep interest the chaplains felt in his welfare and of their prayers in his behalf. Lee replied, "I sincerely thank you for that, and I can only say that I am a poor sinner, trusting in Christ alone for salvation and that I need all the prayers you can offer for me."[1] These were not mere words.

Lee took a great interest in the revival among the men of the Army of Northern Virginia and was immensely pleased to hear of his men looking to Christ for salvation and blessing. Lee himself never failed to attend the preaching that went on in the camps when his duties did not absolutely preclude his doing so. His Christian faith was integral to his life and truly Lee cannot be understood apart from this great overriding fact.

At the end of November 1863, when the army was camped at Mine Run, a battle was expected at any moment. Lee and a number of his staff officers were riding down the line of battle when they came upon a party of soldiers engaged in prayer. Already the sharp-shooting for the upcoming battle had begun along the skirmish-line and the artillery had just begun to fire. When Lee saw these men, however, he immediately dismounted and, uncovering his head, joined the men in prayer. The rest of his staff followed the example of their chieftain. One can only imagine the surprise of the privates when the prayers were finished to find that they had just led their beloved commander before the throne of grace.

Lee always believed in and practiced regular church attendance. He was a faithful member of the Episcopal church in Lexington, sitting in his pew—the second row from the pulpit and directly in front of the chancel—every Sunday. He read the Bible privately on a daily basis. His private devotional time was often extended, particularly during periods of special joy or sorrow.

His view of the war was shaped by his consciousness of God's justice and man's sin. Lee wrote to Mrs. Lee in February of 1862, "I hope God will at last crown our efforts with success. But the contest must be long and severe, and the whole country must go through much suffering. It is necessary we should be humbled and taught to be less boastful, less selfish and more devoted to right and justice to all the world."[2]

One of the best assessments of Lee's character is given to us by Edward Clifford Gordon, his aide at Washington College. Gordon worked at Lee's side for three years and spent hundreds of hours with him. He captured the essence of General Lee in these words:

> *Intellectually he was cast in a gigantic mold. Naturally he was possessed of strong passions. He loved excitement, particularly the excitement of war. He loved grandeur. But all these appetites and powers were brought under the control of his judgment and made subservient to his Christian faith. This made him habitually unselfish and ever willing to sacrifice himself on the altar of duty and in the service of his fellows...He is an epistle, written of God and designed by God to teach the people of this country that earthly success is not the criterion of merit, nor the measure of true greatness.*[3]

One biographer has noted, "As a former newspaper editor and writer of countless short historical biographies, I searched diligently for a flaw in Lee's character. I found none. I cannot say that of any other person I've read about or researched. I kept asking myself, 'Why? What was his secret?'...His secret was that he found the source of his strength and commitment in Christ."[4]

This was the judgment of those who knew him best. William Jones wrote,

> *If I have ever come in contact with a sincere, devout Christian,—one who, seeing himself to be a sinner, trusted alone in the merits of Christ,—who humbly tried to walk the path of duty, "looking unto Jesus the author and finisher of our faith," and whose piety was constantly exemplified in his daily life, that man was the world's great soldier, and model man, Robert Edward Lee.*[5]

WORSHIP

*Above all things, learn at once to worship your
Creator and to do His will as revealed in His Holy
Book.*

-R. E. Lee in a letter to a child that had
been named after him

*T*he first question of the Westminster Assembly's
Shorter Catechism asks, "What is man's chief end?"
And the answer is given, "Man's chief end is to glorify God
and to enjoy Him forever." The ultimate purpose for man's
existence is to bring honor to God, to acknowledge Him and
give Him praise, thanksgiving, and obedience. This purpose
finds its central expression in worship.

The word "worship" is derived from the Old English word
"worthship." It means to recognize the worth of another and
respond accordingly. To worship God is to recognize God's
worth. A man who refuses to worship is a man who refuses
to acknowledge the most basic fact of all: that we live and
move and have our being in God.

To Lee, worship was essential. A correspondent from Georgia once announced to the general the birth of a new son—to whom the father had given the name Robert Lee. The general carefully penned a reply—written to the little baby—with many kindly paragraphs full of encouragement, and concluded with this admonition, "Above all things, learn at once to worship your Creator and to do His will as revealed in His Holy Book."[6]

What he was careful to recommend to others, he followed himself. During the war, Lee made it a practice to encourage the chaplains in their labors and always attended upon their preaching when not called away by other responsibilities. And he was no disinterested participant, either. Lee's response to the faithful preaching of the Word revealed his love for the Savior. A correspondent from Richmond noted an occasion when he was present at a service—under the leadership of Pastor Benjamin T. Lacey—when both Lee and Jackson were moved to tears by the preaching.

The same high regard for the worship of God was evidenced in Lee while he was president of Washington College. Attendance at chapel services, though never compulsory, was as important in Lee's eyes as any class. The president was always prompt for the service and especially enjoyed it when there was vigorous and clear preaching of the Gospel. Lee once remarked to the Reverend William Jones after one of the sermons at the chapel,

> *It was a noble sermon—one of the very best I
> have ever heard—and the beauty of it was that
> the preacher gave our young men the very
> marrow of the Gospel, and with a simple
> earnestness that must have reached their hearts
> and done them good.[7]*

Lee believed not only in the importance of public worship on the Lord's Day, but he was also very careful to maintain family worship. He began every day with private devotions. In his view, "No day should be lived unless it was begun with a prayer of thankfulness and an intercession for guidance." Afterwards he held family prayers. So important were these times that the general always insisted that the family meet promptly at the appointed hour, that they might begin prayers without delay.

Before "Rooney" Lee's fiancée came for her first visit in the Lee home, Rooney told her of his father's insistence on promptness at family prayers. During a stay of three weeks, she was not late even one time. She later said that as a result of her diligence she rose greatly in the general's estimation. It was her opinion ever afterward that not even General Washington himself would have the entire good opinion of General Lee if he had been late for morning prayers![8] In Lee's view, the one who was not conscientious about his obligation to worship God would not be conscientious about less important things.

To Lee, God was to be honored before and above all. And this honor was not merely a duty to be promptly performed but the happy privilege of one who had received the goodness of God, and it was the overwhelming sense of the goodness of God which produced in Lee a pervasive sense of gratitude and indebtedness which never left him.

THE BIBLE

The Bible is the Book of Books.

–R. E. Lee

Our Savior noted that "man does not live by bread alone, but by every word that proceeds out of the mouth of God." (Matthew 4:4) To the child of God nothing is more precious than the book of God. So it was for General Lee.

Though Lee was a diligent student, most of his adult life was providentially so ordered to leave little time for leisurely reading. He was never too busy, however, to read the Scriptures. Even in the midst of the most active of campaigns, Lee found time to read some portion of God's Word. In peacetime, every day began and ended with the Word. Lee said that the Bible is "a book which supplies the place of all others and cannot be replaced by any other." [9]

The Scriptures were his comfort and delight:

> *I prefer the Bible to any other book. There is enough in that to satisfy the most ardent thirst*

for knowledge; to open the way to true wisdom;
and to teach the only road to salvation and
eternal happiness. It is not above human com-
prehension, and is sufficient to satisfy all its
desires.[10]

Lee once received the gift of a beautiful edition of the
Bible from a group of English donors headed by A. W.
Beresford Hope. In his letter thanking Mr. Hope for this precious gift, Lee said, "I must ask the favour of you to thank
them [i.e., the donors] most heartily for their kindness in providing me with a book in comparison with which all others
in my eyes are of minor importance, and which in all my per-
plexities has never failed to give me light and strength."[11]

He believed the Bible to be the written, inspired, and
infallible Word of God. He once remarked, "There are many
things in the old Book which I may never be able to explain,
but I accept it as the infallible Word of God, and receive its
teachings as inspired by the Holy Ghost."

Lee always manifested a lively concern to promote the
distribution of the Bible to others. During the war, he encouraged the distribution of Bibles among his men and then
encouraged them to make good use of the Scriptures. After
arriving in Lexington, he was called upon to accept the post
of president of the newly revived Rockbridge County Bible
Society. Honored by the opportunity, he accepted the post and
continued to serve till the day of his death. He was desirous,
he said, "of cooperating in any way I can in extending the
inestimable knowledge of the priceless truths of the Bible."[12]

Each evening the Lee household followed the same routine: the general first read to Mrs. Lee, and then closed the day
with a portion from God's Word and, of course, prayer. Toward
the end of his life he more and more focused his reading in

two books: the Bible and the Protestant Episcopal Prayer Book. The most worn page in his copy of the prayer book, marked by a small strip of paper, is the one containing the Psalter for the thirtieth day (Psalm 144): "Blessed be the Lord my strength: who teacheth my hands to war, and my fingers to fight."[13] The great warrior knew well that his most important weapon in this life was the sword of the Spirit.

A Devoted Husband

Husbands, love your wives even as Christ loved the Church and gave Himself for it.

–Ephesians 5:25

St. Paul's admonition was not lost on Robert E. Lee. From the day he first took Mary Custis to be his bride, he devoted himself to her sacrificially. Mrs. Lee never enjoyed complete health after the birth of Mary, her second child, in 1835. She developed a pelvic infection that was not treated properly, and from that time on she experienced a steady decline in her physical well-being. By 1857, when Lee returned home from Texas upon the death of Mr. Custis, Mrs. Lee had become an invalid. Due to the ravages of arthritis, she had lost the use of her right arm and hand. Kept awake by the pain, she was seldom able to get a full night's rest and she was barely able to move about the house under her own power. At the age of forty-nine, she had become an old woman.

Though Lee was truly shocked over his wife's condition (she had made no mention of the deterioration in her health in her letters to him), it only caused him to become more devoted to her as he sought to comfort and uphold her in her affliction. In fact, the severe suffering Mrs. Lee was called to endure in God's providence deepened the Lees' love for one another. The sight of Mrs. Lee's suffering drew forth more of her husband's love, and the love he gave strengthened her love for him. He delighted to pamper her; she delighted to honor him.

Even during the horrors of war, Lee never forgot her. Their thirty-third anniversary occurred on June 30, 1864, during the siege of Petersburg. In spite of the tension and worries of battle, General Lee found time to write his wife:

> *Do you recollect what a happy day thirty-three years ago this was? How many hopes and pleasures it gave birth to. God has been very merciful and kind to us...I pray that he may continue his mercy and blessings to us and give us a little peace and rest together in this world and finally gather us and all he has given us around His throne in the world to come.*[14]

Her well-being was never far from his mind. Lee wrote to his daughter Mildred five days later and expressed his love for his wife and his desire to be with her:

> *My Precious Life:*
> *I received this morning by your brother, your note, and am very glad to hear your mother is better. I sent immediately to try and find some lemons, but could only procure two—sent to me by a kind lady, Mrs. Kirkland, in Petersburg...I found one in my valise, dried up,*

*which I also send, as it may be of some value. I
also put up some early apples, which you can
roast for your mother, and one pear. This is all
the fruit I can get.*

*You must go to market every morning and see
if you cannot find some fresh fruit for her...Tell
her lemonade is not as palatable or digestible
as buttermilk. Try and get some for her–with
ice it is delicious, and very nutritious. I hope
she will continue to improve, and be soon well
and leave the heated city...Tell her I can only
think of her and pray for her much, but cannot
now see the day when we shall be together
once more. I think of you, long for you, pray for
you: it is all I can do. Think sometimes of your
devoted father,*

R. E. Lee.[15]

As a man conscious of his responsibilities to his wife, Lee
sought to assist her in becoming more faithful in her duties.
This was especially his concern in regard to her training of
the children. Mrs. Lee was not the disciplinarian that her husband was. Robert, Jr., once noted, "My mother I could
sometimes circumvent, and at times took liberties with her
orders, construing them to suit myself; but exact obedience to
every mandate of my father was a part of my life and being
at that time." [16]

While Lee was on assignment out West, rumors reached
him that his little boy was being spoiled by all the attention
he was receiving. This pampering, coupled with a notable lack
of chastisement, had contributed to his reputation of being
"unmanageable." Lee was quick to seek to remedy the situation, writing to Mrs. Lee on October 16, 1837:

*Our dear little boy seems to have among his
friends the reputation of being hard to manage,
a distinction not at all desirable, as it indicates
self-will and obstinacy. Perhaps these are qualities which he really possesses, and he may have
a better right to them than I am willing to
acknowledge; but it is our duty, if possible, to
counteract them and assist him to bring them
under control. I have endeavored in my inter-
course with him, to require nothing but what
was in my opinion necessary or proper...I have
also tried to show him that I was firm in my
demands, and constant in their enforcement,
and that he must comply with them; and I let
him see that I look to their execution, in order
to relieve him as much as possible from the
temptation to break them...You must assist me
in my attempts, and we must endeavor to com-
bine the mildness and forbearance of the
mother with the sternness and perhaps unrea-
sonableness of the father... I pray God to
watch over and direct our efforts in guarding
our little son, that we may bring him up in the
way that he should go.*[17]

These gentle admonitions had their desired effect, and
Mrs. Lee sought to become more faithful in bringing needed
checks to the self-will of her son. Later, after the general's
death, Mrs. Lee wrote to her son Fitzhugh concerning his son
Robert:

*I am glad to hear my darling little Rob is
becoming so sweet and good. Don't spoil him. I*

fear he will have too many indulgences to
make a great & self-controlled spirit essential to
a great & good man; but we must pray that
God will direct him in all his ways & teach
him early to love & serve Him.[18]

There was never any question about who was the head of
the house. Nothing was more respected than the word of the
general. But, in later years, Mrs. Lee delighted in showing her
wifely mastery over her husband and he, it should be noted,
took pleasure—in these innocent instances—of showing her
honor.

She retained for herself the final approval of every sculp-
ture, painting, or photograph of her husband. No
representation of the famous general could be "officially" dis-
tributed without her imprimatur. After the sculptor E. V.
Valentine had completed a bust of the general, therefore, he
had it transported to the Lee residence for the required
approval of the mistress of the house.

Mrs. Lee had decided to make the judging of the bust a
minor event, and had invited several of her friends to join her
for the occasion. All were seated and ready to examine the
work of art. Mrs. Lee called for her husband to come and
stand beside the bust so that they all could compare it with
the "real article." Lee dutifully did so and for the next few tor-
tuous minutes obeyed each command from his wife to turn to
the left or right or full face, as Mr. Valentine turned the bust.
After a most careful scrutiny, Mrs. Lee announced herself
delighted and dismissed her faithful husband, who retreated
without complaint or protest, happy to have been of service to
her.

Lee was ever solicitous of his wife's well-being, seeking to
be sure that everything that might contribute to her comfort

was provided. After the war, he delighted to be with her. Most evenings were spent quietly, she knitting, and he reading to her. Before retiring, he always read her a portion of the Scripture, and then they prayed together. He purchased a small carriage for her so she would have the opportunity for fresh air without too much discomfort. He often claimed the privilege of taking her on rides around the countryside.

His love for his wife became a shining example to the young men at the college in Lexington. Mrs. Lee's room was on the first floor of the house and opened out on the large porch that extended around three sides of the house. It was the general's custom every afternoon, weather permitting, to roll her out on the porch in her chair. Many of the students, knowing the hour of this ritual, would arrange to be walking—very slowly—by the president's house at the appointed time in order to get a glimpse of their hero serving his invalid bride. Stooping down to kiss her cheek, making sure that she was comfortable, patting her on the shoulder, his great pleasure in her company was clearly manifest. Lee's attentiveness and solicitude provide a picture of what St. Peter meant when he called upon husbands to honor their wives as "the weaker vessel." (I Peter 3:7)

The love of a man causes his wife to flourish. Without question, it was her husband's love that kept Mrs. Lee from bitter despair at the end of her days. Ill health, the loss of children, family home, and estate would all have conspired to embitter a woman with a less obedient husband. But Mary Lee was known for her contentment, kindness, grace, thoughtfulness, hospitality, and joy. She was a testimony to the blessings of having a husband who loves his wife as Christ loves the Church.

A Godly Wife

My Mother was a hero, as veritable a one as my Father.

—Mildred Lee

King Lemuel's mother knew what was important. Riches, fame, and power are fine, in their place, she taught her son, but nothing excels the value of a "woman who fears the Lord." (Proverbs 31:30) Accordingly, the wise king noted, "House and riches are the inheritance of fathers: but a prudent wife is from the Lord." (Proverbs 19:14) Men who are blessed with godly wives know their value to be above gold and silver. Robert E. Lee was no exception.

When he married "the belle of Arlington" he was gaining much more than a formal connection to the family of George Washington. Mary Custis had the good providence to have a godly mother who took care to train her not only in the womanly arts, but also in the disciplines of the Spirit. Mary had received from her mother a love for the Word of God and a reverence for the truth that leads to righteousness. Wealth and prestige are notorious for causing shipwreck in the lives of children born into such circumstances. However, Mary—trained to understand that all things come from God—never allowed her privileges to blind her to her responsibilities.

There was in her, as in her husband, a humility born of grace. She was never known to despise those whom the world would view as "beneath her rank," and she cared about their best interests. After arriving at Fort Monroe with Robert, she found to her great distress that the room in which worship was held on the Lord's Day had no seats provided for the blacks of the community. She wrote to her mother that there "are no seats provided in the room...for the blacks, consequently they never go." As a result, Mary doubled her efforts in the spiritual instruction of her maid Cassy[19]. Mrs. Lee, like many other Christians in the South, was quite committed to teaching her servants to read in order that they might study God's Word on their own. In letters to her mother, she regularly reported on the progress of the servants, "Margaret and Meniday get their lessons every week & Dick has gotten through the first reader."[20]

While at West Point with her husband, she faithfully taught a "Sunday school" for blacks. She mentions in letters to her mother her desire for the conversion of those around her—the blacks, the soldiers, friends, and family. The quality of the sermons was also carefully recorded:

> *Dr. Ducachet preached two excellent sermons last Sunday. The one in the morning was particularly addressed to young officers....It was a faithful sermon, and the one at night more so, from the text "What shall it profit a man if he gain the whole world and lose his own soul?" on what he gives in exchange for his soul.*

*I was glad to see the house crowded and some
very attentive hearers, particularly among the
soldiers. I hope some good may have been
done.*[21]

As a faithful mother, she did not overlook the spiritual
welfare of her own children. Upon hearing of Annie's conversion, Mrs. Lee wrote joyfully to her daughter:

*It is very late my precious little daughter, but I
cannot let another day pass without telling you
the real happiness your letter afforded me, you
for whom I have felt so anxious to hear that
God had sent his spirit into your heart &
drawn you to himself. Remember what He says,
"Those who seek me early shall find me." the
promises of God are sure & cannot fail.
Therefore seek Him with all your heart... You
must pray for your sister & for your brothers
who are out of the fold of Christ. Think what a
happiness to your Mother to be able to present
all her children at the throne of God & to be
able to say, "Here I am Lord & the children
Thou hast given me." Pray for your Mother that
she may be more faithful in her prayers &
example...*[22]

"There is no such thing as an indolent Christian!" Mrs.
Lee loved to remind her daughters and friends. Though
afflicted severely with crippling arthritis, she yet followed this
maxim. Throughout the war, Mrs. Lee kept herself and the
girls of the household busy knitting socks and other items for
the destitute soldiers of the South. A lady visitor to her house

during the war made this observation: "Her room was like an industrial school—everyone was busy. Her daughters were all there plying their needles, with several other ladies…When we came out someone said, 'Did you see how the Lees spend their time? What a rebuke to taffy parties!'"[23] In one three-month stretch—March, April, and May of 1863—Mrs. Lee sent over two hundred pairs of socks for distribution to the Stonewall Brigade.

In Lexington, Mrs. Lee became house mother to all the boys at the college, especially the homesick ones. She would often invite them to the Lee home and sorely missed them when they didn't come. When she heard of a boy who was far from home, she took special interest in him, "frequently telling him to bring to her any of his clothing which might need mending."[24]

Her love for her husband was unstinting and constant in spite of their frequent separations. Her anxiety for his well-being was only calmed by her trust in the Lord of Hosts. During the Mexican War, she wrote:

> *I do so long for tidings of you & yet always feel afraid to hear. May God in his mercy preserve & keep you now and ever. Life is at the best a fleeting current; whether it glides smoothly on or rushes in a turbid course, its end is the same, the great ocean of eternity…May God prepare us all.*[25]

Though she was reared in the lap of privilege, she never viewed it a sacrifice to live within the limits of a military officer's meager salary. No one would ever have known that she came from one of the most prominent families in the country. Her cheerful hospitality made all feel welcome. After the war provisions were slender—the bounty and abundance of prior days now only a memory—yet Mrs. Lee never complained. The same blessing was said before every meal, regardless of its sparse nature: "God bless us and make us truly grateful for these and all thy mercies, and be pleased to continue them to us." [26]

During the war, and afterward, she suffered the loss of nearly all her earthly possessions, not least of which was her beloved Arlington. She quietly submitted to God's providence. No doubt the example of his wife taught Lee unforgettable lessons about contentment in the face of great disappointment. One hears her own words coming through in his letters. Writing to General Edward G. W. Butler about the new wife of his son Fitzhugh, Lee says:

> *I fear she will find it both rough and uninviting at first, for we have to depend mainly on our own hands now for all we receive. Young people, however, can make themselves very happy, and we must all be content with the bare necessaries of life, if we can maintain clean hands and clear consciences.*[27]

A great influence upon her husband and those around her was her constant submission to the wise disposal of God. Pain threw her into the arms of her heavenly Father:

> *I do not improve at all in walking & have to be lifted in & out of a carriage by 2 men & the physicians do not give me hope that I shall be any better—sad is it not to renounce all hope. I can only pray & strive for submission to God's holy will.*[28]

Her disappointments were many, not the least of which was the defeat of her beloved South. Here again, she willingly bowed before the wisdom of the Sovereign, "Tho' it has not pleased Almighty God to crown our exertions with success in the way & manner we expected, yet we must still trust & pray not that *our will* but His may be done in Heaven & in earth." [29]

The loss of her faithful husband was the heaviest of all that she endured. Yet even in this loss, we see that, for Mrs. Lee, the grace of God was sufficient: "God knows the best time for us to leave this world & we must never question either His love or wisdom." To General Butler, who had written to comfort her in "the untimely death" of her husband, she replied,

> *You speak of my husband's "untimely death."*
> *We must not deem that untimely which God*
> *ordains. He knows the best time to take us from*
> *this world; and can we question either his love*
> *or wisdom? How often are we taken from the*
> *evil to come. How much of care and sorrows*
> *are those spared who die young. Even the hea-*
> *then considers such the favorites of the gods;*
> *and to the Christian what is death but a trans-*
> *lation to eternal life. Pray that we may all live*
> *so that death will have no terrors for us.* [30]

God has said that when two marry, they are no longer two but one. Each is used as an instrument of His grace in the life of the other. It was this example of faith and love that stirred and encouraged Lee throughout his life. He was a better man because of the companion God gave him. So it is. A good wife is truly the most valuable asset any man can have. "Whoso findeth a wife findeth a good *thing*, and obtaineth favour of the Lord." (Proverbs 18:22)

Marital Fidelity

*You do not know how much I have missed
you…my dear Mary. To be alone in a crowd is very
solitary.*

　　　　　　　　　　　–R. E. Lee to his wife, June 5, 1839

It is interesting to note that throughout his life Lee delighted in the company of women. He wrote to his friend Henry Kayser when he was around thirty-five years old, "You are right in my interest in pretty women—it is strange that I do not lose it with age. But I perceive no diminution."[31] This was not hidden from his wife Mary. Indeed, she wrote of her husband after his death, "No one enjoyed the society of ladies more than himself. It seemed the greatest recreation in his toilsome life."[32]

Lee kept in check what could have been a disastrous temptation, and thus his enjoyment of women was never anything more than an "interest." He was always most circumspect in his actions in order to avoid even the appearance of impropriety.

At the time of Lee's tour of duty in New York, one mode of transportation in the city during the winter was by sleigh. He recorded this incident with the sleigh "Oregon" in 1846:

> *I did not learn how many passengers it carried. But they went "the whole or none." The girls returning from school were the prettiest sight; held on each others laps with their bags of books and smiling faces. Indeed there was no lack of customers at sixpence a ride, and you might be accommodated with a lady in your lap in the bargain. Think of a man of my forbidding countenance having such an offer. But I peeped under her veil before accepting and though I really could not find fault either with her appearance or age, after a little demurring preferred giving her my seat. I thought it would not sound well if repeated in the latitude of Washington, that I had ridden down [Broadway] with a strange woman in my lap.*[33]

Lee's self-deprecation notwithstanding, he was considered to be quite a handsome man. As a result, he faced far more serious temptations than the one recounted above. While he was stationed in Texas—a full two thousand miles away from his wife—in what he once referred to as "a desert of dullness," an incident occurred which demonstrates Lee's strict devotion to moral purity and marital fidelity. In San Antonio he met an attractive young lady who was more than a little attracted to him. He told the story himself in a letter to his wife:

*I was invited to her house to a musical party,
but declined. About a week afterwards I
thought it incumbent on me to return the com-
pliment by a call. I found the house and made
myself as agreeable as I could for about 5 minutes, and when I rose to depart she took me out
in her garden to see her corn and potatoes by
starlight! But she had waked the wrong
passenger. I told her I had no knowledge of
horticulture, and took no interest in agriculture
in Texas. I have not seen her since.*[34]

He never allowed his interest in women to be expressed
in any immoral or indecent way. He was the perfect gentleman and he always remained the faithful husband. Marriage,
for Lee, was not a hindrance to joy but the God-ordained
means of true happiness and contentment. "I would not be
unmarried for all you could offer me,"[35] he once wrote to a
friend, and he meant it.

FATHERHOOD

I pray God to watch over and direct our efforts in guarding our dear little son, that we may bring him up in the way he should go.
    –R.E. Lee in a letter to his wife, October 16, 1837

A favorite maxim of the Puritans was, "The father is the mirror by which the child dresses himself." In spite of all that is often said to the contrary, we know this to be so. The greatest influence we will ever have is that which we have on the children that God has given us.

This reality was impressed upon thirty-three-year-old Robert Lee one winter's day eight years after the birth of his son Custis. Lee was now the father of four: Custis, who was eight; Mary, six; Fitzhugh, who was approaching his fourth birthday; and Annie, who was still in the cradle. One afternoon Lee took Custis for a walk in the snow, holding him by the hand. When they had walked for a short way, Custis dropped his father's hand and fell behind. In a few minutes Lee looked back over his shoulder and saw Custis imitating his every movement. Walking as his father walked, head and shoulders erect, with all the grace and dignity the eight-year-old could muster, he was struggling to walk in the very footprints his father had left behind in the snow.

Lee said later, "When I saw this, I said to myself, 'It behooves me to walk very straight, when this fellow is already following in my tracks.'"[36]

God has put within our children the desire to be like us. It is one of those wonderfully terrifying blessings God gives—wonderful that our children would desire to be like us, terrifying when we consider the damage we might do by our example. No father can safely ignore this reality, as Lee learned in the early days of fatherhood.

Though he was often called away from home by the exigencies of war and service in the army, Lee was not a detached, out-of-touch father. He wrote home regularly, addressing each of his children with specific concerns, encouragements, admonitions, and exhortations to faithfulness. He called upon them to be diligent and conscientious in their studies. He exhorted them to honor their mother. He encouraged them to be good examples to those around them. And most of all, reminded them of his love for them and their duties to God.

"I shall not feel my long separation from you," he once wrote the two older boys on his way to Mexico,

> *if I find that my absence has been of no injury to you, and that you have both grown in goodness and knowledge, as well as stature. But, ah! How much I will suffer on my return if the reverse has occurred! You enter all my thoughts, into all my prayers; and on you, in part, will depend whether I shall be happy or miserable as you know how much I love you. You must do all in your power to save me pain.*[37]

Lee often expressed his grief at having to be away from his wife and children. Even so, he remained involved to a high degree with their training, as a letter to his wife Mary on June 5, 1839, attests:

> *I hope you are all well and will continue so; and therefore must again urge you to be very prudent and careful of those dear children. If I could only get a squeeze at that little fellow turning up his sweet mouth to "keeze Baba!" You must not let him run wild in my absence, and will have to exercise firm authority over all of them. This will not require severity, or even strictness, but constant attention, and an unwavering course. Mildness and forbearance, tempered by firmness and judgment, will strengthen their affection for you, while it will maintain your control over them.*[38]

Lee was careful to remind all his children that he constantly monitored their progress in all areas, especially when he had to be away. On November 30, 1845, he wrote from Mexico to one of his sons:

> *I received last night, my dear son, your letter of the 25th inst. And was much gratified to perceive the evident improvement in your writing and spelling and to learn that you were getting on well in your studies. You must endeavor to learn, in order to compensate me for the pain I suffer in being separated from you, and let nothing discourage or deter you from endeavoring to acquire virtue and knowledge.*

> *I am pleased with your progress so far, and the*
> *last report sent me by Mr. Smith gave you a very*
> *good standing in all your studies. I was sur-*
> *prised to see that you were lower in algebra*
> *than in any other. How was that?—for I*
> *thought you had some talent for*
> *mathematics...*[39]

His concern for their education was thoroughly practical in the best sense of the word. He eschewed "empty" learning, learning that was impressive when measured by the world's standards, but in reality more disabling than profitable to the student. Instead, he desired his children to be trained to live faithfully in God's world. It was this concern that prompted his advice to Mildred to avoid "romance novels." Lee was not one to believe that holy entertainment was evil, but he did not want his daughter to be swept away by "romanticism." He wrote, "Read history and works of truth—not novels and romances." It was his long-held conviction that "romances" did not portray the realities of the world and would ultimately be harmful in forming the views and tastes of youth. Years before, he had written his wife, reminding her to guard Fitzhugh from such things:

> *Let him never touch a novel. They print beauty*
> *more charming than nature, and describe hap-*
> *piness that never exists. They will teach him to*
> *sigh after that which has no reality, to despise*
> *the little good that is granted us in this world*
> *and to expect more than is given.*[40]

Lee desired his children to grow in godly character. On March 31, 1846, he wrote,

I cannot go to bed, my dear son, without writ-
ing you a few lines to thank you for your letter,
which gave me great pleasure. I am glad to
hear you are well, and hope you are learning to
read and write, and that the next letter you will
be able to write yourself. I want to see you very
much, and to tell you all that has happened
since you went away. I do not think that I ever
told you of a fine boy I heard of in my travels
this winter...

After relating the story of a young man whose father was killed by a falling limb in the woods and found by his son, who manfully brought his father's body home, Lee continued,

You and Custis must take great care of your
kind mother and dear sisters when your father
is dead. To do that you must learn to be good.
Be true, kind, and generous, and pray earnestly
to God to enable you to "keep his command-
ments, and walk in the same all the days of
your life."[41]

The spiritual interests of the children were never forgotten. In June, 1860, when Lee was stationed in Texas, he received word from home that Robert was preparing for confirmation. In a letter Lee wrote to Mrs. Anna Fitzhugh we see something of his holy desires for the spiritual well-being of his children,

I know you will sympathize in the joy I feel at
the impression made by a merciful God upon
the youthful heart of dear little Rob. May He

that has opened his eyes to the blessing of
Salvation, taught him the way, and put in his
heart the good resolution he has formed, enable
him to do all things to secure and accomplish
it.[42]

Lee took fatherhood seriously and, as a consequence, won the hearts of all his children. His influence upon the lives of his sons was evident to a remarkable degree. Custis Lee graduated first in his class at West Point, became an accomplished officer in the Corps of Engineers, and during the War Between the States was an aide to President Davis, a brigadier, and then a major-general in the army. After the war, Custis became professor of engineering at the Virginia Military Institute, and later succeeded his father as president of Washington and Lee University.

Fitzhugh graduated from Harvard and was appointed lieutenant in the United States Army by the special application of General Winfield Scott. When the war broke out, he resigned from the U.S. Army and raised a cavalry company, of which he was made captain. He received steady promotions until he became major-general in the Confederate Cavalry Corps.

Robert was a student at the University of Virginia when the war broke out and promptly enlisted in the Rockbridge Artillery, where he served faithfully until he was given a position on his brother's staff in December, 1862. He eventually rose to the rank of captain. After the war, Robert became a successful planter and a leading citizen.

LOVE FOR CHILDREN

I have not had so pleasant a visit for a long time.
–R. E. Lee after a visit from three small girls

*C*hildren always received Lee's special attention and were a cherished entertainment during the war and afterward. "Yesterday afternoon," he wrote Mrs. Lee during the war, "three little girls walked into my room, each with a small basket. The eldest carried some fresh eggs laid by her own hens; the second, some pickles made by her mother; the third, some popcorn grown in her garden."

Lee was greatly moved by this incident, one of many that demonstrated the generosity of the Southern people who, at this particular time, were suffering great privation themselves. Knowing this, Lee sought whenever possible to refuse their kindnesses, but in so doing, he ran the hazard of provoking such great disappointment that more often than not he was forced to accept the sacrificial offerings of love—as he did in the case of the three little girls. Lee continued in his letter to his wife, "I fortunately was able to fill their baskets with apples and begged them to bring me nothing but kisses and to keep the eggs, corn, etc, for themselves." [43]

While living in Lexington after the war, he procured Christmas presents for all the children of his acquaintance. It was his delight to ride through the town—like a kindly, grey-clad St. Nicholas—distributing tokens of his love to his little friends. Children felt no reluctance to come into his presence. His kindness and gentleness made them instinctively view him as a friend.

Once during the college commencement exercises, a child lost his parents in the crowded auditorium. General Lee, who was sitting on the platform, got the child's attention and motioned for him to come up to the platform and join him. This the child did and, sitting down on the floor at Lee's feet, he leaned over, put his head against the General's knee, and went fast asleep. The ceremony called for Lee to stand as he congratulated the winners of prizes and handed diplomas to the graduates. But rather than risk disturbing his sleeping young friend, he performed this part of the ceremony seated. [44]

The children of Lexington viewed Lee as their best friend. Once, a young boy of five years was exhorted by his pastor to go out and find others to bring to Sunday school, that they might be taught about the Savior and God's Word. He immediately thought of the one whom he loved the most, and ran to General Lee early one Sunday morning—begging the general to accompany him to his church and be his "Sunday Scholar."

Lee gently refused, reminding the boy that he had obligations at his own congregation. Seeing the boy's disappointment, however, and noticing as well that a few college students had stopped to listen to his response, Lee enlarged his reply:

> *Ah, C___, we must all try to be good
> Christians—that is the most important thing. I
> can't go to your Sunday-school to be your new
> scholar today, but I am very glad that you
> asked me. It shows that you are zealous in a
> good cause, and I hope that you will continue
> to be so as you grow up. And I don't want you
> to think that I consider myself too old to be a
> Sunday-school scholar. No one ever becomes
> too old to study the precious truths of the
> Bible![45]*

The last comment, no doubt, was as much for the benefit of the other young men who were listening as for the child himself.

The old general often became the supreme judge in all manner of disputes among the children of Lexington. To them the word of General Lee held all the authority of Sinai. One day while sitting in his office at the college, a little boy with flushed cheeks pushed open the door—without knocking—and marched up to the general's desk. Lee took off his reading glasses and asked him what he wanted.

With great indignation the boy said that his father had fought in the Confederate army and had died in battle, but because his mother was from the state of New York, his playmates kept calling him a "Yankee." Unable to find relief elsewhere, he had decided take his complaint to headquarters.

Lee responded with equal indignation, "The next boy that calls you 'Yankee,' send him to me." This greatly satisfied the young complainant and he retired armed with a threat that was sure to strike terror in the hearts of all who heard it.[46]

Lee's picture was in nearly every home in the South and the children all came to think of him and love him as one of their own relations. This was especially so for the children of his old soldiers. In their homes, Lee was spoken of so often and with such affection that the children revered him as the most important man in all of history and, consequently, held him in considerable awe. Once, in the summer of 1867, Lee and one of his daughters were taking a ride to the beautiful Peaks of Otter and came across some children playing near the road. When the children saw General Lee, they scattered into the woods. Lee called to them to come back to the road and asked, "Why are you running away? Are you afraid of me?"

"Oh no sir," said one of the girls, "we are not afraid of you; but we are not dressed nice enough to see you."

"Why, who do you think I am?" asked Lee.

"You are General Lee—we knew you by your picture. Father was one of your soldiers." [47]

It was surely improper to appear before General Lee in anything less than your scrubbed-up best!

Lee's death was as much the occasion of grief to the children as to any of his closest companions. Many of the citizens of the town noted that when the news of General Lee's death was heard, the children were as deeply affected as any of the adults. There was literally "no joy" in the town as Lee's young friends were too sad even to play. Dr. William Jones noted,

> *I have never seen children manifest more sincere grief at the death of a near relative than that exhibited by the children of Lexington at the death of General Lee. The schools were all closed, their usual sports were abandoned, and the children mingled their tears with those of*

> *strong men and women as they realized that*
> *their kind, dearly loved friend had gone from*
> *among them.*[48]

He was gone from them but he would never be forgotten by them.

AUDACITY

*There is always a hazard in military movements,
but we must decide between the positions of inaction and the risk of action.*

—R. E. Lee

*J*ust after Lee took command of the Army of Northern
Virginia, Major E. P. Alexander was riding with
Colonel Joseph Ives, who had been Lee's engineer in South
Carolina and was at that time on President Davis' staff.
Alexander had some questions about Lee's boldness. Lee had
been nicknamed the "King of Spades" in mock honor of the
importance he placed on digging earthen fortifications, and
most of the men at that time thought Lee too gentlemanly to
fight the sort of war necessary to win.

As the two men rode together, the conversation came
around to Lee. Major Alexander asked, "Has General Lee the
audacity that is going to be required for our inferior force to
meet the enemy's superior force—to take the aggressive and
to run risks and take chances?" At this question, Ives stopped

his horse, turned so he could look Alexander in the face, and replied, "Alexander, if there is one man in either army, Confederate or Federal, head and shoulders above every other in *audacity*, it is General Lee! His name might be Audacity." [49]

Indeed, it was so. Seldom has a man in less favorable circumstances made more audacious moves. To this day his actions hold students of military strategy spellbound. Yet it is important to note that audacity is not folly. Lee took chances, but not foolish chances; bold chances, but not brash chances. His moves were taken with the knowledge of his men, the knowledge of his situation, the knowledge of the prospects for the immediate future, and the knowledge of his foe. They were chances which almost invariably succeeded.

Caution is necessary in any endeavor—up to a certain point. But in the situation in which the Southern army found itself, undue caution would have bred pessimism and pessimism would have led to despair. Lee did not allow this to happen. He avoided the twin pitfalls of rashness and timidity. "Nothing is easier than for a soldier to be rash and to tell himself he is original. Nothing is more difficult than for him to be daring and at the same time to avoid rashness." [50]

He was not paralyzed by opposition and formidable obstacles. He was concerned to do what had the best chance for success and not what was considered safe. Lesser men would have been prone to play it safe—which would have, under the circumstances, meant certain (and quick) defeat.

His willingness to take calculated risks can be attributed—more than anything else—to his serene confidence in God. God promises in His Word to protect, provide, and to work all things together for the good of His people. This to Lee meant that after carefully considering the situation, seeking sound counsel, and committing the whole to God, he could have confidence to take the initiative and act decisively.

The idea of taking initiative, of courageously striking out to do what must be done though all the world think it folly, is one of the rarest of qualities among men today. Yet this is surely one of the marks of the man of faith. He is not the dare-devil, but neither is he paralyzed by the possibility of failure.

Lee's confidence had a great influence upon his troops. The men realized that Lee would make them fight when they had to, but always when there was the greatest opportunity for success, and never when unnecessary risks were involved. The men thus judged that any time Lee asked them to do something, he could be trusted. They knew they would never be asked to do anything merely to gain their general a reputation.

Lee's audacity brought failure as well as glorious success. He came to be convinced that his men could and would do anything, including what proved to be impossible and thus, toward the end of the war, he may have expected too much of them. But had he not been a man of audacity from the beginning, the South would have been immediately overwhelmed by the more numerous and better equipped troops called into action by the North.

Calculated audacity founded upon trust in God is the formula for holy warfare as well. We must not be paralyzed by the numbers or the wealth or the power of the foe. We must trust in the God of armies, believing that He who is for us is greater than those who are against us.

COURAGE

*For myself, I intend to die sword in hand rather than
to yield.*

–R. E. Lee

Once at Petersburg, one of the Negro cooks, who
were so numerous in the Southern army, came up
to greet General Lee.

"General Lee, I been wantin' to see you for a long time.
I's a soldier."

"Ah," said Lee, "to what army do you belong—to the
Union army or to the Southern army?"

"Oh, General, I belong to your army."

"Well, have you been shot?"

"No sah, I ain't been shot yet."

"How is that? Nearly all our men get shot."

"Why, General," the cook replied, "I ain't been shot 'case I
stays back whar de generals stay."[51]

Lee loved to repeat this story, but there was little truth in
it as far as his own conduct was concerned. Lee was not a

general who remained "safely back" behind the lines. He was too much of a soldier for that. His men were dear to him and he was often so caught up in their efforts that he moved unconsciously to join them.

In the battle of the Wilderness, when it appeared that the Southern army would be overrun, a group of approximately twenty men came up to fill the gap that had been made in the lines. Lee called to them excitedly, "Who are you, my boys?" "Texas boys," the men yelled back. They were from Hood's Texas brigade and they had come just at the critical time. "Hurrah for Texas! Hurrah for Texas!" shouted Lee, waving his hat.

In the excitement he called to them to form a line of battle. As the men obediently formed, General Lee rode to the left, preparing to lead the men on a counter charge into the Union forces! The charge began and Lee spurred Traveller so that he followed close behind the infantry. Only then did the men realize what was happening. "Go back, General Lee, go back!" they cried. Lee ignored their cries. The men slackened their pace and said, "We won't go on unless you go back!" Lee did not hear them. Caught up in the spirit of battle, his face was set like a flint upon the enemy's front.

General Maxie Gregg tried to head him off—to no avail. A tall sergeant grabbed the reins of Traveller but Lee kept going forward. Finally Colonel Venable arrived, caught up with Lee, and shouted into his ear that it might be best to turn aside and give Longstreet his orders—since that general had just arrived upon the scene. Finally, Lee slowly began to pull back on Traveller. His eyes were still fixed upon the front but he no longer headed in that direction. He waved his hat to encourage the charging Texans and returned to the rear.[52]

At a critical point in the battle, at Spotsylvania Courthouse, Lee rode to the center of the line and quietly turned Traveller toward the enemy's front. The line was drawing considerable fire from the Union forces, so much that anyone who was exposed was in danger. General Gordon turned and saw to his surprise that General Lee was preparing to join the upcoming charge! He rushed toward the general and exclaimed, "General Lee, this is no place for you. Go back, General; we will drive them back. These men are Virginians and Georgians. They have never failed. They never will. Will you, boys?"

"No, no! General Lee to the rear; Lee to the rear!" the men cried. "Go back, General Lee, we won't charge until you go back!"

Gordon and some of his men put their horses between General Lee and the enemy and Gordon, leaning forward, caught hold of Traveller's bridle to lead him back. At that moment the crowding of the ranks preparing to charge pushed him behind Lee. Upon this, a sergeant of the Forty-ninth Virginia seized Lee's horse and led him back.[53]

Later in the same action, Lee found himself in range of cannon, and the exploding shot all around him made Traveller so excited that he began to rear wildly. Lee sought to calm him down to no avail. Once more Traveller reared up, just as a round passed under his girth only a few inches from Lee's stirrup. Had Traveller not been up in the air, Lee would have been hit.

When the veterans saw what had happened, the familiar cry arose for the third time in that day's battle: "Go back! For God's sake, go back!" Lee was determined to be a part of the action, but realized again the necessity for obeying the orders of his men. "If you will promise me to drive those people from our works, I will go back." The men shouted their promise and Lee retired to the rear again.[54]

Lee exposed himself to enemy fire so often on this campaign that he drew many protests about his carelessness from general officers as well as men in the ranks. He would reply to these numerous admonitions, "I wish I knew where my place is on the battlefield; wherever I go some one tells me it is not the place for me." [55]

Some of Lee's actions nearly defy belief. During the fighting around Petersburg, Lee found himself in an exposed position under intense fire. He ordered the men around him to seek shelter, and then stepped out into the open to pick up a baby sparrow that had fallen from a tree. Returning the sparrow to its nest, Lee followed his men to shelter.

Courage is not the absence of fear. Courage is the ability to do your duty in the face of fear. Indeed, we can say that courage is inescapably tied to fear. One of J. E. B. Stuart's favorite sayings was, "Fear God and you shall have nothing else to fear!" Lee would have heartily agreed. Courage is rooted in right fear, the fear of God.

DUTY

Do your duty in all things... You cannot do more;
you should never wish to do less.

–R. E. Lee

*I*t was once said of the great Christian writer and
teacher, John Bunyan, that if you pricked him anywhere, he would bleed *bibleline.* Similarly, it could be said
that if one were to prick Lee anywhere, one would find devotion to duty flowing forth. Indeed, his entire life could be
summarized, as Charles Flood has said, "as one long response
to the call of duty." If this were not so astonishingly and
unavoidably true it could be omitted here. Without question,
however, "duty" was the polestar of his life.

It is likely not true that Lee made the statement so often
attributed to him, that "Duty is the sublimest word in the
English language." But there is no question that his view of
duty was equal to this sentiment. Faithfulness to duty domi-
nates his life wherever you look: at home as a child caring for
his mother; at West Point, incurring not a single demerit; in

the army of the United States, serving with nobility and grace; at the head of the Southern forces, leading with boldness and fortitude; as president of Washington College, quietly molding the lives of young men. "Duty" echoes throughout Lee's life.

After the fall of Mexico City, when the army was celebrating the victory—with great joy and relief—in the emperor's palace, someone arose to propose a toast to the captain of the Engineers, who had been the one to find a way for the army to take the city. It was only then that the men noticed that Robert E. Lee, the captain of the Engineers, was not present. Major John Magruder was immediately dispatched to find the him and bring him to the hall to receive his honors.

After an extended search, Magruder finally found Captain Lee in a remote, quiet room in the palace, busily working on a map! It was his responsibility to make maps of the area and he had not yet finished this task. Magruder reproached Lee for ignoring the festivities. Lee calmly responded by pointing to his instruments. Magruder was incredulous.

"But this is mere drudgery! Make somebody else do it and come with me."

"No," replied Lee, "no, I am but doing my duty." [56]

Only his manifest sincerity saved him from being ridiculed for self-righteousness. Magruder knew Lee well enough to know that this was indeed his strict view of the matter and no amount of words would sway him.

This was a quality of Lee from his youth. It was said of him as a young student that his "specialty was finishing up." He completed what he began and fulfilled his responsibilities to the full. It later became a maxim with him, "You cannot be a true man until you learn to obey." [57]

It was important faithfully to fulfill your duty without any dissimulation or justification of your failure. "Private and public life are subject to the same rules; and truth and manliness are two qualities that will carry you through this world much better than policy, or tact, or expediency, or any other word that was ever devised to conceal or mystify a deviation from a straight line." [58]

It was his sense of duty that guided him in the national crisis of 1860-61, when the states of the South were seceding from the Union and the choice was set before him to remain loyal to the Union or to his native state. It is true that in 1860 Lee's sentiments were decidedly against secession. He wrote to his son in January, 1861,

> *The framers of our Constitution never*
> *exhausted so much labor, wisdom, and forbear-*
> *ance in its formation, and surrounded it with*
> *so many guards and securities, if it was*
> *intended to be broken by every member of the*
> *Confederacy at will. It was intended for "perpet-*
> *ual union," so expressed in the preamble, and*
> *for the establishment of a government, not a*
> *compact, which can only be dissolved by revo-*
> *lution, or the consent of all the people in*
> *convention assembled. It is idle to talk of seces-*
> *sion.*[59]

With such convictions, one would think that Lee would have been greatly tempted to accept the position of commanding general of the army of the United States. It was not so. Indeed, though he wrestled with the consequences of his choice, the choice he had to make was clear. Lee never gave any thought to a response other than that of loyalty to his native state. When Lincoln offered him—through the intermediation of Francis Preston Blair—supreme command of the Union forces, Lee responded, "Mr. Blair, I look upon secession as anarchy. If I owned the four millions of slaves in the South, I would sacrifice them all to the Union—but how can I draw my sword upon Virginia, my native state?"[60] This position was also maintained in his conversation with General Scott.

Thus, when Virginia seceded on April 17, 1861, the decision for Lee was made. He knew that many men would outrank him in the Southern armies. He had an appreciation for the fearful odds the South would face and the great uncertainty of a contest with the North that few in the South had. He knew that his estate and home would likely become the property of the Northern government, given its proximity to the capitol. If he chose for the Union, he could retain all and have rank, glory, and wealth besides. But he would not have had honor. He wrote to his sister, "With all my devotion to the Union, and the feeling of loyalty and duty of an American citizen, I have not been able to make up my mind to raise my hand against my relatives, my children, my home."[61]

After the war, in speaking to his former lieutenant, General Wade Hampton, he described his decision in these terms, "I did only what my duty demanded; I could have taken no other course without dishonor. And if all were to be done over again, I should act in precisely the same manner."[62]

Some things are more important than worldly reputation, prosperity, and personal ease. Fearing God and living faithfully, keeping a clear conscience before God and man, cannot be replaced by worldly fame or riches. It is a lesson that all men need to learn.

Submission to God's Will

God disposes. This ought to satisfy us.

-R. E. Lee

*T*here are some truths that are like anchors to the soul. They hold us up in times of deep grief and tense crisis. One such truth is that of the absolute sovereignty of God—that He has "ordained all things, whatsoever comes to pass." (Ephesians 1:11) This truth means that all that occurs is the fruit of the infinite wisdom, grace, and goodness of God. Nothing is meaningless. The great comfort that is derived from this glorious reality is impossible to describe: it can only be observed. The life of Lee gave him much occasion to lean on these truths.

Perhaps the greatest sorrow for a parent is losing a child. This Lee experienced during the war in a most unexpected way. He did not lose a son who was involved on the battlefield, but one of his daughters who was safe at home. After the battle of Second Manassas in October, 1862, Lee was recuperating from an injury he had received when news arrived from home that Annie, his second daughter, had become ill with typhoid fever. On October 20, shortly after this news, the message came that she had died. She was twenty-three years old. It was totally unexpected and a great blow to her father.

After receiving the letter, Lee went over the official correspondence of the morning with his secretary, Major Walter Taylor. When their business was finished and Major Taylor had left his tent, Lee gave vent to his sorrow. When Taylor suddenly came back into the tent a few minutes later, he was shocked to find the general weeping.

As soon as Lee could control himself, he sent word to his sons and wrote to Mrs. Lee, "I cannot express the anguish I feel at the death of my sweet Annie. To know that I shall never see her again on earth, that her place in our circle which I always hoped one day to enjoy, is forever vacant, is agonizing in the extreme." God's children, however, do not sorrow as the world, which has no hope. "But God in this, as in all things, has mingled mercy with the blow, in selecting that one best prepared to leave us. May you be able to join me in saying 'His will be done.'" [63]

The same truth by which he was comforted he used to comfort others. (II Corinthians 1:4) When Fitzhugh's wife Charlotte died, Lee received the sad news with the same resignation to God's will that he displayed in all things:

> *It has pleased God to take from us one exceedingly dear to us, and we must be resigned to His holy will. She, I trust, will enjoy peace and happiness forever, while we must patiently struggle on under all the ills that may be in store for us. What a glorious thought it is that she has joined her little cherubs and our angel Annie in heaven. Thus is link by link the strong*

chain broken that binds us to earth, and our
passage soothed to another world. Oh, that we
may be at last united in that heaven of rest,
where trouble and sorrow never enter, to join in
an everlasting chorus of praise to our Lord and
Savior![64]

He was ever confident in the wise disposal of God. After the Seven Days battle, during which he suffered the great frustration of opportunities lost and orders ineffectually carried out, Lee continued free of bitter recriminations. He wrote to Mrs. Lee, "Our success has not been so great or complete as we could have desired, but God knows what is best for us."[65]

This same confidence was demonstrated during the tense retreat from Pennsylvania, when there was great doubt whether the army could or would escape. The swollen rivers were blocking their retreat, and their condition was very perilous. Lee never fretted. He wrote to his wife, "I trust that a merciful God our only hope and refuge will not desert us in this hour of need, and will deliver us by his almighty hand, that the whole world may recognize His power and all hearts be lifted up in adoration and praise of His unbounded loving-kindness. We must however, submit to His almighty will, whatever that may be."[66]

Lee's faith was as strong when things were going poorly as when they were going well. After the surrender, Lee wrote to George W. Jones, an old friend, "We failed, we failed, but in the good providence of God apparent failure often proves a blessing."[67]

After the war, Pastor William Jones, in General Lee's presence, was lamenting the unhappy results. Lee responded emphatically, "Yes, all that is very sad, and might be a cause of self-reproach, but that we are conscious that we have humbly tried to do our duty. We may, therefore, with calm satisfaction, trust in God, and leave results to him."[68]

It was his submission to God's will that prevented him from the eroding bitterness and self-reproach which ate away at the lives of many. He knew he had done his best to do his duty and the results had been the will of his Father in heaven. He could not therefore justly complain.

As Freeman notes: "Nothing of his serenity during the war or of his silent labor in defeat can be understood unless one realizes that he submitted himself in all things faithfully to the will of a Divinity which, in his simple faith, was directing wisely the fate of nations and the daily life of His children."[69]

Fighting Bitterness

I believe I may say, looking into my own heart, and speaking in the presence of God, that I have never known one moment of bitterness.

–R. E. Lee

*L*ee has often been praised, and justly so, for his nobility in defeat. It is important to note, however, that this did not come easily for him. Lee, along with many other patriotic Southerners, was very much opposed to secession prior to the outbreak of hostilities. He did not initially think secession lawful and he certainly viewed it as somewhat foolhardy. He loved the Union for which his father had fought so valiantly and did not relish the thought of its demise.

But Lee was a Southerner through and through. And, as a Southerner, he came strongly to embrace the Southern cause of independence. Defeat was thus a difficult pill to swallow. His life had come to be so intertwined with the Southern cause that the very thought of surrender was abhorrent to him. "I would rather die a thousand deaths," he said when he realized there was no choice but to seek terms with General Grant.[70]

Bitterness was a difficult thing to counteract when the harsh Reconstruction Acts began to be applied to the Southern states. Even those in the general's own family could not refrain from expressions of outrage over the injustice administered. Mrs. Lee was an ardent Southern nationalist and, in contrast to her husband, was far less inhibited in making her views known. She was a vehement partisan and didn't mind saying so—even after the war. In a letter to Mrs. R. H. Chilton in December of 1870, she wrote indignantly,

> *It is bad enough to be the victims of tyranny, but when it is wielded by such cowards and base men as Butler, Thaddeus Stevens & Turner it is indeed intolerable. The country that allows such scum to rule them must be fast going to destruction and we shall care little if we are not involved in the crash…They still desire to grind [the South] to dust & wish to effect this purpose by working on the feelings of the low & ignorant negroes many of whom do not even comprehend what a vote means. My indignation cannot be controlled and I wonder our people, helpless and disarmed as they are, can bear it. Oh God how long?*[71]

Even in a brief note to her son Robert, the purpose of which was to encourage him to come to the "Baths" where there were "plenty of pretty girls & a great scarcity of beaux," she couldn't resist putting in a jab at the Reconstruction government and its policies:

*Your Papa told me that he would leave his let-
ter open that I might write you a little note,
dear Rob, & you know I never miss an opportunity & therefore I could not refrain from
placing those few lines in the bundle of papers
even at the risk of Uncle Sam's penitentiary;
but as I neither feel nor owe any allegiance to
him, except what is exacted by force, my conscience does not trouble me. We are protected
neither in person nor property by his laws; nor
do I feel any respect for the military satraps
who rule us.*[72]

Later, after the charges against Jefferson Davis were dropped, Mrs. Lee wrote to Mrs. Lorenzo Lewis:

*I am sure you have all rejoiced in the release of
our President, whose misfortunes & heroic
endurance of them has endeared him so
strongly to every Southern heart & must command the love & respect of Christendom. Those
evil spirits who, like their Father the Devil, can
rejoice in nothing that is pure or lovely will
continue to howl even after their hold upon
him has been wrenched away... What do you
think of Judge Underwood's charge? If it were
not so wicked, it would be perfectly ridiculous.
He is one of the blessed mementoes bequeathed
to us by the "Sainted" Lincoln, for which we
are expected to be grateful; but unfortunately
our Southern hearts are still rebellious.*[73]

There are second-hand reports which indicate that Lee too had far greater frustration in dealing with the defeat and the Reconstruction policies followed by the North than he expressed publicly. The former Governor of Texas, F. W. Stockdale, related an incident which illustrates this. It occurred in August of 1870 at the White Sulpher Springs resort, where Lee often went for health and relaxation. Lee had been requested by the Northern general-turned-politician, W. S. Rosecrans, to gather the former Confederates who were then at the springs for a meeting where he might get to know them and perhaps be able to form a consensus of the "Southern view" of the outcome of the war to take back North.

Lee obliged and the meeting took place in his living room with thirty-one former Confederates (among them General P. G. T. Beauregard and Vice-President A. H. Stephens). All thirty-one men expressed their views in turn. The last man to be asked his view was Governor Stockdale. Believing the replies of his friends somewhat too accommodating to their former foes, Governor Stockdale spoke bluntly of the fact that the South had submitted only because it had little choice and could not be expected to act like a "lap-dog" and lick the hand of the man who kicked it. With a few more equally blunt words, Governor Stockdale made plain the South's displeasure with the policies of the new regime.

When Stockdale finished, Lee stood to end the meeting and the participants filed out. Stockdale later related to the Reverend R. L. Dabney that as he came to the door, Lee pushed it closed in front of him and thanked him for his "brave and true words." Lee then went on to say, according to Stockdale, "Had I foreseen these results of subjugation, I would have preferred to die at Appomattox with my brave men, my sword in this right hand."[74] In light of this incident, it is clear that the Reconstruction measures galled Lee as much as they did his wife.

But however much he may have felt indignation against unjust treatment, Lee consistently counseled patience and caution in response to the measures imposed by the North. The extreme disappointment of the South, coupled with the triumphalism of the more radical element in the North, produced a great deal of ill will among the Southern people. Lee realized that this could lead to nothing profitable and set about to do all he could to bring about reconciliation. The people looked to him for guidance, and his example likely had more influence than anything else in bringing about peaceable feelings.

Conscious of his position as the "representative Southerner," he was careful not to say or to do anything that could be used against the South. He refused to attend political rallies and carefully avoided discussing the war and its issues with any except his closest friends. Publicly, he consistently appealed for reconciliation.

One day at White Sulpher Springs, the general was expressing his grief at finding Southern young people so bitter against the North. He was then asked by one of his young female admirers if he did not feel resentment toward the North. At this Lee paused and in a low voice continued, "I believe I may say looking into my own heart, and speaking as in the presence of God, that I have never known one moment of bitterness or resentment." After another pause he continued,

> *When you go home I want you to take a message to your friends. Tell them from me that it is unworthy of them as women, and especially as Christian women, to cherish feelings of resentment against the North. Tell them that it*

grieves me inexpressibly to know that such a
state of things exists, and that I implore them
to do their part to heal our country's wounds.[75]

In February of 1866, Lee received a letter from Mrs. Jefferson Davis in reference to a fiery and somewhat exaggerated speech made by the radical Republican Schuyler Colfax. Mrs. Davis sought his aid and counsel in responding to this unjust attack upon her husband and the South. Lee's reply indicates his determination to avoid needless controversy:

> *I have never seen Mr. Colfax's speech, and am*
> *therefore ignorant of the statements it con-*
> *tained. Had it, however, come under my notice,*
> *I doubt whether I should have thought it proper*
> *to have replied. I have thought, from the time of*
> *the cessation of hostilities, that silence and*
> *patience on the part of the South was the true*
> *course, and I think so still. Controversy of all*
> *kinds will in my opinion only serve to continue*
> *excitement and passion, and will prevent the*
> *public mind from the acknowledgment and*
> *acceptance of the truth. These considerations*
> *have kept me from replying to accusations*
> *made against myself, and induced me to recom-*
> *mend the same to others.*[76]

None of this is to say, however, that he was unsympathetic with the struggle that many in the South had in following his counsel. He had little sympathy with the ruling party and on more than one occasion said so. After the war, General Longstreet requested Lee's support for the administration's policies. In his reply Lee refused to do so with uncharacteristic bluntness, "I cannot think the course pursued by the dominant political party the best for the interests of the country, and therefore cannot say so, or give them my approval." [77]

As the situation deteriorated after the war and President Johnson's trial for impeachment proceeded, Lee wrote to a friend that he deplored "this grand scheme of centralization of power in the hands of one branch of the government to the ruin of all others, and the annihilation of the Constitution, the liberty of the people and of the country...I grieve for posterity, for American principles and American liberty. Our boasted self government is fast becoming the jeer and laughing-stock of the world." [78]

In a letter to General Jubal Early, Lee expressed his concerns about the way the South was being treated and how the South's position would be represented by the victors. He again counseled quiet patience under the rod:

> *We shall have to be patient and suffer for awhile at least; and all controversy, I think, will only serve to prolong angry and bitter feeling, and postpone the period when reason and charity may resume their sway. At present, the public mind is not prepared to receive the truth.*[79]

It would have taken little encouragement from him to inflame the resentment of the South to active resistance again. Lee knew such a reaction would be the death of the South. If there was any hope for his country (and for the North as well) it lay in humble submission to the tyrannical actions of the radicals while crying out to God to deliver them from the oppressor.

Thus, despite the deplorable situation and the unqualified rulers forced upon the South, Lee saw no alternative but to seek peaceable reformation and avoid lawless revolution. He continued to counsel patient trust in God. God would do what was best and all must rest satisfied in that assurance. All things work together for good. The only legitimate response to affliction and disappointment is humble submission. Bitterness, no matter how understandable, is never justified.

Humility

I know of nothing good I could tell you of myself,
and I fear I should not like to say any evil.

          –R. E. Lee (in a letter to a lady who had
          requested an interview for the purpose of
          gathering materials for his biography)

*L*ee was surely one of the greatest men this country has ever produced and few had more apparent reason for pride than he: born of a distinguished family; allied by marriage to perhaps the most famous family in this country; recipient of honors for distinguished military service; a household word on two continents. It would certainly have been understandable if Lee had fallen into a certain haughtiness of manner, or at least demonstrated a self-consciousness of his superiority. Yet, few have ever displayed more sincere modesty and humility than Lee.

The unwise and unfounded boasting of some in the South—prior to and during the war—always troubled Lee.

On Christmas Day, 1862, after the battle of Fredericksburg, Lee wrote of God's blessing upon his armies: "What should have become of us without His crowning help and protection?" He continued to Mrs. Lee, "Oh, if our people would only recognize it and cease from vain self-boasting and adulation, how strong would be my belief in final success and happiness to our country!...I pray that, on this day when only peace and good-will are preached to mankind, better thoughts may fill the hearts of our enemies and turn them to peace."[80] Confidence he always encouraged, cockiness he consistently opposed. The two must never be confused.

Lee never bothered about "gold lace and feathers" in his military dress. His common uniform during the war was a suit of gray, without any ornament, and no insignia of rank other than three stars on his collar, which every Confederate colonel had a right to wear. Once he was asked why he did not wear the full insignia of his rank. "Oh," Lee replied, "I do not care for display. And the truth is, that the rank of colonel is about as high as I ought ever to have gotten; or, perhaps, I might manage a good cavalry brigade if I had the right kind of subordinates."[81]

On one of the advances of the army, a farmer rode up to a bivouac where Lee was sitting and addressed him as "colonel," not guessing his identity. Lee put him at his ease and chatted with him for some time. At length the planter told the "colonel" that he had come to the army in the hope of seeing General Lee and wondered if it was possible for him to do so. "I am General Lee," his host replied, "and I am most happy to have met you."[82] Lee never gave the least indication that he was insulted over not being recognized.

Lee cared little for the "pomp and circumstance" of war. He never quibbled over military etiquette when it came to his men. Visitors were often amazed over the relationship that existed between them. Love and respect were never more closely and amiably mixed.

Lee always returned the salutations of the men. Every cheer received an acknowledgment. Even the often incredibly unmilitary greetings he received were welcomed (to the great shock of the foreign military observers who often rode with him). One old soldier greeted him on the line one day by saying, "Howdy do dad!" Lee never hesitated in his reply, "Howdy do, my man!" [83]

The degree to which he was indifferent to his own honor is astonishing. After the war, Lee often received distinguished visitors from the North into his home in Lexington. Assuming that the Lees—like many prominent families in the North—had household servants, their guests, after retiring to bed, would often leave boots and shoes outside their bedroom doors to be cleaned and "blacked." Many a night it was the general who stayed up after all others had retired and—in order not to embarrass his guests—collected the boots and cleaned and polished them himself. [84]

His humility was expressed in his concern to remember the names of those whom he met. Lee had a phenomenal memory. When serving both at West Point and at Washington College, he could remember the name of every student, even though most years there were between two and three hundred of them. The same was true for most of his military acquaintances. Major Hudson Lee was present at a reception held in General Lee's honor in Charleston, South Carolina. As soon as he entered the room, General Lee called out "I have a crow to pick with you, Major." Lee said he had seen Major Lee in Richmond during a review in that city and he noticed that Major Lee had not spoken to him. The young man was taken aback for he had only met General Lee two or three times and did not feel that he would be missed in such a large gathering.[85]

The Reverend William Jones relates that he knew of only one incident (which occurred sometime after the war) in which the general failed to remember a name. It occurred at a reception for General Lee. Lee was speaking with a gentleman when Pastor Jones walked up to join them. Strangely, the general did not introduce the man to Pastor Jones and when Jones later inquired as to the man's name, General Lee replied, "I am ashamed to say, sir, that I do not know the name of that gentleman. And I am so sure that I ought to know him that I would be sorry for him to find out that I do not recognize him." Jones took it upon himself to find out the man's name and returned to Lee to give him the information. The next day Lee confided to Jones,

> *I was really very much ashamed at not know-*
> *ing that gentleman yesterday. I ought to have*
> *recognized him at once. He spent at least an*
> *hour in my quarters in the City of Mexico just*
> *after its occupation by the American army [this*
> *occurred around 30 years previous], and*
> *although I have never seen him since (and had*
> *never seen him before) he made a very agree-*
> *able impression upon me, and I ought not to*
> *have forgotten him.*[86]

Humility enables a man to be utterly self-forgetful. Once, in the process of recommending an officer for a promotion, Lee was urged not to do so by a member of his staff. It seems that the man had often spoken very disparagingly of the general when not in his presence and that, so the staff officer thought, should disqualify him from promotion. Lee replied,

"The question is not what he thinks or is pleased to say about me, but what I think of him. I have a high opinion of this officer as a soldier, and shall most unquestionably recommend his promotion, and do all in my power to secure it." [87]

The citizens of the South had all confidence that their forces would be victorious against all odds. This confidence was nearly always based upon the fact of Lee's presence. Upon hearing of how assured the citizens of the South were in victory because of their unbounded trust in him, Lee responded, "I tremble for my country when I hear of confidence expressed in me. I know too well my weakness, and that our only hope is in God." [88]

His humility was demonstrated by his response to the mistreatment he received. Both during and after the war, General Lee had much provocation to bitterness. His homes and lands were confiscated and destroyed. He was slandered often in national journals and indicted for treason after being promised immunity. And yet amid all this he never once uttered a word of bitterness but, on the contrary, often gently chastised others who fell victim to the temptation.

After General Lee was indicted for treason and rebellion, a prominent Southern pastor was visiting in the Lee home and expressed great bitterness over the action. The general pleasantly remarked, "Well, it matters little what they may do to me. I am old and have but a short time to live anyhow." Lee then changed the subject of conversation and nothing more was said.

Later, as the pastor arose to leave, Lee followed him to the door and remarked,

> *Doctor, there is a good old book which I read*
> *and you preach from, which says, "Love your*
> *enemies, bless them that persecute you, do good*
> *to them that hate you, and pray for them which*

despitefully use you." Do you think your
remarks this evening were quite in the spirit of
that teaching?

The pastor was abashed at Lee's observation and asked forgiveness for his bitter expressions. To this Lee replied, "I have fought against the people of the North because I believed they were seeking to wrest from the South dearest rights. But I have never cherished toward them bitter or vindictive feelings, and have never seen the day when I did not pray for them." [89]

One day during the war, as his men were scouting the numbers of the Union army, one of his subordinates, realizing the vast numbers of Union forces, exclaimed in bitter tones, "I wish those people were all dead!" To which General Lee replied, "How can you say so General? Now I wish that they were all at home attending to their own business and leaving us to do the same!" [90]

His concern for others dominated his later life. Prestigious offers for honor and position poured in to Lee after the war. His response to them is most instructive. He was once offered the nomination for governor of Virginia (which would have meant sure election) yet he refused, giving these reasons: 1) that he was unqualified for the position; 2) that political offices should not be offered or accepted "as a means of rewarding individuals for supposed former services;" and 3) chiefly, because he feared his nomination (and election) might bring more repercussions upon the South in general and Virginia in particular. "I cannot consent to become the instrument of bringing distress upon those whose prosperity and happiness are so dear to me." [91] Lee's view was that no personal honor should be received which might bring harm to others.

One stands in awe over such noble self-abnegation. What made Lee like this? Only one answer is sufficient: Lee understood that his gifts were from God and not a result of his own efforts. Ever mindful of the words of the apostle Paul to the haughty Corinthians (I Corinthians 4:7), he understood that he had nothing that he had not been given.

SELF-CONTROL

I cannot consent to place in the control of others
one who cannot control himself.

–R. E. Lee

So central to Lee was the call of duty that he lived in such a way that he could be ready at a moment's notice for this call. For this reason he felt it his obligation to live a disciplined, sober life. His study habits while a student; his faithfulness in caring for his invalid mother and later, his invalid wife; his devotion to strict obedience in carrying out orders; his honorable conduct among friends and enemies; all testify to the trait of self-government.

Throughout his life he never used tobacco and strictly avoided whiskey or brandy, though he occasionally drank a glass of wine. This he did not out of some mistaken idea of their "sinfulness," but because he feared falling under their dominion. He once wrote to his son Fitzhugh, "I think it better to avoid it [whiskey] altogether, as you do, as its temperate use is so difficult." [92] It was for this reason that he so strongly promoted temperance, especially among his soldiers.

On more than one occasion he refused to promote men who were known to be addicted to alcohol. "I cannot consent to place in the control of others one who cannot control himself."[93] Once, during the siege at Petersburg, Lee walked in on a number of young officers of his staff who were earnestly discussing a mathematical problem—a stone jug and two tin cups on the table beside them. He made no comment, but next morning when one of the officers mentioned the fact that he had experienced strange dreams the night before, the general observed, "when young gentlemen discuss at midnight mathematical problems, the unknown quantities in which are a stone jug and tin cups, they may expect to have strange dreams."[94]

Mrs. Lee loved to tell the story of Lee's return from the Mexican War. Prior to departing, he had been given a bottle of brandy by a friend, to be used in case of sickness. Though Lee may well have had legitimate reason to use it, he brought the bottle back after the war—unopened. When a friend commented on his determination not to partake of strong spirits, Lee responded that he knew he should inevitably make many mistakes, and he determined that at least they should not be blamed to intemperance.[95]

In a similar incident, in the spring of 1861, during an inspection tour of Norfolk, Lee was forced by a friend to take two bottles of brandy. The man insisted, saying he was sure that Lee would "be certain to need it" and then would likely find it very difficult to find such high quality brandy as this. Lee at first declined, but because of the man's insistence, decided to yield to his request. At the close of the war he met a brother of this same man and said to him, "Tell your brother that I kept the brandy he gave me all through the war, and should have it yet, but that I was obliged to use it last summer in a severe illness of one of my daughters."[96]

Self-control is essential if we are to live to the glory of God. Without it we are defenseless against temptation. ("He that *hath* no rule over his own spirit *is like* a city *that is* broken down, *and* without walls." Proverbs 25:28.) Usefulness is dependent upon learning to live by principle rather than lust. This was a hallmark of Lee's life.

Self-Denial

God's will ought to be our aim, and I am quite contented that His designs should be accomplished and not mine.

–R. E. Lee

*L*ee took seriously our Lord's command to consider others as more important than ourselves and, consequently, was self-forgetful to an astonishing degree.

After Virginia seceded from the Union and joined the Confederacy, Lee was left, by an oversight, without commission or rank in the Confederate army. All, including President Davis, merely assumed he would come into his proper rank, but no one actually communicated with Lee himself. Rather than complaining, pouting, or bearing offense, Lee never said a word about his situation. He was busy securing positions for his staff and arranging to enlist in the Confederate army as a *private* in the cavalry, when the oversight was discovered by some friends and the situation rectified.

This was not a display of false humility designed to embarrass others. Lee had earlier declared to A. H. Stephens, the vice-president of the Confederacy, in a private interview, that he was willing to do whatever he could to help the Southern cause, including enlisting as a private soldier.[97]

Though he dreaded writing, he carefully responded to every gift and expression of kindness that the people of the South showed him. This was his practice even during the war. He acknowledged every present sent him, "from a mattress to a prayer book."[98]

It was unthinkable for Lee to use his rank as an occasion for special privileges. It is said that during the war, Lee rarely slept in a house (even though nearly every house in the South would have counted it an honor to accommodate him). He never allowed his allotment from the commissary to be greater than that given to his men, and often he took less than they. Jones tells us that "not infrequently he would sit down to a dinner meager in quality and scant in quantity."[99]

Though he loved good food, he was always content with his small portion and would often end up sharing even that with visitors who happened to be present. General Ewell mentioned after the war that once, during the evacuation of Petersburg, he had been at Lee's headquarters, and had been unable to stay for dinner. At this, Lee had insisted that Ewell take *his* dinner—which Ewell found to be two small, cold sweet potatoes, one of General Lee's favorite foods.[100]

During the War, Lee often received gifts of special treats and luxuries for his enjoyment, but he seldom consumed them himself. At Christmas in 1864, some friends sent him a saddle of mutton. Somehow it never reached the general, and when he learned of it he said, "If the soldiers got it, I shall be content. I can do very well without it. In fact, I should rather they should have it than I."[101]

During the siege of Petersburg, at a special Christmas dinner to which he had been invited, he was embarrassed that the hostess discovered him not eating his portion of turkey. When asked about it, he said he wanted to save his portion so that he could carry it to one of his staff officers who had been very ill and had eaten nothing "but corn bread and sweet-potato coffee." Later, a barrel of turkeys arrived at camp—one for each officer—courtesy of his generous host in Petersburg. Upon seeing the gift, Lee ordered his turkey sent to the hospital and, says Freeman, pronounced his purpose in such a spirit that the other officers "sadly repacked the barrel" and sent all its contents (i.e., their turkeys!) to the convalescents as well.[102]

While the army was in Petersburg, the wife of Judge W. W. Crump, a distinguished jurist of Richmond, sent daily for three months, by a special messenger, fresh bread for the general's mess. He finally wrote this dear lady, "Although it is very delicious I must beg you to cease sending it. I cannot consent to tax you so heavily. In these times no one can supply their families and furnish the Army too. We have a plenty to eat and our appetites are so good that they do not require tempting."

Lee had a great love for fine things, and had known his share of good things prior to the war. The war, however, left him nearly destitute. Early in the war the federal armies occupied the old Custis family home of Arlington. On Christmas Day of 1861, Lee wrote to one of his daughters,

> *Your old home, if not destroyed by our enemies,*
> *has been so desecrated that I cannot bear to*
> *think of it. I should have preferred it to have*
> *been wiped from the earth, its beautiful hill*
> *sunk, and its sacred trees buried, rather than to*
> *have been degraded by the presence of those*
> *who revel in the ill they do for their own selfish*
> *purposes.*[103]

His gall once expressed however, immediately brought forth a self-rebuke, "You see what a poor sinner I am and how unworthy to possess what was given me; for that reason it has been taken away. I pray for a better spirit, and that the hearts of our enemies may be changed." [104]

Arlington was confiscated during the war by the federal government for "delinquent taxes." Lee sent the money to pay the tax bill but it was refused by the federal officer since, he explained, the owner had not appeared *in person* to pay it. Thus, the Lees lost their home and it became the property of the United States.

The furnishings of Arlington were taken by marauding federal soldiers and others. Many family heirlooms were lost, as well as furniture and possessions which had belonged to General Washington himself. After the war, on the initiative of Congressman James May from Illinois, it was arranged for Mrs. Lee to recover some of the items that had been taken from Arlington. This effort had the support of President Johnson, who viewed it a very small thing to do for the woman who had lost her family home and the eleven hundred acres of land which went with it.

Just as the transfer of these articles was about to take place, *The Washington Evening Express* ran a story about it. The article was filled with inaccuracies and was highly inflammatory. The Lees were represented as traitors who were seeking to steal the priceless possessions of the father of our country away from the people of the nation. This set the radicals afire. They saw in this an opportunity not only to give another insult to the South but to stick their fingers in the eyes of the outgoing, "traitorous" president that they had failed to impeach. A resolution was quickly passed to forbid the transfer of any of Mrs. Lee's family possessions, saying that these articles were now the property of the federal government and "to deliver the same to the Rebel General Robert E. Lee is an insult to the loyal people of the United States." [105]

Lee's response was typical: "[The relics] were valuable to Mrs. Lee as having belonged to her great-grandmother and having been bequeathed to her by her father. But as the country desires them, she must give them up. I hope their presence at the capital will keep in the remembrance of all Americans the principles and virtues of Washington." [106]

When he was asked his thoughts about the property stolen by private individuals who had not returned it, he replied,

> *From what I have learned a great many things formerly belonging to General Washington… were carried away by individuals and are now scattered over the land. I hope the possessors appreciate them and may imitate the example of their original owners, whose conduct must at times be brought to their recollection by these silent monitors. In this way, they will accomplish good to the country.*[107]

His main concern was always for the civilians of the South and the terrible suffering they were undergoing. On Christmas Day, 1863, he was hosting some foreign dignitaries in his tent and could not forbear mentioning the suffering of the poor families in Virginia—and elsewhere—who had been so terribly mistreated by the enemy. He mentioned specifically how the enemy seemed determined to burn and to harass even when the country was so barren that the Southern army could not draw supplies from it. One of his guests reminded Lee that the Union soldiers had treated Arlington in the same way.

At this, Lee quickly responded, "That I can easily understand and for that I don't care; but I do feel sorry for the poor creatures I see here, starved and driven from their homes for no reason whatsoever." [108]

Once, a short while before his death, a young mother brought her baby to him. He took the infant in his arms and looked at him, and then at her, and slowly said, "Teach him he must deny himself." [109] It was a lesson well learned by Robert E. Lee. Douglas Freeman says, "Had his life been epitomized in one sentence of the Book he read so often, it would have been in the words, 'If any man will come after me, let him deny himself, and take up his cross daily, and follow me.'" [110]

Refusal to Follow Self-Interest

Our country requires now everyone to put forth all his ability, regardless of self.

—R. E. Lee

*L*ee never sought self-promotion. He refused to put himself forward in the manner others did, seeking recognition and honor. After the Mexican War, when many were pressing their own names forward for notice, he refused to do so. Before leaving Mexico he even discouraged others from making any attempt in his behalf to gain a promotion for him.

> *I hope my friends will give themselves no annoyance on my account or any concern about the distribution of favors. I know how these things are awarded at Washington, and how the President will be besieged by clamorous claimants. I do not wish to be numbered among them. Such as he can conscientiously*

*bestow, I shall gratefully receive, and have no
doubt that those will exceed my deserts.*[111]

Time after time, in his life, he was given offers that would
have been greatly to his advantage, but he refused them
because he believed it improper to accept those opportunities
with only his own advantage in view. If anything was perceived
to be contrary to duty and honor, it was rejected out of hand.

One of the most unusual opportunities came after the
war with Mexico. Cuban revolutionaries had long desired to
throw off Spanish domination because of misrule. Around the
fall of 1849 the Cuban revolutionary junta met in New York
and decided upon a new assault upon the island. Some of the
Cuban leaders had offered the opportunity to command the
expedition to General William J. Worth, who had been considering resigning from the army. General Worth, however,
died before he made a final decision.

The Cubans then turned to Jefferson Davis, who at the
time was a prominent senator from Mississippi and chairman
of the Committee on Military Affairs in Washington. Davis
refused the offer, but suggested that they approach Lee with
it. The Cubans then went to Baltimore where they made the
same offer to Lee.

Without question this matter opened a door for recognition and fame. Lee would have full command of the entire
operation. It would have been viewed at the time by the people of this country in the most favorable light possible.
Opposition to Spain was high. Success would mean fame, fortune, and a place in history akin to other successful liberators.
Lee could become the George Washington of Cuba.

But before any of these considerations were addressed,
Lee had to settle the matter in light of personal honor. He
had been educated at the expense of the people of his own

country and state to serve in their defense. Was it proper to consider a commission from a foreign country when under commission to your own? He debated the question in his mind and came to a conclusion, but decided to consult with Davis before making his decision final. It is not known what Jefferson Davis' counsel was, but Lee declined the offer.

It is another of those amazing moments in history when the course of the world hinges upon a man's decision. Had Lee accepted this offer from Cuba, how different would the history of this nation have been? We know only that his sense of honor kept him here.

Prior to the war with the North, Lee's name was often overlooked for promotion. Once Mrs. Lee wrote him to complain that he had again been passed by. His response is instructive:

> *We are all in the hands of a kind God, who will do for us what is best, and more than we deserve, and we have only to endeavor to deserve more, and to do our duty to him and ourselves. May we all deserve His mercy, His care, and protection. Do not give yourself any anxiety about the appointment of the brigadier. If it is on my account that you feel an interest in it, I beg you will discard it from your thoughts. You will be sure to be disappointed; nor is it right to indulge improper and useless hopes. It besides looks like presumption to expect it.*[112]

Lee's life after the war was one of cheerful frugality. He did without joyfully, hoping by his example to encourage the people of the region who were suffering so horribly. However, he could have lived in style: many offers came to Lee which would have made his life one of luxury and prominence. He rejected all these offers because he felt he had to remain in his native country and do all he could to rebuild its lost fortunes.

One offer came from England: Lee was invited to be the life-guest of a generous nobleman and recipient of an annuity of 3,000 pounds. The country of Romania offered him the command of the Romanian army, with promises of a generous salary and rich accommodations. He refused, saying he could not desert his native state in the time of her necessity.

Publishers offered Lee over $100,000 for the copyright to his memoirs. It is most probably due to this, ironically, that Lee never wrote his memoirs. He thought it would be monstrous for him to make money from the struggle that had caused so much grief to his people and nation.[113]

Repeated business offers poured in. The Knickerbocker Life Insurance Company offered him a salary of $10,000 as supervisor of agencies.[114] While Lee was in Lexington, another life insurance company offered him a similar sum to become the president of their company. Lee told the agent that he could not give up his position at the college and did not see how he could do justice to both positions if he did not. At this the agent responded, "But, general, we do not want you to discharge any duties. We simply wish the use of your name; *that* will abundantly compensate us." "Excuse me sir," Lee immediately responded, "I cannot consent to receive pay for services I do not render."[115]

The polestar of the modern era, "Look out for number one," was never consulted by Lee. He was guided by the star of Jacob, "Whoso saveth his life shall lose it, but he that loseth his life for my sake, shall find it."

HUMOR

A merry heart doeth good like a medicine.
                                        –Proverbs 17:22

*L*ee's quiet good humor was a trait that never left him. He was one who rejoiced in all good things and never felt somberness was a requirement for holiness.

During the war, when the newspapers were particularly vehement and unyielding in their criticism of the conduct of the Southern effort, Lee spoke of the matter to Senator B. H. Hill. Too big a man to be peevish, the situation did afford a fine opportunity to fling a barb back at the media, and Lee did not let the opportunity pass:

"We made a great mistake, Mr. Hill, in the beginning of our struggle, and I fear, in spite of all we can do, it will prove to be a fatal mistake."

The senator was shocked to hear this admission. "What mistake is that, general?"

"Why sir," replied Lee, "in the beginning we appointed all our worst generals to command the armies, and all our best generals to edit the newspapers!"

After a pause, Lee solemnly continued:

> *I have no ambition but to serve the*
> *Confederacy and do all I can to win our inde-*
> *pendence. I am willing to serve in any capacity*
> *to which the authorities may assign me. I have*
> *done the best I could in the field, and have not*
> *succeeded as I should wish. I am willing to*
> *yield my place to these best generals, and I will*
> *do my best for the cause in editing a newspa-*
> *per.*[116]

In a similar vein, Lee once remarked to one of his generals,

> *Even as poor a soldier as I am can generally*
> *discover mistakes after it is all over. But if I*
> *could only induce these wise gentlemen who*
> *see them so clearly beforehand to communicate*
> *with me in advance, instead of waiting until*
> *the evil has come upon us, to let me know that*
> *they knew all the time, it would be far better*
> *for my reputation, and (what is of more conse-*
> *quence) far better for the cause.*[117]

Lee enjoyed teasing men whom he knew could use a little loosening up. Once the "German Goliath" Major Heros
von Borcke, of J. E. B. Stuart's staff, bought a carriage in order
to obtain the horses. Being on the thrifty side, von Borcke
decided to put the carriage in service as a baggage wagon.
This brought no little teasing from Lee, who seldom saw von
Borcke without asking the whereabouts of his carriage.
During a minor engagement when von Borcke happened to
be with Lee, the general turned to him and remarked dryly,

"If we only had your carriage, what a splendid opportunity to charge the enemy with it!"[118]

John Hood was another favorite target of Lee's jibes. One day Hood called upon Lee while Lee was engaged in conversation with Colonel Chilton about the misconduct of some of the troops, who had burned fence rails for their fires. Hood felt compelled to defend his troops against these charges, which he did with no little indignity. He was quite put out that his men might be thought capable of acting so dishonorably. Lee allowed Hood to finish and then replied, "Ah, General Hood, when you Texans come about, the chickens have to roost mighty high."[119]

Lee's humor showed itself sometimes at the most unexpected times. During the last retreat when provisions were low and tensions were high, the general was seeking to find a place called the "Stone Chimneys" on his map. A young officer asserted that where they then were was in fact the place so marked. He remembered distinctly, he said with authority, when these chimneys were built. Lee noted the officer's comments and then said pleasantly, "I was waiting for the guide to come up that we might ascertain from him, but I suppose we had as well go on. If you remember when the chimneys were built, this is not the place. The stone chimneys mentioned on this map were built before you were."[120]

After the war, Lee received a letter from a group of spiritualists who asked his opinion on some military question. Colonel William Preston Johnston, a member of the faculty at Washington College, describes Lee's reply. "He wrote," said Col. Johnston, "a most courteous letter in which he said that the question was one about which military critics would differ, that his own judgment about such matters was but poor at best, and that inasmuch as they had power to consult (through their mediums) Caesar, Alexander, Napoleon,

Wellington, and all of the other great captains who have ever lived, he could not think of obtruding his opinion into such company." [121]

When Lee was president of Washington College, the greatest dread of the students was to be called into his office for their misdeeds. One student, who had been too careless in his attendance upon his classes, was called into Lee's office. When asked by the general to explain his truancy, he was terror-stricken and all the reasons he had carefully prepared to give the general evaporated from his memory. He "stammered out" a story about being violently ill. Realizing, however, that he in fact was "the picture of health," he changed his excuse and began to explain that his boots had been at the shoemaker's. Lee interrupted, "Stop, Mr. _____, stop sir! One good reason is enough." [122]

Lee delighted in humor that was self-effacing. During his "Southern tour" Lee stayed at the homestead of Dr. Prosser Tabb. Overwhelmed by the beautiful gardens on the place, Lee heaped praise upon the gardener. When Dr. Tabb told Lee that this gentleman had been in the Army of Northern Virginia and had fought to the end at Appomattox, Lee at once doubled his praise of the man.

But the man responded unpretentiously, "Yes, General, I stuck to the army, but if you had in your entire command a greater coward than I was, you ought to have had him shot." Lee was so amused by this response that he would often repeat it and would always add, "That sort of coward makes a good soldier." [123]

Lee loved to poke fun at his children, especially the girls. Once, after receiving a letter from Mildred that was peculiarly difficult to read because of her hurried handwriting, Lee responded with the following:

My Precious Life:

I received yesterday your letter of the 4th. We held a family council over it. It was passed from eager hand to hand, and attracted wondering eyes and mysterious looks. It produced few words, but a deal of thinking, and the conclusion arrived at, I believe unanimously, was that there was a great fund of amusement and information in it, if it could be extracted. I have therefore, determined to put it carefully away till your return, then seize a leisure day and get you to interpret it. Your mother's commentary, in a suppressed soliloquy, was that you had succeeded in writing a wretched hand. Agnes thought it would keep this cold weather—her thoughts running on jellies and oysters in the store-room. But I, indignant at such aspersions upon your accomplishments, retained your epistle and read in an elevated tone an interesting narrative of travels in sundry countries, describing gorgeous scenery, hair-breadth events by flood and field, not a word of which, they declared, was in your letter. Your return I hope will prove the correctness of my version of your annals.[124]

Lee kept a merry heart even in the midst of his sorrow and physical pain and weariness. The above letter was written in January, 1870, when he was beginning to experience great discomfort from his heart condition. Yet, in spite of all, he endured without complaint and, according to his son Robert, "was uniformly bright and cheerful." Testimony, no doubt, to the medical counsel of the Great Physician.

Kindness

*My experience of men has neither disposed me to
think worse of them nor indisposed me to serve
them.*

–R. E. Lee

*L*ee's kindness was not that forced, artificial sort one
often sees in people who believe their reputation
depends upon how nice they appear to be before others.
Rather it was the natural outflow of the heart of a man who
sought constantly to esteem others better than himself. One
of the remarkable manifestations of this was Lee's kindness
toward his men.

The couriers who carried out the dangerous duty of bringing vital communications through the lines were always objects
of his admiration and concern. His common practice upon
receiving their messages was to offer to them whatever he had
available for refreshment. Most of the time, it was only a cup of
water, and, says Freeman, he would "proffer it in the same tones
he would have employed in addressing the President." [125]

The horrors and sorrows of war were not forgotten by the great general. Often, after a battle, Lee would spend many hours sending notes of condolence to the families of those men who had been killed, wounded, or captured. Victory as well as defeat comes at a high cost.

Lee was always careful to show many small kindnesses to his officers. This was especially the case if an officer was visited in camp by his wife. Lee saw to it that they received a demonstration of his good will. He would in some way show his respect for the officer in front of his wife so that she would have another reason to honor her man.

Not just officers but common soldiers were always given great consideration. Whether they received his assistance, his compassionate inquiry about their well-being, or a cup of cold water in his tent, Lee treated them with open affection and great respect at all times. It was his view that the privates—men who fought without the incentive of rank or fame—were the most meritorious class of the army and that they deserved and should receive the utmost respect and consideration. Every private who appealed to him got a sympathetic hearing.

One day he saw a man standing near his tent. "Come in Captain," he said, "come in and take a seat."

"I'm no captain, General," the soldier replied, "I'm nothing but a private."

"Come in sir," Lee replied, "come in and take a seat. You ought to be a captain." [126]

One old soldier loved to tell of his most precious memory of the war. He had joined the army at the age of fifteen, serving in Parker's Battery under the command of Colonel Stephen D. Lee. A year he later became one of Colonel Lee's couriers. During the battle of Sharpsburg, Colonel Lee stopped under an apple tree full of delicious ripe apples and requested this man to take some of the apples to General Lee. He ripped out the bottom of his coat pocket in order to fill the entire side of his coat with apples and rode to Lee's headquarters.

When he arrived, he presented the apples to General Lee with the compliments of his commanding officer. General Lee thanked him heartily and then said, "Now, sir, won't you sit down and eat one of these apples with me?" The youth of sixteen readily agreed and sat eating with Lee—as much honored by Lee as if he had been a head of state.[127]

In the winter of 1864, as Lee journeyed by train to Richmond for a meeting with President Davis, a wounded soldier got up in the crowded train car and struggled to put on his overcoat. Though he put his teeth as well as his good arm in service, he could not accomplish the task. Lee, observing this, arose and assisted him into his coat, and with a few kind words returned to his seat.[128]

Lee was quick to make amends when he offended others. He lived by this rule:

> *The gentleman does not needlessly and unnec-*
> *essarily remind an offender of a wrong he may*
> *have committed against him. He can not only*
> *forgive, he can forget; and he strives for that*
> *nobleness of self and mildness of character*
> *which imparts sufficient strength to let the past*
> *be but the past. A true man of honor feels hum-*
> *bled himself when he cannot help humbling*
> *others.*[129]

In the aftermath of Gettysburg—when all emotions were high—Major Charles Venable, one of Lee's staff, reported in great disgust and in a loud voice how badly things were going with the portion of the army at Williamsport. Lee rebuked him sternly for speaking of such an important matter in a tone that could easily be overheard by the soldiers. Lee's manner was so severe that Venable was hurt and offended.

Lee realized immediately that he had offended his faithful staff officer and later requested that Venable join him in his tent for a glass of buttermilk. This failed in its purpose, as Venable continued to pout. At dawn the next day, when the staff was with General Lee, Venable lay down and went to sleep. A storm was coming and Lee took off his own poncho and quietly put it over the sleeping officer. When the major awoke and found what Lee had done, he soon forgot his pique.[130]

This consideration for his men was duplicated in his kindness toward the people of the South. After the war, the daughter of the Reverend Dr. Joseph Clay Stiles was visiting with the Lees. The general had earlier that day seen her father pass the house wearing a rather shabby hat, and Lee had called to Dr. Stiles from his porch, but the pastor—not hearing him—had passed on. Knowing how difficult it was to obtain a new hat, or anything else for that matter, Lee determined to do what he could for his old friend.

He later entered the room where his daughters and their guest were sitting and asked Dr. Stiles' daughter, "Miss Josie, has your father a good hat?" Uncertain of the purpose of the question, the girl did not answer immediately. General Lee continued, "Tell your father he is too good a rebel to wear such a bad hat as I saw on his head today, and I am too good a rebel to keep two hats as good as both mine are. I don't think a good rebel ought to have two good articles of one kind in these hard times. This was my dress-parade hat. Take it please and if your father has not a good hat, give him this one with my compliments." That hat became the prized possession of this Southern family for many years afterward and, in fact, was worn by Major Robert Stiles, the son of Dr. Stiles, at the unveiling of the monument to General Lee in Richmond on May 29, 1890.[131]

Once, upon hearing that one of his former chaplains was going to make a tour of the Southern states, Lee told him: "You will meet many of my old soldiers during your trip, and I wish you to tell then that I often think of them, try every day to pray for them and am always gratified to hear of their prosperity."[132] This was no exaggeration. He always remembered his men.

Love to Enemies

*Those who oppose our purposes are not always to
be regarded as our enemies.*

–R. E. Lee

*L*ee's men were not the only ones who were the recipients of his love and compassion. These were extended to the enemy as well. Once during the Spotsylvania campaign, a general of the infantry was hotly berating the cavalry for allowing the Union general, Phil Sheridan, to destroy a food depot: "If I were in command of this army, I would notify General Grant that, inasmuch as he had sent his cavalry to the rear and destroyed our rations, I should not give his prisoners whom we hold a morsel of food, and if he wanted to save them from starvation, he would have to send rations here to them!"

At that moment, General Lee came up and the general repeated the entire tirade. General Lee turned without breaking stride and said, "The prisoners that we have here, General, are my prisoners; they are not General Grant's prisoners and as long as I have any rations at all I shall divide them with my prisoners." [133] And he did. Lee always saw to it that Union prisoners were treated with respect and courtesy.

Lee understood the importance of showing esteem and honor to others, even to his enemies, and was often called upon to remind others of the same. While in Richmond early in the war, a young father brought his five-year-old to Lee's office to make him a gift of a Bible. Lee's aide protested that the general could not be seen because of the press of business, but Lee, overhearing the conversation, insisted that his guests be admitted. After giving the Bible, the father asked his son, who was sitting on Lee's knee, "What is General Lee going to do with General Scott?"

The boy responded as he had been taught by his father, "He is going to whip him out of his breeches."

Upon this, Lee's manner changed. He stood the boy before him and said, speaking in reality to his father who had put him up to this, "My dear little boy, you should not use such expressions. War is a serious matter, and General Scott is a great and good soldier. None of us can tell what the result of the contest will be." [134]

Lee was ever careful to encourage respect towards the victorious side and felt it to be a sad sign of corruption and lack of self-control if respect were not shown by his friends. Once, during a faculty meeting at Washington College, one of the faculty decided to favor the rest of the professors with his view of the Republican candidate for president, U. S. Grant. Not surprisingly, his was not a flattering portrayal.

When he had finished his scathing attack on the former general, Lee replied sternly, "Sir, if you ever again presume to speak disrespectfully of General Grant in my presence, either you or I will sever his connection with this university." [135]

In Lee's eyes, there was only one Grant: the Grant of Appomattox, who had treated his men so justly. He was for the rest of his life indebted to Grant for his willingness to make the surrender as easy as possible upon the Army of Northern Virginia and did not hesitate to defend the general in the presence of others.

Once while Lee was on vacation at the White Sulphur Springs, the rumor spread through the hotel that General and Mrs. Grant had secured reservations and were expected to arrive in a few days. One of the young girls whom Lee had befriended had become tired of hearing the admonition that she should be friendly to every Northerner in sight and appealed to the general to get his views. "Well, General Lee, they say General Grant is coming here next week; what will you do then?" Her boldness mortified her friends who, said one, "would gladly have slain her on the spot." But Lee was unperturbed: "If General Grant comes I shall welcome him to my home, show him all the courtesy that is due from one gentleman to another, and try to do everything in my power to make his stay here agreeable."[136] To Lee, any other course of action would have been unthinkable.

Among the infamous Reconstruction measures taken by the U.S. Congress after the war was an act disenfranchising all citizens who had supported the Confederate government. This law, of course, effectively disenfranchised all the white citizenry of the South. The Southern people were outraged. Some friends were visiting in General Lee's home soon afterwards and became rather animated in their denunciations of their old enemies. After listening quietly to the bitter expressions of anger and indignation, Lee turned to a table near him—on which was the manuscript of his father's life that he was editing—and began to read these lines:

> Learn from yon Orient shell to love thy foe,
> And store with pearls the hand that brings thee
> woe;

Free like yon rock, from base, vindictive pride,
Emblaze with gems the wrist that rends thy
side.
Mark where yon tree rewards the stony shower,
With fruit nectarious or the balmy flower;
All Nature cries aloud: shall men do less
Than love the smiter, and the railer bless?

He then stated, "These lines were written in Arabia, and by a Mahomedan, the Poet of Shiraz, the immortal Hafiz; and ought not we, who profess to be governed by the principles of Christianity, to rise at least to the standard of this Mahomedan poet, and learn to forgive our enemies?"[137] From anyone else such a rebuke might appear self-righteous, but not from Lee.

While Lee was president of Washington College, he was seen by the Reverend William Jones speaking at his gate with a stranger to whom, before parting, he gave some money. Reverend Jones inquired who the stranger was. "One of our old soldiers," replied Lee. "To whose command did he belong?" Pastor Jones asked. "Oh," said Lee, "he was one of those who fought against us. But we are all one now, and must make no difference in our treatment of them."[138]

The Love of His Men

I love you just as much as ever, General Lee!
                    –an unnamed Confederate soldier upon
                                hearing of the surrender

There may never have been a commanding general in the history of the world who had a bigger place in the hearts of his men than R. E. Lee. This, no doubt, was one of the chief ingredients in his ability to lead and motivate. Their confidence in his judgment, their certainty of his love and care for them provoked in them a corresponding love for him that is remarkable in any time, much less in time of war.

Lee never appeared among the men without being greeted with enthusiastic cheers and many other manifestations of love and affection. Once while riding alone—which he often did—Lee met a ragged private. The man immediately took off his hat and stood as reverently as if he had entered the presence of a king. Seeing this, Lee immediately took off his own hat, greeting the man with all courtesy and extending to him his respects. As Lee rode on, the soldier could not contain himself, and exclaimed: "God bless Marse Robert! I wish he was emperor of this country, and that I was his carriage-driver." [139]

Lee once came across a soldier from Georgia whose right arm had been badly wounded. Lee never failed to give a word of encouragement and comfort to his men when wounded, and so addressed this man, "I grieve for you, my poor fellow, can I do anything for you?"

"Yes sir!" replied the private, "You can shake hands with me, general, if you will consent to take my *left* hand."

Lee quickly dismounted and warmly shook the man's left hand, speaking more words of comfort. Rather than being disheartened, the man was left with a sense of privilege that he should have the honor of suffering under such a leader. [140]

The respect and confidence his men had in him was a key ingredient in keeping them in the field under the terrible conditions the Southern army faced. William Jones remarks:

> *Time and again have I seen these brave men—many of them the very elite of Southern society, who had been raised in luxury, and never knew what want was before—ragged, barefooted, and hungry, and almost ready to break out into open revolt at the idea that their sufferings were due to the inefficiency of the quartermaster and commissary departments. But a single word from General Lee, assuring the men that the supply department was doing all that it could to relieve their wants, would act like a charm, and the magic words, "Marse Robert says so," would hush every murmur and complaint.* [141]

After the war, Lee related what he called the oddest encounter he ever had with one of his old soldiers. During one of his frequent rides into the country surrounding Lexington, Lee met one of the old veterans in a section of deep forest. The veteran at once recognized his former commander and stopped his horse. "General Lee," he said, "I am powerful glad to see you, and I feel like cheering you." Lee told the man that as they were alone in the forest that would be quite unnecessary, but the soldier insisted and immediately began waving his hat above his head and giving forth at the top of his lungs, "Hurrah for General Lee!" He followed this exclamation with the old rebel yell. Lee began to resume his ride but the old soldier continued his tribute to his beloved leader. Lee said he traveled some distance before he could no longer hear this hearty cheer.[142]

One night during the war, the men were discussing some of the new-cast theories of atheism, especially those found in the new book by Charles Darwin. The discussion went back and forth for a time, when finally one of the impatient contenders for the old faith blurted out, "Well boys, the rest of us may have developed from monkeys; but I tell you *none less than God could have made such a man as Marse Robert.*"[143]

LOVE FOR HIS MEN

*No commander was ever more careful and never
had care for the comfort of an army given rise to
greater devotion.*

–Colonel A. L. Long

*A*fter the war a friend asked General Lee why he
did not make his escape before the surrender,
when that course was open to him. Lee responded that he was
unwilling to separate his fate from that of the men who had
fought under him for so long. This answer is the key to the
loyalty Lee inspired in his men. He truly loved them. Indeed,
the respect Lee enjoyed in their eyes was only rivaled by the
respect he himself had for them. The men were his chief pride
and his first obligation. As long as he lived, Lee considered
those who served in the Southern army as the most honorable of men.

Unlike many notable military leaders in history who
sought first to secure their own fame regardless of the fate of
those under them, Lee often put his reputation at risk in order

to preserve his men. Many of the criticisms one hears of his military strategy and errors in judgment are explained by his concern for them. He would not unnecessarily endanger them.

His letters are filled with expressions of concern for his soldiers. He regularly wrote to President Davis reporting shortages of food, clothing, shoes, and other provisions. His efforts in their behalf were untiring. But his concern was not merely expressed in these "public" ways; he often mentioned his men in his letters to his wife. On September 26, 1861, Lee wrote:

> *It is raining heavily. The men are all exposed on the mountain, with the enemy opposite to us. We are without tents, and for two nights I have lain buttoned up in my overcoat. To-day my tent came up and I am in it. Yet I fear I shall not sleep for thinking of the poor men.*[144]

Though often quite careless of his own safety, he was almost ferocious to keep his men from exposing themselves to unnecessary danger. Once near Farmville, in Virginia, he sat for some time on a horse near a section of Chamberlayne's battery, which was engaged in shelling the enemy. Thomas G. Jones tells the story:

> *He was quite exposed. Receiving a report from a staff officer, General Lee gave him a message in reply, and as he started off said to him: "You rode up on the wrong side of the hill and unnecessarily exposed yourself. Why did you not come up on the other side?" The officer said he was ashamed to shelter himself when his commander was so exposed. General Lee*

remarked to him quite sharply: "It is my duty to be here; I must see. Your duty does not require you to see, or to expose yourself when there is no occasion for it. Ride back the way I tell you!"[145]

Lee once found it necessary to caution one of the veterans who had entered Washington College against working too hard on his studies. The man defended himself by saying, "I am so impatient to make up for the time I lost in the army." Lee responded with a vehemence only a little below anger, "Mr. Humphreys, however long you live and whatever you accomplish, you will find that the time you spent in the Confederate army was the most profitably spent portion of your life. Never again speak of having lost time in the army!" [146]

Lee's affection for his men never waned. One of his chief concerns after the war was the welfare of his veterans. He loved to hear of their prosperity and when he heard of them zealously seeking to rebuild their lives, as they had once fought with high zeal for their independence, he was overcome with joy. An associate at Washington College once told the general of a maimed and once-affluent veteran he had seen ploughing a field with a cheerful spirit, thankful to God that He had preserved to him one arm with which to work. "What a noble fellow!" Lee exclaimed. "But it is just like one of our soldiers! The world has never seen nobler men than those who belonged to the Army of Northern Virginia." [147]

It was this sincere love and esteem for his men that stirred their loyalty and affection for him. Colonel A. L. Long well summarized the relationship that existed between Lee and his men in this way:

[T]he feeling for him was one of love, not of awe or dread. They could approach him with the assurance that they would be received with kindness and consideration, and that any just complaint would receive proper attention. There was no condescension in his manner, but he was ever simple, kind, and sympathetic, and his men, while having unbounded faith in him as a leader, almost worshiped him as a man. These relations of affection and mutual confidence between the army and its commander had much to do with the undaunted bravery displayed by the men, and bore a due share in the many victories they gained.[148]

MORALE

Forward! Charge! and remember your promise to
General Lee!

—J. B. Gordon to his men at Spotsylvania
Court House, May, 1864

*T*he love and respect given to Lee is especially remarkable considering the nature of the Confederate army and the conditions under which it fought. Most of the soldiers were from rural areas of the South and had little formal military experience. Once described as "a voluntary association of gentlemen organized to drive out the Yankees," the men of the Army of Northern Virginia were physically tough but nearly totally uninstructed in military tactics and procedure.

They entered the army with high hopes of fame and glory and within a few months realized just how deluded those dreams were. They were almost constantly outnumbered two to one or even more and had to fight most battles with distinctly inferior weapons and equipment. To keep such an army in the field much less in high morale and battle-ready may well be Lee's greatest military accomplishment. He did it by implementing a number of basic things:

Lee's first task was to establish order within the army, increasing discipline and letting all the men know that insubordination would be dealt with justly. Next, he put an end to favoritism in details. All were treated equally. Third, he kept the men occupied. Army life is often quite boring. It is during the times of inactivity that men begin to think of all the problems, inconveniences, and troubles that they have to face. Lee saw to it that such times were few. The Southern army was put to work digging—digging trenches, digging earth works for protection, digging, digging, and digging some more. The men complained, referring to Lee as the "King of Spades," but they did useful work—for which later they were very grateful—and they had little time to consider other problems.

Fourth, Lee took the offensive, and by his successful aggressiveness, raised morale. Fifth, he reorganized the supply service. The irregular—and wretched—rations the soldiers had been receiving were upgraded and made regular. Lee sought to insure that the men were as well cared for as was possible under the circumstances. Sixth, he removed men who proved themselves incapable of their duties, but, most importantly, he was always careful to remove them in such a manner as not to disgrace them publicly. He believed that if a man were humiliated publicly the demoralizing effects on the rest of the men would be severe.

In establishing all of these measures, as well as through his own conduct among the men, Lee showed his sincere concern for them. This sincere regard for the men's well-being was evident to all who met the general, and produced in the minds of his troops a respect, confidence, and affection that was invincible. Freeman says, the "men came to believe that whatever he did was right—that whatever he assigned them they could accomplish."

As a result, they would follow him anywhere and do whatever he requested. Once in July of 1862, after the Seven Days, General Jackson was anxious to launch an attack into enemy territory. Not to attack was to repeat the mistake of Manassas, Jackson said, by "allowing the enemy leisure to recover from his defeat and ourselves to suffer by inaction." Lee had not yet responded to Jackson's proposed plan, which made his anxiety even greater—so great that he expressed it to Colonel A. R. Boteler, a member of his staff, who was also a congressman.

Boteler asked what Lee had said in response to Jackson's proposal. "He says nothing," replied Jackson, "Don't think I complain of his silence; he doubtless has good reason for it."

"Then you don't think that General Lee is slow in making up his mind?"

"Slow! By no means, Colonel!" answered Jackson emphatically. "On the contrary his perception is as quick and unerring as his judgment is infallible. But with the vast responsibilities now resting on him, he is perfectly right in withholding a hasty expression of his opinions and purposes."

After a brief pause, Jackson continued, "So great is my confidence in General Lee that I am willing to follow him blindfolded." [149]

Not a bad endorsement from one who also knew something about military strategy and tactics.

The fact that Lee led men who were almost always ill-fed and poorly clothed, badly equipped, and regularly outnumbered makes their loyalty all the more amazing. Never perhaps has there been an army that presented a more pitiful appearance. A boy who lived in Maryland when the army came through described them as "the dirtiest men I ever saw, a most ragged, lean, and hungry set of wolves. Yet there was a dash about them that the Northern men lacked. They rode like circus riders." [150] The "dash" may be attributed almost completely to the pride and confidence they had in their leader.

And what confidence they had! A sergeant in the 1st Georgia remarked, "Gen. Lee has won the confidence of his men. They trust him with the same faith that a child does while in its parent's arms, with no thought of tomorrow. We have been victorious under his leadership in every battle, and expect to still win victory wherever he directs." [151] General E. P. Alexander concurred: "I am sure there can never have been an army with more supreme confidence in its commander than that army had in Gen. Lee. We looked forward to victory under him as confidently as to successive sunrises." [152]

When Field-Marshal Lord Wolseley was visiting Lee, he remarked that he saw no signs of demoralization in the army: "I never saw [an army] composed of finer men, or that looked more like *work* than that portion of General Lee's army which I was fortunate enough to see inspected." This he attributed to the commanding general. Lee, said Wolseley, spoke "as a man proud of his country, and confident of ultimate success under the blessings of the Almighty, whom he glorified for past successes, and whose aid he invoked for all future operations."

A private would later write, "It was remarkable what confidence the men reposed in General Lee; they were ready to follow him wherever he might lead, or order them to go."

This was illustrated in the spring of 1864. The army had been traveling for days with slender provisions and many of the men were utterly exhausted. Lee, bringing up the rear of General Ewell's division, came upon some of the stragglers resting by the roadside. "I know you do not want to be taken prisoner and I know you are tired and sleepy, but the enemy will be along before or by daybreak and if you do not move on you will be taken."

There was a good deal of grumbling among the men and some, further away from the road, gave back sharp responses to this admonition. "Well you may order us to 'move on, move on' when you are mounted on a horse and have all the rations that the country can afford!" One man replied tartly.

Lee made no answer. Some of the men nearer to him made out his familiar features and exclaimed, "Marse Robert!" This cry brought all alive. "Yes, Marse Robert, we'll move on and go anywhere you say, even to hell!"[153] And that was only the slightest of overstatements.

The men loved Lee as they loved their own fathers and gave him equal respect. Once, during the Cold Harbor campaign, the troops were moving noisily (the Confederate army was not particularly known for moving quietly) down a road when one of the men in the front of the column recognized that General Lee was resting under a tree up ahead. Word instantly passed down the column and, we are told, the men became as quiet as spies so they would not wake their beloved commander.[154]

Lee seldom gave stirring addresses to his men. Indeed, most often he never said anything. His mere appearance was sufficient to stir their hearts to fight. J. E. B. Stuart's aide, the German Heros von Borcke, once described a scene which illustrates this perfectly. Lee was riding along the ranks of his men before ordering them to charge. Von Borcke reported, "He uttered no word. He simply removed his hat and passed bare-headed along the line." Though no words were uttered, von Borcke said it was "the most eloquent address ever delivered." So powerful was the effect that a few minutes later a youth in the line, crying and reloading his musket, was heard to shout through his tears that "any man who would not fight after what General Lee said was a damned coward."

Lee was careful not to allow distress to show in his face. Because he was watched so closely by the troops, he knew that any indication of dismay on his part could send the army into panic. Thus his usual expression was what might be described as a grave calm. Thomas Jones, governor of Alabama in the last part of the nineteenth century, once recalled in an address how Lee's facial expression affected the men:

> *I well remember on the day after Sailor's Creek,*
> *riding by some troops drawn up in line and*
> *momentarily expecting to advance upon the*
> *enemy, who were discussing the truth of the*
> *report that Ewell's corps had been captured*
> *there, and how a private produced conviction*
> *of the falsity of the news by indignantly asking:*
> *"Didn't you see Mars Bob when he rode by just*
> *now? Did he look like Ewell's corps had been*
> *captured?"*[155]

His presence during the war was always enough to hearten the troops no matter how bad their situation. Little changed after the war. While Lee was in Richmond after the surrender, he received a message from a Confederate prisoner held in the Libby Prison in Richmond, requesting that Lee use his influence to seek his and his comrades' release. He closed with these words, "But if you can't, just ride by the Libby, and let us see you and give you a good cheer. We will all feel better after it."[156]

Clearly, there is no more impressive example in the history of modern warfare of the power of personality in creating and sustaining morale than one finds in the person of Robert E. Lee.

Politics

I am of the opinion that all who can should vote for the most intelligent, honest and conscientious men eligible to office.

–R. E. Lee

It is not unusual in our day for men who gain some degree of popularity to go into politics. This seems especially to be the case with regard to military heroes. It is assumed that a man capable of leading men on the field of battle is also capable of leading a country in the civil sphere. This idea is not altogether unfounded. George Washington was not the first military man to be placed in political office, but his obvious ability in the field of politics probably encouraged this notion more than was warranted.

Even though Lee did not lead his country to victory, the respect he gained did open the door to political opportunity. His nomination for the office of governor of Virginia has already been mentioned. What many do not know, however, is that Lee was seriously spoken of as a candidate for president.

The New York Herald in June of 1868 printed an editorial in which Lee was suggested as the perfect candidate for the Democratic party for the office of president—to oppose the Republican incumbent, U. S. Grant. The writer urged the Democrats to forget Union generals as potential nominees:

> *We will recommend a candidate for [the Democrats'] favors. Let it boldly take over the best of all its soldiers, making no palaver or apology. He is a better soldier than any of those they have thought upon and a greater man...For this soldier, with a handful of men whom he had molded into an army, baffled our greater Northern armies for four years; and when opposed by Grant was only worn down by that solid strategy of stupidity that accomplishes its object by mere weight. With one quarter the men Grant had this soldier fought magnificently across the territory of his native state, and fought his army to a stump. There never was such an army or such a campaign, or such a General for illustrating the military genius and possibilities of our people; and this General is the best of all for a Democratic candidate. It is certain that with half as many men as Grant he would have beaten him from the field in Virginia, and he affords the best promise of any soldier for beating him again.*[157]

Of course the recommendation was impossible to carry out, even if the Democrats had been so inclined, for Lee was still not a citizen of the United States. But it is a remarkable testimony to the esteem in which he was held by many.

There is another reason, however, why this suggestion was unrealistic: Lee himself would have laughed aloud over it. Not only would he have recoiled in horror at the potential such a move would have for disruption in the country, but, equally important, he did not view himself as even remotely qualified for civil office. Whatever fame he may have gained in the field of battle was no indication, as far as he was concerned, of his fitness for the civil sphere. His judgment of himself would have made it impossible for him to consider seriously any such proposal.

Lee had little patience with men who forgot the bounds of their abilities and entered spheres for which they were entirely unsuited. This was especially his attitude towards what he called "military statesmen and political generals." This was the phrase he used to describe men who were gifted in the military sciences and consequently judged themselves to be suited to the political arena. It was Lee's observation that the requisite gifts and abilities were not common to both callings and thus, military men were usually not men gifted for the political sphere.

For this reason Lee studiously avoided giving his opinions upon political questions, viewing himself utterly ill-equipped to offer any light in these matters. His thoughts on this were expressed to Senator B. H. Hill when he asked General Lee to give his opinion about whether the capital should be moved from Richmond—an issue that had sparked considerable controversy. Lee replied, "That is a political question, Mr. Hill, and you politicians must determine it; I shall endeavor to take care of the army, and you must make the laws and control the government."

Hill would not be put off so easily. "Ah, general, but you will have to change that rule, and form and express political opinions; for, if we establish our independence, the people will make you Mr. Davis' successor.

"Never sir," Lee replied firmly, "That I will never permit. Whatever talents I may possess (and they are but limited) are military talents. My education and training are military. I think the military and civil talents are distinct, if not different, and full duty in either sphere is about as much as one man can qualify himself to perform. I shall not do the people the injustice to accept high civil office with whose questions it has not been my business to become familiar."

Hill continued to pursue his prey. "Well, but general, history does not sustain your view. Caesar, and Frederick of Prussia, and Bonaparte, were great statesmen, as well as great generals."

"And great tyrants," Lee quickly responded. "I speak of the proper rule in republics, where, I think, we should have neither military statesmen nor political generals."

One more time Hill entered the fray, this time with what he considered his "ace in the hole": "But Washington was both, and yet not a tyrant."

At this Lee smiled, "Washington was an exception to all rule, and there was none like him."

Hill later revealed that to this remark he could not reply, but did think, "Surely Washington is no longer the only exception, for one like him, if not greater, is here." [158]

STATES' RIGHTS

*I fear the liberties of our country will be buried in
the tomb of a great nation.*

–R. E. Lee

*I*t has often been noted that Lee's opinion of secession
at the time of the outbreak of the war was unfavor-
able. "Secession is nothing less than revolution," he stated in
a letter to one of his sons. He submitted to Virginia's secession
because he viewed himself a citizen of the state and thus, the
state had first call upon his allegiance. But it is equally clear
that when Lee stated his opinion in 1861, he had not carefully
considered the constitutional arguments on this subject.

During the war, however, he reached a different opinion
about the Southern cause. He never mentioned what it was
that convinced him, whether his own reading or the debates
that went on constantly in the camps, but he came to
embrace the Southern constitutional argument and was obviously convinced by it. He wrote in January, 1866, "All that the
South has ever desired was that the Union, as established by

our forefathers, should be preserved; and that the government, as originally organized, should be administered in purity and truth." This letter was written to the great constitutional scholar, Chauncey Burr, whose book, *The Federal Government: Its True Nature and Character* (published in 1865), is one of the more thorough defenses of the original structure of the federal union as a *voluntary* union of sovereign states. Lee goes on to thank Mr. Burr for his "advocacy of right and liberty." [159]

In describing his own actions, he stated in a letter to Captain James May in July of the same year, "I had no other guide nor had I any other object than the defense of those principles of American liberty upon which the constitutions of the several States were originally founded." Lee goes on to say that unless these principles are strictly observed, "I fear there will be an end to Republican government in this country." [160]

In a letter to George W. Jones, in March of 1869, Lee referred to his prior position on secession, "I was not in favor of secession, and was opposed to war; in fact,...I was for the Constitution and the Union established by our forefathers. No one now is more in favor of that Constitution and that Union; and, as far as I know, it is that for which the South has all along contended...." [161] Here it appears Lee views his former opposition to secession more strategic than principled. Many in the South opposed secession not because it was in their view illegal, but because it was unwise. Lee here seems to say that he, too, was among that group, as he goes on to insist that the South had ever supported the Constitution and Union "as established by our forefathers."

Perhaps the clearest evidence of Lee's change of view in regard to secession is found in his letter to Lord (John Dalberg) Acton. Lord Acton had written to Lee to request his view on how "the current politics of America" should be understood. In his response, Lee gave the most thorough explanation we have of his views on states' rights and secession:

> *I have considered the preservation of the constitutional power of the General Government to be the foundation of our peace and safety at home and abroad, I yet believe that the maintenance of the rights and authority reserved to the states and to the people, not only essential to the adjustment and balance of the general system, but the safeguard to the continuance of a free government. I consider it as the chief source of stability to our political system, whereas the consolidation of the states into one vast republic, sure to be aggressive abroad and despotic at home, will be the certain precursor of that ruin which has overwhelmed all those that have preceded it.*

After referring to the papers of Washington and Jefferson wherein "consolidation and centralisation of power" is denounced, Lee mentions the position of the New England states on the matter of secession, noting that they did not always oppose the concept. The states meeting in the Hartford Convention of 1814, threatened secession over the Louisiana Purchase. It had long been the view that the right of the states to govern themselves included the right to withdraw peaceably from the Union. The South, said Lee, simply maintained the old view of the Union:

> *The South has contended only for the supremacy of the constitution, and the just*

> *administration of the laws made in pursuance*
> *to it. Virginia to the last made great efforts to*
> *save the union, and urged harmony and com-*
> *promise.*[162]

The responsibility for the war, in Lee's mind, rested with the radical Republicans and not with the states who sought merely to preserve their rights by secession. This letter seems to give irrefutable evidence to the fact that Lee's views had at the least matured to the point that he no longer viewed secession as "revolution" in the sense that it was an illegal and unauthorized action. He still maintained that secession was not the best alternative at the time and seemed to indicate that had the South been more patient, a compromise might have been worked out, but as to the right of self-preservation secured by the right of secession, apparently there was no question in Lee's mind that it was legitimate.

SLAVERY

If the slaves of the South were mine, I would
surrender them all without a struggle, to avert this
war.

–R. E. Lee

*L*ee, like all other Southerners of his day, had lived around slavery all his life. He seems never to have owned more than six slaves, most of them inherited upon the death of his wife's father. His will, written in 1846, indicated that at that time he had legal title to a Negro woman named Nancy and her children.

He was virtually a life-long supporter of gradual emancipation and willingly released his slaves prior to the war. His views on the institution, however, were molded by the fact that his experience with slaves had been largely benevolent. Most Southerners strove to treat their slaves with respect and provide them with a sufficiency of goods for a comfortable, though—by modern standards—spare existence. Evidence from plantation records indicates that the average slave in the

South had a higher standard of living than the average poor white of the region. Indeed, one study concluded that the living conditions of the average Southern slave were in some ways better than those of the average working man living in New York City in 1900.[163]

Lee was not unaware of the mistreatment some slaves received, but his greater objection to the institution was the potential problems it posed to the society as a whole, rather than merely to the slaves themselves. He wrote,

> *In this enlightened age, there are few I believe, but what will acknowledge, that slavery as an institution, is a moral and political evil in any Country. It is useless to expatiate on its disadvantages. I think it however a greater evil to the white than to the black race, and while my feelings are strongly enlisted in behalf of the latter, my sympathies are more strong for the former. The blacks are immeasurably better off here than in Africa, morally, socially, and physically.[164]*

The last statement may sound strange to modern ears, but this was the commonly accepted sentiment of that day. It was based on realities that have been forgotten today. The conditions that prevailed in Africa in the fifteenth through the nineteenth centuries were horrible. Most of the blacks purchased by the New England and foreign slave traders were purchased from African slave dealers. Africa, like any other pagan country, was permeated by the cruelty and barbarism typical of unbelieving cultures. Slavery was widespread within the continent long before the Portuguese arrived in the fifteenth century and initiated the international trade. The fact was (and is) easily demonstrable that, taken as a whole, there is no question that blacks in this country, slavery notwithstanding, were "immeasurably better off" in nearly every way.

In Lee's view, however, emancipation could only be accomplished successfully if it was gradual. Time was needed for the sanctifying effects of Christianity to work in the black race and fit its people for freedom.

> *Their emancipation will sooner result from the*
> *mild and melting influence of Christianity,*
> *than the storms and tempests of fiery*
> *Controversy. This influence though slow, is*
> *sure. The doctrines and miracles of our Saviour*
> *have required nearly two thousand years, to*
> *convert but a small part of the human race,*
> *and even among Christian nations, what gross*
> *errors still exist! While we see the course of the*
> *final abolition of human slavery is onward,*
> *and we give it the aid of our prayers and all*
> *justifiable means in our power, we must leave*
> *the progress as well as the result in his hands*
> *who sees the end; who chooses to work by slow*
> *influences; and with whom two thousand years*
> *are but as a single day.*[165]

Abolitionism was not the best answer.

> *Although the Abolitionist must know this, and*
> *must see that he has neither the right or power*
> *of operating except by moral means and sua-*
> *sion, and if he means well to the slave, he must*
> *not create angry feelings in the Master; that*
> *although he may approve the mode by which it*

> *pleases Providence to accomplish its purposes,*
> *the result will nevertheless be the same; that the*
> *reasons he gives for interference in what he has*
> *no concern, holds good for every kind of inter-*
> *ference with our neighbours when we*
> *disapprove their conduct; Still I fear he will per-*
> *severe in his evil course. Is it not strange that*
> *the descendants of those pilgrim fathers who*
> *crossed the Atlantic to preserve their own free-*
> *dom of opinion, have always proved themselves*
> *intolerant of the spiritual liberty of others?*[166]

This view was not unique to Lee. It is safe to say that the vast majority of Southerners believed slavery existed by the will of God and would be abolished when He so willed. The effect of this view was not to make them passive (over four-fifths of the anti-slavery societies in this nation prior to 1830 existed in the South), but rather to guard them from revolutionary measures in dealing with the institution.

Once Lee was asked his opinion of the view being set forth in the North that the war was fought over the issue of slavery. Dr. John Leyburn, who raised the issue with Lee, gives us this account:

> *On this point he seemed not only indignant but*
> *hurt. He said it was not true. He declared that,*
> *for himself, he had emancipated most of his*
> *slaves years before the war, and had sent to*
> *Liberia those that were willing to go; that the*
> *latter were writing back most affectionate let-*
> *ters to him, some of which he received through*
> *the lines during the war.*[167]

Lee went on to say, "So far from engaging in a war to perpetuate slavery, I am rejoiced that slavery is abolished. I believe it will be greatly for the interests of the South. So fully am I satisfied of this, as regards Virginia especially, that I would cheerfully have lost all I have lost by the war, and have suffered all I have suffered, to have this object attained."

He then spoke of the misrepresentation the South had suffered at the hands of Northern writers. "Doctor," he said, "I think some of you gentlemen that use the pen should see that justice is done us." [168]

Lee was once interviewed by the Englishman, Herbert C. Saunders. During the interview, Mr. Saunders asked Lee about his views of slavery. Mr. Saunders later wrote,

> *On the subject of slavery, he assured me that he had always been in favour of the emancipation of the negroes, and that in Virginia the feeling had been strongly inclining in the same direction, till the ill-judged enthusiasm (amounting to rancour) of the abolitionists in the North had turned the Southern tide of feeling in the other direction.*[169]

Though Lee and the South in general were anti-slavery, they were not fooled by the rhetoric flowing from the radical abolitionists of New England. Such rhetoric rang more than a little hollow when one remembered that many of the abolitionists came from families made wealthy by the slave trade. They sought not merely the end of slavery but the destruction of the South and thus, received little sympathy even from those who were otherwise favorably disposed to their cause.

RACE RELATIONS

*Let no motive of worldly interest induce you to act
an unkind or ungenerous part towards them.*
                              –Mrs. R. E. Lee, to her cousin,
                              on the treatment of slaves

*W*ith the presence of slavery, the South was
indeed a caste society, but it is important to
remember that it was not a compartmentalized or segregated
society. There were specific roles for blacks and whites and
each race "knew its place," as it were, but what is often overlooked is the high level of interaction that was a common and
everyday experience. The two races whose lives were intertwined in the old South were more intimate and dependent
upon each other than any two races in any country in the
world. This mutual dependence produced an intimacy and
trust between the white and black races that has seldom if
ever existed anywhere in history.

Northerners were often shocked and offended by the
familiarity that existed as a matter of course between the

whites and blacks of the old South. This was one of the surprising and unintended consequences of slavery. Slavery, as it operated in the pervasively Christian society which was the old South, was not an adversarial relationship founded upon racial animosity. In fact, it bred on the whole, not contempt but, over time, mutual respect. This produced a mutual esteem of the sort that always results when men give themselves to a common cause.

The credit for this startling reality must go to the Christian faith. Historic Christianity enabled men who were different in nearly every way to live and work together, to be friends and, often, intimates.

This relationship of trust and esteem which existed between the races received its greatest expression (and perhaps its greatest promotion) when the sectional tensions between the North and South broke out in war. The expected black slave revolt didn't happen. (Indeed, very few of the things the abolitionists thought would take place did so.) The predominant response on the part of the black population of the South was quite the opposite of revolt. Dr. Edward C. Smith, of American University, has noted that without black support, the South could never have held out for four years against one of the most powerful military machines of the nineteenth century.[170]

Blacks not only worked the farms and plantations of the South, supplying food to the troops, but also filled positions in factories, in mines (digging coal, iron, and saltpeter), in hospitals, in munitions plants, and in naval shipyards. In addition to this "indirect" support, there was also the more direct support given by black men to the military. It is impossible to get accurate figures, but the estimates of the number of blacks who served in the Southern armies vary from 50,000 to 90,000. The South, therefore, had a greater percentage of blacks serving in the army than did the North. And it should be noted that blacks in the Southern army were not segregated from whites, as they were in the Northern army. Further, they received the same rations, provisions, and compensation as the white soldiers. This is in direct contrast to the common practice of the Union army.

The Confederate veterans did not view these black partisans as lesser men or lesser soldiers. They were viewed and treated as equals and, considering the circumstances of their service, they were esteemed as honored compatriots. In 1913, at the fiftieth anniversary of the battle of Gettysburg, thousands of veterans converged on the little Pennsylvania town. The committee for housing had made arrangements for the black Union soldiers, but were completely unprepared when hundreds of black Confederate veterans began showing up. As they had made no provisions for their housing, the black Southerners were given straw pallets in the main tent of the compound.

When the white Southerners heard about this arrangement, a delegation was sent to the main tent to gather up all the black soldiers and bring them down to the Southern encampment, where they were put up in the tents of the white Southerners and given every provision.[171] Whatever may have been the sense of superiority that had existed prior to the war, it was no longer in existence afterwards—at least among the soldiers. The war had made them brothers in a common cause and they could not be parted.

These and other incidents raise the question of what might have been the relationship between the races had the South won the war. There can be little question that the support given by the black population of the South would have had a significant impact on race relations. The war had demonstrated the mutual dependence of each race upon the other. As it was, the loyalty and love demonstrated in the crisis was never forgotten by some. The impact would have undoubtedly been culture-wide had there not been the disruption of the Reconstruction.

With the Reconstruction, however, a wedge was driven between the races that has yet to be removed. The policies enforced on the South by the Union produced a bitterness, mistrust, envy, and hatred that had never existed on any wide scale prior to the war.

Lee had never held any animosity for blacks—slave or free. But his role in promoting reconciliation during the difficult times in the aftermath of the war must not be overlooked.

One of the most revealing incidents demonstrating Lee's desire for reconciliation occurred at St. Paul's Church in Richmond on a Sunday in June, two months after Appomattox. The congregation had gathered as usual to hear Dr. Charles Minnegerode preach and afterward to administer Communion.

When the time came for Communion, Dr. Minnegerode read the order from the liturgy. At the invitation, the first man down the aisle was a tall, well dressed, and very black man. Colonel T. L. Broun, of Charleston, West Virginia, was present that morning and recorded what happened:

> *This was a great surprise and shock to the communicants and others present. Its effect upon the communicants was startling, and for several moments they retained their seats in solemn silence and did not move, being deeply chagrined at this attempt to inaugurate the "new regime" to offend and humiliate them during their most devoted Church services. Dr. Minnegerode was evidently embarrassed.*

> *Gen. Robert E. Lee was present, and, ignoring*
> *the action and presence of the negro, arose in*
> *his usual dignified and self-possessed manner,*
> *walked up the aisle to the chancel rail, and rev-*
> *erently knelt down to partake of the*
> *communion, and not far from the negro. This*
> *lofty conception of duty by Gen. Lee under such*
> *provoking and irritating circumstances had a*
> *magic effect upon the other communicants*
> *(including the writer), who went forward to the*
> *communion table.*[172]

The painful and often misguided efforts to make us a "color-blind" society have failed largely because we are being forced to ignore personal character. And in such a situation, skin color is a poor substitute.

The unity and companionship that existed between the races in the South prior to the war was the fruit of a common faith. The deterioration of this spiritual unity greatly contributed to the division that occurred between the races after the war. The lesson Lee symbolically enacted at the communion rail in St. Paul's church that Sunday in Richmond is that only in Christ can there be any true harmony between the races. In Him alone is there "neither Jew nor Greek, neither male nor female, bond or free."

TRUST IN GOD

My whole trust is in God, and I am ready for what-
ever He may ordain.

–R. E. Lee

*T*here are many times in our lives when we are able
to see the merciful providence of God in a most clear
and marvelous way. The life of Robert E. Lee is full of examples of such times and Lee himself was quick to note them.

During the Mexican War, Lee and Pierre G. T. Beauregard
were chosen by General Winfield Scott to make reconnaissance of Vera Cruz to determine the most advantageous
positions for the artillery. On the nineteenth of March, 1847,
Lee and Beauregard were returning from the front along a
narrow path that had been cut through the thick undergrowth
in the area. As they came to a turn in the path they were chal-
lenged by the call of a young, inexperienced sentinel: "Who
goes there?"

"Friends," said Lee.

"Officers," called Beauregard.

But before they could get the words out of their mouths, the sentinel, believing them to be Mexicans, fired his gun at point blank range at Lee. The bullet passed between the inside of his left arm and his upper chest, singeing his uniform. Had the soldier fired two inches to his left, the entire history of this nation would no doubt have been quite different. As it was, Lee escaped without a scratch.

Later in the same campaign, Lee and his guide, John Fitzwalter, were on reconnaissance in an effort to find an alternative route to the road which traversed the deadly pass at Cerro Gordo, which was protected by six pieces of Mexican artillery. Lee and his companion scouted out the ridges north of the river and satisfied themselves that the army could cut a path across them and so circumvent the pass.

In climbing one of the ridges, Lee came to a spring surrounded by tall trees and dense, lush undergrowth. As he was examining the area around the spring, he heard Spanish-speaking voices. Realizing that Mexican soldiers were rapidly approaching, he and Fitzwalter hid under the scrub-covered trunk of a fallen tree. The soldiers stayed around the spring all afternoon—talking, drinking from the spring, generally killing time. All the while Lee and his companion were forced to lie motionless under the tree trunk. Several times the Mexicans nearly stepped on them. Two of the enemy soldiers actually sat down on the trunk itself. This was, without doubt, the longest day of Lee's life. Had the soldiers poked around in the bushes or noticed American footprints in the soft soil, it would have meant instant death. Soon darkness fell and the Mexicans began to descend the ridge, and Lee and Fitzwalter were finally able to slip away undetected.

The information gathered was invaluable to the army's advance. The troops were able to travel around the northern end of Cerro Gordo, attack the enemy from the rear, and capture the Jalapa road.

Lee consistently showed the most amazing calm and self-control during the most fearful times. The explanation for this, as Freeman points out, can only be his implicit trust in God.

His calm during battle was often startling to others. Once Lee was prevailed upon by a Mr. W. E. Fox to enjoy his hospitality, since the general had ridden into his yard to observe enemy movements. Lee thanked Mr. Fox, but replied that he would only be there a few minutes. Mr. Fox then requested him to take some refreshment. Again, Lee expressed his appreciation but refused. Realizing that Mr. Fox was hurt by his refusal, however, the general consented to have a drink of some buttermilk and took his seat on the man's porch.

Just as the general began to drink, a Union artillery officer from across the valley spotted him on the porch and fired a round shot. It passed within a few feet of the general and imbedded itself in the door frame of the house. To Mr. Fox's amazement, the general finished his milk as if nothing had happened, thanked him, and then rode away, explaining that he felt it best to leave lest his presence provoke an attack upon the house.[173]

In victory, Lee was careful to give the glory and credit to God. His official reports and letters are filled with these expressions. But he was also careful to remind his men of the same reality. Colonel Charles Marshall, Lee's military secretary, relates how this characterized Lee:

> *We recall him as he appeared in the hour of victory, grand, imposing, awe-inspiring, yet self-forgetful and humble. We recall the great scenes of his triumph, when we hailed him victor on many a bloody field, and when above the paeans of victory we listened with reverence to*

> *his voice as he ascribed "all glory to the Lord of*
> *hosts, from whom all glories are." We remember*
> *that grand magnanimity that never stooped to*
> *pluck the meaner things that grow nearest the*
> *earth upon the tree of victory, but which, with*
> *eyes turned to the stars, and hands raised*
> *toward heaven, gathered golden fruits of mercy,*
> *pity, and holy charity, that ripen on its topmost*
> *bough beneath the approving smile of the great*
> *God of battles.*[174]

What was true of Lee in victory was also true of him in defeat. After the disaster at Gettysburg, Lee ordered a day of fasting on the 21st of August, 1863. He addressed his men with these words:

> *Soldiers! we have sinned against Almighty God.*
> *We have forgotten His signal mercies, and have*
> *cultivated a revengeful, haughty, and boastful*
> *spirit. We have not remembered that the*
> *defenders of a just cause should be pure in his*
> *eyes; that 'our times are in His hands'; and we*
> *have relied too much on our own arms for the*
> *achievement of our independence. God is our*
> *only refuge and our strength. Let us humble*
> *ourselves before Him. Let us confess our many*
> *sins and beseech Him to give us a higher*
> *courage, a purer patriotism, and more deter-*
> *mined will; that He will convert the hearts of*
> *our enemies; that He will hasten the time when*
> *war, with its sorrows and sufferings, shall cease,*
> *and that He will give us a name and place*
> *among the nations of the earth.*[175]

Lee's trust in God was unshakable. This trust was all the more remarkable because Lee always faced the reality of every situation, no matter how desperate. He saw the real dangers and reckoned with them in the light of the promises of God. Before the final campaign, when Grant had amassed an army five times larger than his own, he wrote to his son Robert,

> *Our country demands all our strength, all our energies. To resist the powerful combination now forming against us will require every man at his place. If victorious, we have everything to hope for in the future. If defeated, nothing will be left for us to live for. My whole trust is in God, and I am ready for whatever He may ordain.*[176]

EFFECTIVE GENERALSHIP

Whatever happens, know this—that no men ever fought better than those who have stood by me.

—R. E. Lee

*L*ee was without question one of the greatest generals of all time. Shortly before the war, General Winfield Scott was asked by one of his friends, "Whom do you regard as the greatest living soldier?" Scott never hesitated in his reply, "Colonel Robert E. Lee is not only the greatest soldier of America, but the greatest soldier now living in the world. This is my deliberate conviction, from a full knowledge of his extraordinary abilities, and if the occasion ever arises Lee will win this place in the estimation of the whole world." [177]

Scott's words were prophetic: Lee became one of the greatest leaders of all time. But what makes a man a leader? No doubt there are many qualities, but in Lee certain characteristics stand out.[178]

First, Lee possessed both high intelligence and physical strength. Without question, he was a military genius. Often to his opponents it seemed that he was privy not only to their counsels of war but to their thoughts as well! He had a remarkable ability to analyze the battle situation, taking into account the men and materiel of both sides, the geographical situation, the morale, the weather conditions, and the disposition of the respective forces. He was then able to arrive at a correct judgment of what the opponent would likely do, and know what plan he must devise to prevent the enemy from taking the advantage.

Without his amazing physical endurance Lee's military genius would have been useless, because he would have been unable to endure not only the rigors of battle but the great privations of the war. But Lee was an astonishment to both friend and foe for his ability to operate on little rest and yet remain alert and strong in body and mind.

Secondly, Lee never underestimated his adversary. Regardless of the ability of the opposing commander, Lee did not presume upon any lack of competence as he made his plan: he never assumed that his opponent would blunder by overlooking a strategic advantage. "It is always proper to assume that the enemy will do what he should do," was one of his standard rules. He operated on the assumption that the enemy's plan would be sound, but that the execution of it would result in failure (as a result of *his* battle plan).

Third, Lee was scrupulously just in his dealings with his men. He always gave his officers the benefit of the doubt. He never praised them except when he was sure they deserved it, but neither did he rebuke them unless he was certain they merited it. He was careful to avoid unnecessary criticism and bore with the weaknesses of his men.

After the disaster at Gettysburg, Lee requested General Pickett to change his report, which contained some fairly harsh criticism of others for not giving his men the support necessary to gain a victory. Lee remonstrated, "You and your men have covered yourself with glory, but we have the enemy to fight and must carefully at this critical moment, guard against dissensions which the reflections in your report would create. I will therefore, suggest that you destroy both copy and original, substituting one confined to casualties merely. I hope yet all will be well." [179]

Later, he explained his rationale to General A. P. Hill, who was outraged over the performance of one of his officers:

> *These men are not an army, they are citizens defending their country. General Wright is not a soldier; he's a lawyer. I cannot do many things that I could do with a trained army. The soldiers know their duties better than the general officers do, and they have fought magnificently. Sometimes I would like to mask troops and then deploy them but if I were to give the proper order, the general officers would not understand it; so I have to make the best of what I have and lose much time in making dispositions. You understand all this, but if you humiliated General Wright, the people of Georgia would not understand. Besides, whom would you put in his place? You'll have to do what I do: When a man makes a mistake, I call him to my tent, talk to him, and use the authority of my position to make him do the right things the next time.* [180]

Fourth, Lee was a great leader because he never lost control of himself. A man cannot govern others if he is unable to govern himself. Lee was always sober. During the times of greatest disaster, he did not panic. During the times of great victory, he did not allow the triumph to cloud his judgment. The men depended upon him to make the best judgment and he nearly always did so. This quality points us to the most basic characteristic of the able leader: his spiritual strength.

Lee's spiritual stamina was most clearly illustrated during the nightmarish retreat from Petersburg. One of Lee's young staff officers described his demeanor during this tense and dreadful time:

> *Self-contained and serene, he acted as one who was conscious of having accomplished all that was possible in the line of duty, and who was undisturbed by the adverse conditions in which he found himself. There was no apparent excitement and no sign of apprehension as he issued his orders for the retreat of his sadly reduced army and the relinquishment of the position so long and successfully held against the greatly superior force opposed to him... It was a striking illustration of Christian fortitude, the result of an habitual endeavor to faithfully perform the duties of one's station, and of unquestioning trust in the decrees of an all-wise Creator...[181]*

Lee was nearly imperturbable not because he was incapable of emotion or of terror, but because his trust in the Almighty's care and keeping was deep and unshakable. In other words, Lee was a true man possessed with true manliness. That quality, though often not specifically identifiable by others, inspires a confidence that is irresistible.

CIVILIZED WARFARE

Human virtue should be equal to human calamity.

–R. E. Lee

*T*he phrase "civilized warfare" sounds hopelessly anachronistic to an age where the word "civilization" has become a term with nothing more than an historic meaning. The idea of civilized warfare is distinctively Christian, arising out of the Christianization of Europe during the Middle Ages.

Warfare among sinful men was assumed to be inevitable, but Christianity insists that even warfare be carried on honorably. War is to be conducted between armies; civilians and non-combatants are to be treated with dignity and respect. War is to be waged with self-control. Only those who have no respect for the image of God in man can fight without regard to basic "rules" of justice and humanity. In this way, civilizations could survive war, for war was a contest between combatants, not an unrestrained attack on the culture.

This view was deeply ingrained in the Southern psyche. War, to the majority of Southerners, was looked upon as an "elaborate ceremonial, a gigantic tournament, with the Lord of Hosts as umpire and judge." It was above all to be an "affair of honor." [182]

Thus, when John Pope announced his commitment to total war, the reaction of the South was universal indignation. The arrogant and incompetent Pope took command of the Northern forces, assuring his troops that he was "accustomed to see only the backs of his enemies." This sort of braggadocio brought a good deal of ridicule from both North and South, but his other orders were no laughing matter.

One of his orders directed his troops to live off the country in which they operated and to reimburse only the loyal citizens. Given the situation of the South, this was virtually a license to steal. Another order required each community to make good the damage done by guerrillas and threatened instant destruction of any house from which any Northern soldier was shot. Another required the arrest of all male noncombatants within federal lines. These were to be exiled if they refused to take a loyalty oath and promise good behavior. Anyone who returned to his home after being exiled was subject to execution.

A subordinate of Pope, Brigadier General A. von Steinwher, arrested five citizens of the town of Luray, Virginia, with the announcement that whenever a guerrilla killed one of his soldiers, one of these hostages would be shot in retaliation. This was to be done unless the guerrilla was handed over to the federal commander.

Such policies astonished and infuriated Lee. "No civilized nation within my knowledge has ever carried on wars as the United States government has against us." [183] Perhaps his strongest language was directed against Pope and the measures he ordered against the civilians of the South. In one of his dispatches, he referred to Pope as a "miscreant." He remarked in a letter to his wife about his nephew Louis Marshall, who had sided with the North, "I could forgive [his] fighting against us, but not his joining Pope."[184]

Later, when the Northern General E. V. Sumner first threatened and then bombarded the city and civilians of Fredericksburg on the grounds that his troops had been fired upon from the streets, Lee was again astounded. As one hundred federal guns poured shells of destruction indiscriminately into the city, Lee remarked, "These people delight to destroy the weak and those who can make no defense; it just suits them!"[185]

When Pope's and Sumner's activities were seconded by Sherman, Sheridan, Hunter, and others, it seemed to the people of the South that one of the pillars of civilization had been taken away. Barbarism now reigned unrestrained. Richard Weaver has observed that it was not so much the loss of property that embittered the South, but the moral affront to the tradition of Christendom that made the insult outlive the injury. This spirit is expressed by the character Cindy Lou Bethany in Claire Booth's *Kiss the Boys Good-bye.* When her Northern guest reminds her that the South lost the War, Cindy Lou responds, "Yes, but you cheated." To the South, the North won, but won unfairly and most of all, dishonorably.[186]

By the time of the Gettysburg campaign, pressure had arisen in the South to begin retaliatory actions against the citizens of the North that they might experience the same suffering that the South had felt under the hand of Northern troops. Newspapers carried accounts of the desolation brought about by federal armies. The orders of Pope, Butler, and others were printed and read with outrage and cries for retaliation arose from every quarter. Lee was steadfastly opposed to such actions.

It was a simple matter of obedience to Lee, who stated, "I cannot hope that Heaven will prosper our cause when we are violating its laws. I shall, therefore, carry on the war in Pennsylvania without offending the sanctions of a high civilization and of Christianity."[187] God's honor was more important than effective military strategy or tactics if those tactics involved sin. Lee was expressing the old view of "limited warfare" that had been dominant in the Christian West—a view that was rapidly becoming obsolete.

It was this deep-seated conviction that is reflected in Lee's General Orders No. 73 to his men as they traveled North:

> *It must be remembered that we make war only upon armed men, and that we cannot take vengeance for the wrongs our people have suffered without lowering ourselves in the eyes of all whose abhorrence has been excited by the atrocities of our enemies, and offending against Him to whom vengeance belongeth, without whose favor and support our efforts must all prove in vain.*
>
> *The commanding general therefore earnestly exhorts the troops to abstain with most scrupulous care from unnecessary or wanton injury to private property, and he enjoins upon all officers to arrest and bring to summary punishment all who shall in any way offend against the orders on this subject.*[188]

These orders were sincerely written and vigorously enforced, in spite of protests from some in the South. By daily reminders and the strict example of the commanding officers, Lee prevented the destruction or looting of property. General

Lee himself once dismounted to replace a fence rail which had not been put back into place after the army had passed.

An illustration of how seriously the officers took Lee's orders is seen in an incident that occurred when General John B. Gordon's brigade entered York, Pennsylvania, in 1863. There was initially a great panic among the people, who feared that the Southern troops would carry out widespread retaliation. General Gordon, however, addressed a large number of women who had gathered in the street:

> *Our Southern homes have been pillaged, sacked, and burned; our mothers, wives, and little ones, driven forth amid the brutal insults of your soldiers. Is it any wonder that we fight with desperation? A natural revenge would prompt us to retaliate in kind, but we scorn to war on women and children. We are fighting for the God-given rights of liberty and independence, as handed down to us in the Constitution by our fathers. So fear not: if a torch is applied to a single dwelling, or an insult offered to a female of your town by a soldier of this command, point me out the man, and you shall have his life.*[189]

There were no charges of rape and very few accusations of plundering. The chief problem, as noted by one Northern writer, was preventing the hot, bareheaded soldiers from snatching the hats from the heads of bystanders as they marched by. This did happen, and when it was reported, the officers sought in vain to find the offending men, but "with the similarity of the men and the necessity for the column to keep moving on, not a single one was detected."[190]

The advent of total war revealed a creeping cancer in the bones of our culture. As Richard Weaver has noted, "The deeper the foundations of a civilization, the more war seems to be formalized or even ritualized, and the failure to hold it within bounds is a sign of some antecedent weakening on the part of that civilization."[191] Total war is a symptom of a deep disease in the heart of a culture. So it has proven to be for our nation.

Part III:
The Legacy of Robert Edward Lee

৵৹   ৵৹   ৵৹

*Get correct views of life, and learn to see the world in its
true light. It will enable you to live pleasantly, to do good,
and, when summoned away, to leave without regret.*

*There is a true glory and a true honor; the glory of duty
done—the honor of the integrity of principle.*

–Robert E. Lee

Lee's Accomplishments as a Commander

Lee is the greatest military genius in America.
                                        –General Winfield Scott

*L*ee's accomplishment in carrying on the war for the Confederacy has yet, perhaps, to be fully appreciated. When viewed in the light of the obstacles he faced, it is incredible to contemplate. Consider:

Never once in any major engagement did he meet the Union army on equal terms as far as men and war materiel. Never once was he strong enough to follow up his victories. Lack of food or provisions, the death of officers, the necessity to reorganize were ever-present impediments. Freeman notes that Lee never enjoyed an advantage that was not purchased with the blood of men he could not replace.

He always fought with inferior weapons. He was usually as much concerned with finding food as he was with engaging the enemy. His transportation was woefully inadequate. His government could scarcely ever obtain the cooperation of its own states. States rights formed such an important and central part of the thinking of the South that state leaders at times were oblivious to the critical necessity of cooperation. So fervent was state loyalty that in the Confederate hospital in Richmond, the men had to be separated by states to prevent fights from breaking out among them!

Lee fought without benefit of a navy and constantly in the stranglehold of a federal blockade on all major ports in the South. Not only did the enemy control the ports, they also controlled the major waterways which ran through the Confederacy.

In the beginning, he had to combat the overconfidence of the Southern soldiers and the people. At the end, he had to combat their despair. He fought with a largely citizen army. His officers were often untrained men who did not understand military terminology and strategy. He had to conform his strategy to the views of the Confederate leadership that the war was to be a purely defensive struggle. The reluctance on the part of the Confederate leadership to take the offensive was at times very costly.

Lee made many mistakes—among them, overestimating his men, miscalculating the time needed to carry out certain objectives, placing men in positions of leadership who were unequal to the responsibility, and acquiescing to counsel from men whose vision and understanding were inferior to his own. Perhaps his most serious mistake was allowing his gentility and concern for keeping peace among his officers to interfere with needed discipline.

In spite of all this, however, his accomplishments are utterly remarkable. He mobilized Virginia and got this key state ready for war and defendable. He saved the capitol from what looked like certain capture when he took over command in June of 1862. He repulsed four other major offensives against Richmond and delayed a fifth offensive for ten months by his invasion of Pennsylvania. He fought ten major battles, winning six without any dispute and only once, at Gettysburg, suffering definite defeat.

Because of the superior numbers of the Northern force, Lee was never able to pursue a victory without laying himself open to disaster. Lee would compare the war to "a man breasting a wave of the sea, who, as rapidly as he clears a way before him, is enveloped by the very water he has displaced." It was, under any view, a desperate task to attempt. Without question, the Confederacy, with a lesser man, could not have lasted six months. With Lee, she came very close to winning her independence.

THE GREATNESS OF LEE

The dominant party cannot reign forever, and truth and justice will prevail at last.

–R. E. Lee

*T*here are few men in the history of the world who have dominated a nation and left an imprint upon its people in the way that Robert Edward Lee influenced the nation of the Confederate States of America. It is nearly impossible to understand the shadow Lee cast over this country in the last century and the power he exerted by his example. It is certainly true that no one man has ever exerted such influence over the minds of the Southern people.

So great was this influence that every group and every project desired his endorsement. From insurance companies to inventors, from the railroads to the steel industry, from the Ku Klux Klan to the societies established for the education of the Negro—all desired Lee's commendation. To gain Lee's endorsement was tantamount to insuring the success of any venture. If Lee had endorsed the plan put together by a number of prominent Southern loyalists to emigrate to a foreign country, it would have gained great support throughout the South. His refusal to do so meant the death of this project.

In the history of our nation only one other man has even come close to equalling Lee's impact on Southern culture, and that man is George Washington. There is little question that when it comes to understanding the South, you must know Robert E. Lee.

Freeman describes Lee in this way: "What he seemed, he was. He was—a wholly human gentleman, the essential elements of whose positive character were two and only two, simplicity and spirituality." [1] By "simplicity" he means that Lee was a man without dissimulation. What he appeared to be, he was. He was never pretentious, never concerned to give an exaggerated impression of himself and as a consequence, probably ended up in the eyes of most, greater than he was—but not by much.

Field Marshall Viscount Wolseley, commander in chief of the British army, remarked after interviewing Lee:

> *I have met many great men of my time, but Lee alone impressed me with the feeling that I was in the presence of a man who was cast in a grander mold and made of different and finer metal than all other men... When Americans can review the history of the War Between the States with calm impartiality,...I believe he will be regarded not only as the most prominent figure of the Confederacy, but as the greatest American of the 19th century...* [2]

It is difficult for us, in these egalitarian times, to comprehend the awe in which General Lee was held. Professor James

J. White once accompanied General Lee on a brief outing from the college. Overtaken by darkness, they were forced to spend the night at a farmhouse along the road. To White's dismay, the generous and hospitable hostess had only one bed for both him and the general. White related that he spent the entire night sitting on the rail of the bed, fearful of disturbing the general's rest. Privately, the professor admitted afterwards, that he "would as soon have thought of sleeping with the Archangel Gabriel as with General Lee!"[3]

Lee had his sins and failures. But it is not the sins of the man you remember. What we see here is the amazing evidence of what God can do by His grace with sinners.

The story of Lee is the story of a generation of plain, honest, hard-working, God-fearing men, most of whom will never be remembered. But they deserve remembrance. They believed in principle over convenience. They were willing to stand for the right even though it was almost certain to fail. They were willing to defend sacred principles and the righteous cause—even though they might perish in the process. If it was right, it was to be done regardless of the consequences.

General Lee was once asked by Bishop Joseph P. B. Wilmer (at the beginning of the war) how he expected to win given the overwhelming advantages of the North. Was he, asked the bishop, "looking to divided counsels in the North, or to foreign interposition?" Lee replied, "My reliance is in the help of God." "Are you sanguine of the result?" asked the bishop. "At present I am not concerned with results. God's will ought to be our aim, and I am quite contented that His designs should be accomplished and not mine."[4]

Lee's attitude had not changed at the end of the war. A day or two before the surrender, Lee said to General Pendleton,

*I have never believed we could, against the
gigantic combination for our subjugation, make
good in the long run our independence unless
foreign powers should, directly or indirectly
assist us…But such considerations really
made with me no difference. We had, I was
satisfied, sacred principles to maintain and
rights to defend, for which we were in duty
bound to do our best, even if we perished in
the endeavor.*[5]

Faithfulness, to Lee, was essential whether or not success
was granted.

Lee and the men who followed him believed that ultimately righteousness would prevail. In our day, it would be easy to despair. But the example of Lee teaches us differently. It reminds us of God's power and grace and His willingness to bring glory to Himself through those who love Him above all else.

At the close of his life, General Lee wrote to a friend in an effort to encourage him about the sad events they had endured. He acknowledged his failures and errors, but went on to say that in spite of these he did not despair of the future:

*The truth is this: The march of Providence is so
slow and our desires so impatient; the work of
progress is so immense and our means of aiding it so feeble; the life of humanity is so long,
that of the individual so brief, that we often see
only the ebb of the advancing wave and are
thus discouraged. It is history that teaches us to
hope.*[6]

There it is. Lee understood that during certain seasons in the history of the world, the tide of God's purposes appears to be receding rather than advancing. Our lives are often too short to see the ends we desire. Thus, it may be our lot to see only "the ebb of the advancing wave," but we must remind ourselves that what we see is actually an *advancing* wave. "All things work together for good," not just for the individual, but for the entirety of the Church of Jesus Christ. We have been assured by the One unto whom all authority in heaven and earth has been granted that "the gates of Hell shall not prevail" against the Church. (Matthew 16:18) Thus it is that history, because it is the record of His victory, teaches us to hope.

The Lessons of Leadership

- A leader is indebted to the legacy of his parents. "My son, hear the instruction of your father, and do not forsake the law of your mother." (Proverbs 1:8)
- The most important ingredient in manliness is Christianity. "Fear God and keep His commandments, for this is the whole duty of man." (Ecclesiastes 12:13)
- A man who is not conscientious in the worship of God will be conscientious in little else. "The fear of the Lord is the beginning of wisdom." (Proverbs 1:7)
- A love for the Scriptures equips a man for leadership. "Man does not live by bread alone." (Deuteronomy 8:3)
- The choice of a wife is essential to the success or failure of a man's life. No man can be what God commands him to be apart from a faithful helper. "It is not good for man to be alone." (Genesis 2:18)
- Faithfulness to the marriage covenant is essential to a lifetime of usefulness. "Fornicators and adulterers God will judge." (Hebrews 13:4)
- Our greatest influence will be exercised in the home. A man is not qualified to lead others if he fails to lead his own house. "Fathers, provoke not your children to anger but bring them up in the nurture and admonition of the Lord." (Ephesians 6:4)
- Leaders care about the future and thus understand the importance of being a faithful example to the children. "Let no one despise your youth, but be an example to the believers in word, in conduct, in love, in spirit, in faith, in purity." (I Timothy 4:12)

- ❧ Leadership means taking initiative to do what must be done though all the world think it folly. "Commit your way unto the Lord and He shall bring it to pass." (Psalm 37:5)

- ❧ Courage is not the absence of fear, but the willingness to do one's duty in the face of fear. "What time I am afraid, I will trust in Thee." (Psalm 56:3)

- ❧ No one can be a true man until he learns to obey and faithfully complete the task assigned to him. "He who is faithful in little is faithful in much." (Luke 16:10)

- ❧ In the good providence of God, apparent failure often proves a blessing. "God causes all things to work together for good." (Romans 8:28)

- ❧ Bitterness against other men must be counteracted by remembering what we deserve from the hand of God. "Be angry, yet do not sin." (Ephesians 4:26)

- ❧ Humility is indispensable to usefulness because it teaches a man that he is not indispensable. "Humble yourself under the mighty hand of God that He might exalt you in due time." (I Peter 5:6)

- ❧ No man is fit to govern others if he cannot govern himself. "As a city broken down and without walls, so is a man who has no rule over his own spirit." (Proverbs 25:28)

- ❧ A man unwilling to deny himself is a slave to the world and not a leader of it. "If any man will come after Me let him deny himself, take up his cross daily, and follow Me." (Matthew 16:24)

- ❧ The one who seeks his own has made an idol of self and is thus incapable of loving and serving others. "He who seeks to save his life shall lose it." (Matthew 10:39)

- ❧ A man who cannot laugh sees little of God's purposes and understand nothing of Christ's victory. "He who sits in the heavens laughs." (Psalm 2:4)

- ❧ Sincere kindness endears us to our friends and softens the hearts even of our enemies. "Be kind one to another, tenderhearted, forgiving one another even as God, for Christ's sake has forgiven you." (Ephesians 4:32)

❧ Those who oppose our purposes are not always our enemies. "Love your enemies, do good to them that despitefully use you." (Matthew 5:44)

❧ Genuine love for others provokes undying loyalty. "Love one another." (I John 3:11)

❧ Organization, just administration, activity, and initiative are essential in the maintenance of morale. "Laying aside every weight and the sin which does so easily entangle us, let us run with patience the race that is set before us." (Hebrews 12:1-2)

❧ Knowing the limits of your abilities and the extent of your gifts is vital to avoiding useless and ineffectual pursuits. "Love is not puffed up." (I Corinthians 13:4)

❧ Understanding the history of our nation guards one from endorsing the political fads of contemporary fanatics. "Do not remove the ancient landmarks." (Proverbs 22:28)

❧ Love for a region or people does not mean justifying their sins. "You that love the Lord, hate evil." (Psalm 97:10)

❧ Love for the brethren is not to be confined within racial boundaries. "There is neither Jew nor Greek,… there is neither male nor female; for you are all one in Christ Jesus." (Galatians 3:27-28)

❧ The root of courage, the foundation of serenity, and the basis for perseverance is trust in God. "Trust in the Lord with all your heart and do not lean on your own understanding." (Proverbs 3:5-6)

❧ Discernment, refusal to underestimate the foe, justice, and self-control are non-negotiable ingredients to effective leadership. "The men of Issachar understood the times and knew what Israel was to do." (I Chronicles 12:32)

❧ Virtue should be equal to calamity. "By mercy and truth iniquity is covered." (Proverbs 16:6)

BIBLIOGRAPHY

Books and articles on Robert E. Lee:

Bradford, Gamaliel, Jr. "Lee in Battle," *Jubilee: One Hundred Years of the Atlantic.* Boston: Little, Brown and Company, 1957.

————. *Lee the American.* Boston: Houghton Mifflin, 1929.

Clemmons, Ronald T., ed. *Military Order of the Stars and Bars Papers, vol. 1, "General Robert Edward Lee—The Southern Diadem."* Murfreesboro, TN: Military Order of the Stars and Bars, 1995.

Davis, Burke. *Gray Fox: Robert E. Lee and the Civil War.* New York: Rinehart, 1956; New York: The Fairfax Press, 1981.

Flood, Charles Bracelen. *Lee: The Last Years.* Boston: Houghton Mifflin Company, 1981.

Freeman, Douglas Southall. *Douglas Southall Freeman on Leadership.* Edited by Stuart W. Smith. Shippensburg, PA: White Mane Publishing Company, Inc., 1993.

————. *Lee of Virginia.* New York: Charles Scribner's Sons, 1958.

————, ed. *Lee's Dispatches*. Rev. ed. Baton Rouge: Louisiana State University Press, 1994.

————. *R. E. Lee*. 4 vols. New York: Charles Scribner's Sons, 1947.

Jones, J. William. *Life and Letters of Robert Edward Lee, Soldier and Man*. 1909. Reprint, Harrisonburg, VA: Sprinkle Publications, 1978.

————. *Personal Reminiscences of General Robert E. Lee*. 1874. Reprint, Richmond, VA: United States Historical Society Press, 1989.

Lee, Robert E., Jr. *Recollections and Letters of General Robert E. Lee*. 1904. Reprint, Garden City, New York: Garden City Publishing Company, Inc., 1924.

Long, A. L. *Memoirs of Robert E. Lee*. 1886. Reprint, Secaucus, NJ: The Blue and Grey Press, 1983.

McCabe, James D., Jr. *Life and Campaigns of General Robert E. Lee*. Atlanta: National Publishing Company, 1870.

MacDonald, Rose Mortimer Ellzey. *Mrs. Robert E. Lee*. Boston: Ginn and Co., 1939. Arlington, VA: Robert B. Poisal Publisher, 1973.

Page, Thomas Nelson. *Robert E. Lee: Man and Soldier*. 2 vols. New York: Charles Scribner's Sons, 1912.

Roland, Charles P. *Reflections on Lee: A Historian's Assessment*. Mechanicsburg, PA: Stackpole Books, 1995.

Stiles, Robert. *Four Years Under Marse Robert.* 1903, Reprint, Dayton, OH: Morningside Bookshop, 1977.

Tower, R. Lockwood, ed. *Lee's Adjutant: The Wartime Letters of Colonel Walter Herron Taylor, 1862-1865.* Columbia, SC: The University of South Carolina Press, 1995.

Other works of related interest:

Alexander, Edward Porter. *Fighting for the Confederacy.* Edited by Gary W. Gallagher. Chapel Hill: The University of North Carolina Press, 1989.

Barrow, Charles Kelly, J. H. Segars and R. B. Rosenburg, eds. *Forgotten Confederates: An Anthology About Black Southerners.* Atlanta, GA: Southern Heritage Press, 1995.

Bennett, W. W. *The Great Revival in the Confederate Armies.* 1877. Reprint, Harrisonburg, VA: Sprinkle Publications, 1976.

Blackford, W. W. *War Years With Jeb Stuart.* 1945. Reprint, Baton Rouge, LA: Louisiana State University Press, 1993.

Bowers, Claude. *The Tragic Era.* Cambridge, MA: The Riverside Press, 1929.

Dabney, Robert Lewis. *The Life and Letters of General Thomas J. (Stonewall) Jackson.* 1865. Reprint, Harrisonburg, VA: Sprinkle Publications, 1976.

DeRosa, Marshall L. *The Confederate Constitution of 1861: An Inquiry into American Constitutionalism.* Colombia, MO: University of Missouri Press, 1991.

Foote, Shelby. *The Civil War: A Narrative.* 3 vols. New York: Random House, 1974.

Freeman, Douglas Southall. *Lee's Lieutenants: A Study in Command.* 3 vols. 1942. Reprint, New York: Charles Scribner's Sons, 1970.

Fremantle, Arthur J. L. *Three Months in the Southern States: The 1863 Diary of an English Soldier.* 1863. Reprint, Marshall, VA: Greenhouse Publishing Co., n.d.

Furnas, J. C. *The Road to Harpers Ferry.* New York: William Sloan Associates, 1959.

Gordon, John B. *Reminiscences of the Civil War.* 1903. Reprint, Dayton, OH: Morningside House, Inc., 1993.

Gragg, Rod. *The Illustrated Confederate Reader.* New York: Harper Collins, 1991.

Hummel, Jeffrey Rogers. *Emancipating Slaves, Enslaving Free Men: A History of the American Civil War.* Chicago and La Salle, IL: Open Court, 1996.

Johnson, Thomas Cary. *The Life and Letters of Robert Lewis Dabney.* 1903. Reprint, Edinburgh: Banner of Truth Trust, 1977.

Jones, J. William. *Christ in the Camp.* 1887. Reprint, Harrisonburg, VA: Sprinkle Publications, 1986.

Jordan, Ervin L., Jr. *Black Confederates and Afro-Yankees in Civil War Virginia.* Charlottesville, VA: University Press of Virginia, 1995.

Kennedy, James R. and Walter D. Kennedy. *The South was Right!* Gretna, LA: Pelican Publishing Company, 1994.

Keys, Thomas Bland. *The Uncivil War: Union Army and Navy Excesses in the Official Records.* Biloxi, MS: The Beauvoir Press, 1991.

Lee, Susan P. *Memoirs of William Nelson Pendleton, D.D.* Harrisonburg, VA: Sprinkle Publications, 1991.

Loveland, Anne C. *Southern Evangelicals and the Social Order: 1800-1860.* Baton Rouge, LA: Louisiana State University Press, 1980.

Lytle, Andrew Nelson. *From Eden to Babylon: The Social and Political Essays of Andrew Nelson Lytle.* Washington, D.C.: Regnery Gateway, 1990.

McGlone, John, ed. *Journal of Confederate History,* VII, "The Sword of the Lord and Gideon: Religion in the Confederacy." Murfreesboro, TN: Southern Heritage Press, 1991.

McGuire, Hunter, and George L. Christian. *The Confederate Cause and Conduct in the War Between the States And Other Confederate Papers.* 1907. Reprint, Boonton, NJ: Boonton Bookshop, 1994.

McPherson, James M. *Battle Cry of Freedom: The Civil War Era.* New York: Ballantine Books, 1988.

⸻. *What They Fought For 1861-1865.* Baton Rouge, LA: Louisiana State University Press, 1994.

Rollins, Richard, ed. *Black Southerners in Gray: Essays on Afro-americans in Confederate Armies.* Murfreesboro, TN: Southern Heritage Press, 1994.

Scott, Otto. *The Secret Six.* New York: Times Books, 1979.

Smith, Oran P., ed. *So Good a Cause: A Decade of Southern Partisan.* Columbia, SC: The Foundation for American Education, 1993.

Springer, Francis W. *War for What?* Nashville, TN: Bill Coats, Ltd., 1990.

Tilley, John S. *The Coming of the Glory.* 1945. Reprint, Nashville, TN: Bill Coats, Ltd., 1995.

————. *Facts the Historians Leave Out: A Confederate Primer.* 1951. Reprint, Nashville, TN: Bill Coats, Ltd., 1988.

————. *Lincoln Takes Command.* 1941. Reprint, Nashville, TN: Bill Coats, Ltd., 1991.

Twelve Southerners, *I'll Take My Stand: The South and the Agrarian Tradition.* Harper and Brothers, 1930. Reprint, Baton Rouge, LA: Louisiana State University Press, 1977.

Weaver, Richard. *The Southern Essays of Richard Weaver.* Edited by George M. Curtis, III, and James J. Thompson, Jr. Indianapolis, IN: Liberty Press, 1987.

————. *The Southern Tradition at Bay: A History of Postbellum Thought.* New Rochelle, NY: Arlington House, 1968.

White, H. M. *Rev. William S. White, D. D., And His Times.* Harrisonburg, VA: Sprinkle Publications, 1983.

Wilkins, Steve, and Douglas Wilson. *Southern Slavery As It Was.* Moscow, ID: Canon Press, 1996.

Invaluable information on Lee, the War between the States, and the South in general (some of which has never been published elsewhere) can be found in the following collections:

Battles and Leaders of the Civil War. 4 vols., Secaucus, NJ: Castle, n.d.

Confederate Military History. 16 vols. 1899. Reprint, Harrisonburg, PA: The Archive Society, 1994.

Confederate Veteran (1893-1942). 43 vols. Harrisonburg, PA: The National Historical Society, n.d.

The Southern Historical Society Papers. 52 vols. 1876-1959. Reprint, Millwood, NY: Kraus Reprint Co., 1977.

ENDNOTES

Section 1

1. Charles B. Flood, *Lee, the Last Years* (Boston: Houghton Mifflin Company, 1981), 256.
2. *Ibid.*, 83.
3. *Ibid.*
4. J. William Jones, *Personal Reminiscences*, (Richmond, VA: United States Historical Society Press, 1989, 1874), 448.
5. Flood, *Lee, the Last Years*, 257.
6. Jones, *Personal Reminiscences*, 449.
7. Flood, *Lee, the Last Years*, 259.
8. J. William Jones, *Life and Letters of Robert Edward Lee Soldier and Man* (1909; reprint, Harrisonburg, VA: Sprinkle Publications, 1978), 13.
9. *Ibid.*, 14.
10. *Ibid.*
11. *Ibid.*, 15.
12. Douglas S. Freeman, *R. E. Lee*, 4 vols. (New York: Charles Scribner's Sons, 1947), 1:161.
13. Jones, *Life and Letters*, p.17.
14. A. L. Long, *Memoirs of Robert E. Lee* (1886; reprint, Secaucus, NJ: The Blue and Grey Press, 1983), 21.
15. Freeman, *R. E. Lee*, 1:7.
16. *Ibid.*, 11.
17. *Ibid.*, 13.
18. *Ibid.*, 31.
19. *Ibid.*, 32.
20. Long, *Memoirs*, 22-23.
21. Jones, *Life and Letters*, 23.
22. Earnest Trice Thompson, *Presbyterians in the South* (Richmond, VA: John Knox Press, 1963), 1:12.
23. Freeman, *R. E. Lee*, 1:30-31.
24. Jones, *Life and Letters*, 25.
25. *Ibid.*, 24.
26. Long, *Memoirs*, 25.
27. *Ibid.*, 26.
28. *Ibid.*
29. Freeman, *R. E. Lee*, 1:34.
30. Jones, *Life and Letters*, 26.
31. Freeman, *R. E. Lee*, 1:46.
32. Douglas S. Freeman, *Lee of Virginia* (New York: Charles Scribner's Sons, 1958), 11.
33. *Ibid.*, 16.
34. Freeman, *R. E. Lee*, 1:106.
35. *Ibid.*, 108.
36. *Ibid.*, 109.
37. cited in Freeman, *R. E. Lee*, 1:110.
38. *Ibid.*, 1:148.
39. *Ibid.*, 201-202.
40. *Ibid.*, 294.
41. Jones, *Life and Letters*, 52.
42. *Ibid.*, 53.
43. *Ibid.*, 60-61.
44. *Ibid.*, 58.
45. Freeman, *R. E. Lee*, 1:334-337.

46. Freeman, *R. E. Lee*, 1:337-338.
47. *Confederate Veteran*, (1893-1942) 43 vols. (Harrisonburg, PA: The National Historical Trust, n.d.), 17:160.
48. Jones, *Life and Letters*, 95.
49. *Ibid.*, 100-101.
50. Otto Scott, *The Secret Six* (New York: Times Books, 1979), 288.
51. Freeman, *R. E. Lee*, 1:399.
52. *Ibid.*, 400.
53. James M. McPherson, *Battle Cry of Freedom* (New York: Ballantine Books, 1988), 209-210.
54. For more information on the "Secret Six" see Otto Scott's *The Secret Six*.
55. McPherson, *Battle Cry*, 221.
56. Freeman, *R. E. Lee*, 1:413.
57. *New Orleans Crescent*, quoted in McPherson, *Battle Cry of Freedom*, 231.
58. McPherson, *Battle Cry*, 233.
59. *Ibid.*
60. Jones, *Life and Letters*, 119.
61. *Ibid.*, 120-121.
62. *Ibid.*
63. *Ibid.*
64. Freeman, *R. E. Lee*, 4:303.
65. Lee in a letter to A. G. Brackett, *Battles and Leaders of the Civil War* (Secaucus, NJ: Castle, n.d.), 1:36.
66. Freeman, *R. E. Lee*, 1:426.
67. Robert E. Lee, Jr., *Recollections and Letters of General Robert E. Lee* (1904; reprint, Garden City, NY: Garden City Publishing Co. inc., 1924), 27.
68. *Ibid.*, 27-28.
69. *Ibid.*
70. Freeman, *R. E. Lee*, 1:437.
71. *Ibid.*, 441.
72. R. E. Lee, Jr., *Recollections*, 26.
73. Jones, *Life and Letters*, 139.
74. Quoted in Freeman, *R. E. Lee*, 1:476.
75. Freeman, *R. E. Lee*, 1:468.
76. Jones, *Personal Reminiscences*, 143.
77. Freeman, *R. E. Lee*, 1:572.
78. Long, *Memoirs*, 493-494.
79. Freeman, *R. E. Lee*, 2:74.
80. Joel Cook, *The Siege of Richmond*, 246-247, quoted in Freeman, *R. E. Lee*, 2:88.
81. Quoted in McPherson, *Battle Cry*, 554.
82. McPherson, *Battle Cry*, 558.
83. Freeman, *R. E. Lee*, 2:533.
84. *Ibid.*, 543.
85. R. L. Dabney, *The Life and Letters of General Thomas J. (Stonewall) Jackson* (1865; reprint, Harrisonburg, VA: Sprinkle Publications, 1976), 716.
86. *Ibid.*, 725.
87. Jones, *Personal Remininscences*, 156.
88. Jones, *Life and Letters*, 242.
89. Jones, *Personal Remininscences*, 153.
90. R. E. Lee, Jr., *Recollections*, 94.
91. Jones, *Personal Reminiscences*, 156.
92. *Southern Historical Society Papers*, 26:121.
93. See Douglas Southall Freeman's expert analysis of the battle, in *R. E. Lee*, 3:147-153.
94. Long, *Memoirs*, 277.
95. *Ibid.*, 281.
96. Freeman, *R. E. Lee*, 3:554.
97. Jones, *Life and Letters*, 277-278.
98. *Ibid.*, 283.
99. *Southern Historical Society Papers*, 31:234.
100. Arthur Freemantle, *Three Months in the Southern States: The 1863 Diary of an English Soldier* (1863; reprint, Marshall, VA: Greenhouse Publishing Co., n.d.), 275.
101. Freeman, *R. E. Lee*, 3:146.
102. Letter to Jefferson Davis, 31 July 1863, *Lee's Dispatches*, rev. ed. (Baton Rouge: Louisiana State University Press, 1994), 110.

103. Freeman, *R. E. Lee*, 3:156-157.
104. *Ibid.*, 158.
105. *Ibid.*
106. Jones, *Christ in the Camp* (1887; reprint, Harrisonburg, VA: Sprinkle Publications, 1986) 50.
107. *Ibid.*
108. Freeman, *R. E. Lee*, 3:251.
109. *Ibid.*, 268.
110. Freeman, *Lee of Virginia*, 183.
111. R. E. Lee, Jr., *Recollections*, 143.
112. *Ibid.*, 146.
113. Freeman, *R. E. Lee*, 4:116.
114. Long, *Memoirs*, 421.
115. *Ibid.*, 422.
116. Freeman, *R. E. Lee*, 4:121.
117. Flood, *Lee*, 5-6.
118. *Ibid.*, 8.
119. *Ibid.*, 12.
120. *Southern Historical Society Papers*, 27:96.
121. W. W. Blackford, *War Years With Jeb Stuart* (1945, reprint, Baton Rouge, LA: Louisiana State University Press, 1993), 294-295.
122. Thomas Nelson Page, *Robert E. Lee: Man and Soldier*, 2 vols. (New York: Charles Scribner's Sons, 1912), 2:315.
123. Flood, *Lee*, 37-38.
124. *Confederate Veteran*, 28:459-460.
125. Page, *R. E. Lee*, 2:324.
126. Freeman, *R. E. Lee*, 4:192.
127. Flood, *Lee*, 61-62.
128. *Ibid.*, 58.
129. R. E. Lee, Jr., *Recollections*, 224-225.
130. Flood, *Lee*, 56.
131. Long, *Memoirs*, 439.
132. Jones, *Life and Letters*, 390.
133. Flood, *Lee*, 64-65.
134. Jones, *Personal Reminiscences*, 180.
135. Flood, *Lee*, 83.
136. R. E. Lee, Jr., *Recollections*, 182-183.
137. Jones, *Personal Reminiscences*, 118-119.
138. Page, *Robert E. Lee*, 2:349.
139. Jones, *Personal Reminiscences*, 440.
140. *Ibid.*, 441.
141. Freeman, *R. E. Lee*, 4:426.
142. *Ibid.*, 278.
143. *Ibid.*, 279-280.
144. *Ibid.*, 280.
145. *Ibid.*, 283.
146. *Ibid.*, 283-284.
147. Page, *Robert E. Lee*, 2:344.
148. Flood, *Lee*, 104.
149. Freeman, *R. E. Lee*, 4:286-287.
150. *Ibid.*, 285.
151. Flood, *Lee*, 228.
152. Freeman, *R. E. Lee*, 4:452.
153. R. E. Lee, Jr., *Recollections*, 392.
154. *Ibid.*, 393.
155. *Ibid.*, 395.
156. *Ibid.*, 398.
157. Freeman, *R. E. Lee*, 4:452.
158. *Ibid.*, 455.
159. Flood, *Lee*, 245.
160. Freeman, *R. E. Lee*, 4:458.
161. Flood, *Lee*, 246.

162. Jones, *Personal Reminiscences*, 116.

163. R. E. Lee, Jr., *Recollections*, 433.

164. "Virginians on Olympus," Marshall Fishwick, *The Military Order of the Stars and Bars Papers*, vol. I, General Robert E. Lee—the Southern Diadem (Murfreesboro, TN: Military Orders of the Stars and Bars, 1995), 1:98-99.

Section 2

1. Jones, *Life and Letters*, 467.

2. R. E. Lee, Jr., *Recollections*, 64.

3. Quoted in Flood, *Lee*, 213-214.

4. Lee Roddy, *Robert E. Lee, Gallant Christian Soldier*, Introduction, 1, quoted in "Robert Edward Lee: A Man of Faith," Dr. Larry W. Sizemore, *The Military Order of the Stars & Bars Papers*, 1995, 1:92.

5. Jones, *Life and Letters*, 473.

6. Freeman, *R. E. Lee*, 4:270.

7. Jones, *Personal Reminiscences*, 426.

8. Freeman, *Lee of Virginia*, 230.

9. Jones, *Personal Reminiscences*, 114-115.

10. Freeman, *R. E. Lee*, 4:298.

11. R. E. Lee, Jr., *Recollections*, 217.

12. Jones, *Reminiscences*, 427.

13. Freeman, *R. E. Lee*, 3:242.

14. Rose Mortimer Ellzey MacDonald, *Mrs. Robert E. Lee* (Boston: Ginn and Co., 1939; reprint, Arlington, VA: Robert B. Poisal Publisher, 1973), 178.

15. Long, *Memoirs*, 389.

16. MacDonald, *Mrs. Robert E. Lee*, xviii, xix.

17. Jones, *Personal Reminiscences*, 368-369.

18. MacDonald, *Mrs. Robert E. Lee*, 293.

19. *Ibid.*, 38.

20. *Ibid.*, 54.

21. *Ibid.*, 51.

22. *Ibid.*, 117-118.

23. *Ibid.*, 175.

24. *Ibid.*, 268.

25. *Ibid.*, 121.

26. *Ibid.*, 182-183.

27. *Ibid.*, 251.

28. *Ibid.*, 245-246.

29. *Ibid.*, 197.

30. *Ibid.*, 288-289.

31. Freeman, *R. E. Lee*, 1:198.

32. Flood, *Lee*, 140.

33. Freeman, *R. E. Lee*, 1:198.

34. Flood, *Lee*, 140.

35. Freeman, *R. E. Lee*, 1:198.

36. Long, *Memoirs*, 34.

37. Freeman, *R. E. Lee*, 1:222.

38. Jones, *Life and Letters*, 35.

39. *Ibid.*, 37.

40. Flood, *Lee*, 72.

41. Jones, *Life and Letters*, 39-40.

42. Freeman, *R. E. Lee*, 1:410.

43. *Ibid.*, 3:526-527.

44. *Ibid.*, 4:268-269.

45. Jones, *Reminiscences*, 412-413.

46. Flood, *Lee*, 106.

47. R. E. Lee, Jr., *Recollections*, 271.

48. Jones, *Life and Letters*, 465-466.

49. E. Alexander, *Military Memoirs of a Confederate*, ed., Gary W. Gallagher (Chapel Hill: The University of North Carolina Press, 1989), 110-111.

50. Freeman, *Douglas Southall Freeman on Leadership*, ed., Stuart W. Smith (Shippensburg, PA: White Mane Publishing Co, Inc., 1993), 169.
51. Freeman, *R. E. Lee*, 3:543.
52. "The Campaign from the Wilderness to Petersburg—Address of Colonel C. S. Venable," *Southern Historical Society Papers*, 14:525-526.
53. "The Battle of Spotsylvania Courthouse," *Southern Historical Society Papers*, 32:202-203.
54. "General Lee to the Rear," *Southern Historical Society Papers*, 8:107.
55. Jones, *Life and Letters*, 317.
56. Long, *Memoirs*, 64.
57. Freeman, *R. E. Lee*, 4:288.
58. Jones, *Life and Letters*, 439.
59. Jones, *Personal Reminiscences*, 137.
60. *Ibid*, 138.
61. R. E. Lee, Jr., *Recollections*, 26.
62. Jones, *Personal Reminiscences*, p.142.
63. R. E. Lee, Jr., *Recollections*, 79-80.
64. *Ibid*, 117-118.
65. *Ibid*, 75.
66. *Ibid.*, 102.
67. Jones, *Personal Reminiscences*, 274.
68. Jones, *Life and Letters*, 438.
69. Freeman, *R. E. Lee*, 4:504.
70. Long, *Memoirs*, 421.
71. MacDonald, *Mrs. Robert E. Lee*, 231.
72. *Ibid*, 241.
73. *Ibid*, 249-250.
74. T. C. Johnston, *The Life and Letters of R. L. Dabney* (1903; reprint, Edinburgh: Banner of Truth Trust, 1977), 499-500.
75. Freeman, *R. E. Lee*, 4:329.
76. R. E. Lee, Jr., *Recollections*, 223-224.
77. *Ibid.*, 228.
78. Flood, *Lee*, 186.
79. R. E. Lee, Jr., *Recollections*, 220.
80. *Ibid.*, 88-89.
81. Jones, *Personal Reminiscences*, 148.
82. *Ibid*, 235.
83. Freeman, *R. E. Lee*, 3:395.
84. *Ibid*, 4:411.
85. *Ibid*, 4:285-286,454.
86. Jones, *Life and Letters*, 451.
87. *Ibid*, 449.
88. Freeman, *R. E. Lee*, 2:440.
89. Jones, *Life and Letters*, 401.
90. *Ibid.*
91. Jones, *Personal Reminiscences*, 222.
92. Jones, *Life and Letters*, 94.
93. Long, *Memoirs*, 29.
94. Page, *Robert E. Lee*, 2:358-359.
95. *Ibid*, 359.
96. Jones, *Personal Reminiscences*, 169.
97. *Ibid*, 167.
98. Freeman, *R. E. Lee*, 2:488.
99. Jones, *Life and Letters*, 441.
100. Jones, *Personal Reminiscences*, 171.
101. R. E. Lee, Jr., *Recollections*, 142.
102. Freeman, *R. E. Lee*, 3:528.
103. *Ibid*, 528-529.
104. Jones, *Life and Letters*, 156.
105. Flood, *Lee*, 202.
106. R. E. Lee, Jr., *Recollections*, 337.
107. *Ibid.*

108. Freeman, *R. E. Lee,* 3:216.

109. *Ibid.,* 4:505.

110. *Ibid.*

111. Jones, *Life and Letters,* 57.

112. *Ibid.,* 81.

113. Freeman, *R. E. Lee,* 4:213.

114. Jones, *Life and Letters,* 445.

115. Jones, *Personal Reminiscences,* 174-175.

116. Long, *Memoirs,* 400-401.

117. Jones, *Personal Reminiscences,* 242.

118. Freeman, *R. E. Lee,* 2:486.

119. *Ibid.,* 3:486.

120. Thomas Jones, "The Last Days of the Army of Northern Virginia", *Southern Historical Society Papers,* vol. 21 (Millwood, NY: Kraus Reprint Co., 1979, 1876-1959), 96.

121. R. E. Lee, Jr., *Recollections,* 316.

122. *Ibid.,* 332.

123. Freeman, *R. E. Lee,* 4:462.

124. R. E. Lee, Jr., *Recollections,* 380.

125. Freeman, *R. E. Lee,* 4:183.

126. *Ibid.,* 2:498.

127. Freeman, *Douglas Southall Freeman,* 131-132

128. Jones, *Personal Reminiscences,* 162.

129. *Ibid.,* 163.

130. Long, *Memoirs,* 301.

131. "The Monument to General Robert E. Lee," *Southern Historical Society Papers,* 17:297.

132. Jones, *Personal Reminiscences,* 323.

133. Freeman, *R. E. Lee,* 3:238-239.

134. Jones, *Personal Reminiscences,* 409-410.

135. Flood, *Lee,* 188.

136. *Ibid.,* 167.

137. Jones, *Personal Reminiscences,* 197-198.

138. Page, *Robert E. Lee,* 2:355.

139. Jones, *Personal Reminiscences,* 316.

140. *Ibid.,* 319.

141. *Ibid.,* 315-316.

142. R. E. Lee, Jr., *Recollections,* 372.

143. Jones, *Personal Reminiscences,* 319.

144. R. E. Lee, Jr., *Recollections,* 49.

145. Jones, "The Last Days of the Army of Northern Virginia," *Southern Historical Society Papers,* 21:96-97.

146. Freeman, *R. E. Lee,* 4:276-277.

147. *Ibid.,* 236.

148. R. E. Lee, Jr., *Recollections,* 138.

149. "Stonewall Jackson in Campaign of 1862," Colonel A. R. Boteler, *Southern Historical Society Papers,* 40:180-181.

150. Freeman, *R. E. Lee,* 2:355.

151. "A Marriage Made In Heaven: Robert E. Lee and the Army of Northern Virginia," Philip Katcher, *Military Order of the Stars and Bars Papers,* 1:18-19.

152. Edwars Porter Alexander, *Fighting for the Confederacy,* ed., Gary W. Gallagher (Chapel Hill: The University of North Carolina Press, 1989), 222.

153. Freeman, *R. E. Lee,* 3:347.

154. *Confederate Veteran,* 35:287.

155. Jones, *Southern Historical Society Papers,* 21:96.

156. Freeman, *R. E. Lee,* 4:190.

157. Flood, *Lee,* 188-189.

158. Jones, *Personal Reminiscences,* 223-224.

159. *Ibid.,* 210.

160. *Ibid.,* 218.

161. *Ibid.,* 273.

162. *Selected Writings of Lord Acton,* vol. I (Indianapolis, IN: Liberty Press, 1985), 365-366.

163. See Robert William Fogel and Stanley L. Engerman, *Time on the Cross* (New York: University Press of America, 1984), 115-116.

164. Freeman, *R. E. Lee*, 1:372.
165. *Ibid.*
166. Letter written to Mrs. Lee, December 27, 1856, from the Lee MSS, Library of Congress, quoted in Freeman, *R. E. Lee*, 1:372-373.
167. Freeman, *R. E. Lee*, 4:400.
168. *Ibid.*, 401.
169. R. E. Lee, Jr., *Recollections*, 231.
170. Edward C. Smith, "Calico, Black and Gray: Women and Blacks in the Confederacy," *Civil War*, issue XXIII, 10.
171. Charles Rice, "The black soldiers who served in the Confederate Army are the real forgotten men of the Civil War," *America's Civil War*, 90.
172. *Confederate Veteran*, vol. XIII, August, 1905, 360.
173. Freeman, *R. E. Lee*, 3:352-353.
174. Jones, *Personal Reminiscences*, 149.
175. Jones, *Life and Letters*, 470.
176. Freeman, *R. E. Lee*, 3:268.
177. William Jones, "The Friendship Between Lee and Scott," *Southern Historical Society Papers*, 11:425.
178. For an excellent treatment of Lee's leadership, see Freeman's lectures on Lee in *Douglas Southall Freeman on Leadership*.
179. Freeman, *R. E. Lee*, 3:146.
180. *Ibid.*, 3:331.
181. Freeman, *Lee of Virginia*, 190.
182. See Richard Weaver, "Southern Chivalry and Total War," *The Southern Essays of Richard Weaver*, ed., George M. Curtis (Indianapolis, IN: Liberty Press, 1987), 159-170.
183. Freeman, *R. E. Lee*, 1:621.
184. R. E. Lee, Jr., *Recollections*, 77.
185. Freeman, *R. E. Lee*, 2:446.
186. Weaver, "Southern Chivalry and Total War," *The Southern Essays of Richard Weaver*, 167.
187. "The Battle and Campaign of Gettysburg," *Southern Historical Society Papers*, 26:119.
188. Freeman, *R. E. Lee*, 3:56.
189. Jones, *Personal Reminiscences*, 189-190.
190. Freeman, *R. E. Lee*, 3:57.
191. Weaver, *Southern Essays*, 174.

Section 3

1. Freeman, *R. E. Lee*, 4:494.
2. *Southern Historical Society Papers*, 17:318, 352.
3. Freeman, *R. E. Lee*, 4:430.
4. Jones, Life and Letters, 438.
5. R. E. Lee, Jr., *Recollections*, 151.
6. Freeman, *R. E. Lee*, 4:484.

Printed in the USA
CPSIA information can be obtained
at www.ICGtesting.com
JSHW012018140824
68134JS00033B/2768